For Michael [illegible]

I hope you will derive inspiration and direction from this volume.

[illegible]
Honoch [illegible]

BUILDERS

BUILDERS

Stories and Insights into the Lives of Three Paramount Figures of the Torah Renaissance

by

Hanoch Teller

New York City Publishing Company

Rechov Yehoyariv 4, Arzei Habira, Jerusalem 97354, Israel
hanoch@attglobal.net

12 11 10 9 8 7 6 5 4 3 2 1

Library of Congress Cataloging-in-Publication Data

Teller, Hanoch
Builders: stories and insights of three primary builders of the Torah renaissance: Rabbi Aharon Kotler, Rabbi Yosef Shlomo Kahaneman, Frau Sarah Shenirer / by Hanoch Teller.
p. cm.
ISBN 1-881939-15-3
1. Kotler, Aaron, 1892-1962. 2. Kahaneman, Joseph, 1888-1969. 3. Shenirer, Sarah, 1883-1935. 4. Orthodox Judaism—History—20th century. 5. Rabbis—Biography. I. Title.
BM750.T447 2000
296.8'32'0922—dc21
[B] 00-063816

Distributed by
FELDHEIM PUBLISHERS
200 Airport Executive Park
Nanuet, NY 10954
FELDHEIM PUBLISHERS
POB 35002
Jerusalem, ISRAEL

J. LEHMANN
Hebrew Booksellers
Unit E Viking Industrial Park
Rolling MIll Road
Jarrow Tyne & Wear
NE32 3DP UK

These are the precepts that have no prescribed measure:
the corner of the fields, the first fruit offering, the
pilgrimages, acts of kindness and Torah study...

(פאה א:א)

In tribute, honor and memory to
our parents

Hyman & Bessie Galbut
חיים בן אברהם שיחי'
בתיה בת משה שתחי'

Morris & Reba Kraft
מאיר ב"ר ברוך שיחי'
רבקה בת ישראל ע"ה

May their devotion to God, acts of kindness,
and loving support for their communities
and Torah institutions
serve as a radiant beacon of light
for our children and our children's children
to continue in their righteous paths
for all future generations.

The Galbut Family

Also by
Hanoch Teller

Once Upon a Soul
Soul Survivors
'Souled!'
The Steipler Gaon
Sunset
Courtrooms of the Mind
Above the Bottom Line
Pichifkes
The Bostoner
Bridges of Steel, Ladders of Gold
"Hey, Taxi!"
The Best of StoryLines
Give Peace a Stance
Welcome to the Real World
13 Years
A Matter of Principal
And from Jerusalem, HIS Word
A Midrash and a Maaseh
О ТОМ, ЧТО НА ДУШЕ
ועמך כולם...
It's a Small Word After All
THE MINI Midrash and a Maaseh
E'rase Una Vez...
In an Unrelated Story

APPROBATION OF HAGAON HARAV BARUCH DOV POVARSKY Shlita

RABBI B. D. POVARSKY
45,Ben Zakai Bnei-Brak
Tel. 783538
Israel

ברוך דוב פוברסקי
ר"מ דישיבת פוניבז'
בן זכאי 45, בני ברק
טל. 783538

בס"ד, יום כ"ו אלול תשס"

הנה הלום בא לפני הרב היקר והנעלה ר' חנוך יונתן טל נ"י
מתלמידי ישיבת מיר בעיה"ק ירושלים. אשר רחש לבו דבר טוב
לזכות את הרבים ולחבר חיבורים יקרים בלע"ז בלשוני להרבות תורה.
ודבר. חיבורו באמונה ומהנהגותיהם של גדולי ישראל זיע"א בדברים
המושכים את הלב להתקרב אל אבינו שבשמים ולהתעלות במדות טובות ובמעשים
נשגבים. גם ראיתי בדבר נעלה ספרו הנ"ל כי [illegible] ידו
בשבחו וביקרו נעלתו. דבריהם המלהיבים את הבנים הצעירים אליו
ברורה ונעימה ותועלת רבה. אשר נאמרים בענין ובהשכל בשפה
[illegible]. ואשרנו בכל לב כי יזכהו הש"ת יצ"ו [illegible] עוד לזכות
ובהן לזכות את הרבים ולהוסיף עוד כהנה
והרבות כבוד שמים.

וע"ז באתי עה"ח
ברב יקר
ברוך דוב פוברסקי

APPROBATION OF HAGAON HARAV NOSSON ZVI FINKEL Shlita

ישיבת מיר ירושלים
MIRRER YESHIVAH JERUSALEM
Founded in Mir 1817. In Jerusalem 1944
ב"ה נוסדה במיר בשנת תקע"ז. בירושלים בשנת תש"ד
RABBI N.Z. FINKEL
DEAN
הרב נ.צ. פינקל
ראש הישיבה

בס"ד

כ"ד אלול תש"ס

הנה כבר יצא טבעו של תלמידי ויקירי הרב חנוך יהונתן טלר שליט"א בעולם זה שנים רבות כאומן נפלא להלהיב את הלבבות לחיי תורה ליראת שמים ולמע"ט ומדות טובות. סיפוריו המפורסמים הנאמרים והנכתבים בטוב טעם והיוצאים מלב דואג ומצר על אחיו בני ישראל בכל תפוצותיהם נכנסים אל הלב להרוות צמאונם ולקרב את הרחוקים מדרך הישר ולחזק את הקרובים אלי'. הרב טלר שליט"א הסתופף בישיבתנו הק' תקופה ארוכה מאד בצעירותו וגם לאחר נישואיו ובין כותלי' ספג את תורתו ואת יראתו בסדרי הישיבה ובשיעורים תמידים כסדרם, ומני אז ועד היום קובע שם תפילתו ותורתו. ידי תיכון עמו לתמכו ולחזקו בעבודת קודש זו, יתן ה' שיהי' חלקו בין מצדיקי הרבים לקרבן אל אבינו שבשמים וככוכבים יזהירם לעולם עד ביאת גוא"צ בבא"י.

הכו"ח לכבוד המחבר שליט"א,

נתן צבי פינקל

הרב נתן צבי פינקל
ראש הישיבה

Beth Israel St. P.O.B. 5022 Jerusalem 91050 Tel. 02-5322320 Fax. 02-5323446 ● בית ישראל 3 ת.ד. 5022 ירושלים 91050 טל. 02-5322320 פקס. 02-5323446

APPROBATION OF HAGAON HARAV ELI DOV WACHTFOGEL Shlita

הרב אלי' דוב וואכטפויגעל

RABBI ELI DOV WACHTFOGEL
4 Yeshiva Lane
Fallsburg, N.Y. 12733
914-434-2093

בס"ד עש"ק לסדר ומל ה' אלקך את לבבך תש"ס

למע"כ ידידי וחביבי ש"ב הרב המפורסם חנוך יונתן טלר שליט"א

הנה המחבר הנ"ל קנה לו שם טוב בעולם החרדי בספריו הנכבדים על גדולי אישי ישראל ועל עניני מדות וגם מהסיפורים הנפלאים מעובדות אמונה ובטחון ויצא מזה תועלת רב לדור הצעיר.

ועתה נדבה רוחו להוציא ספר סיפורי מעשיות מהגאון הגדול ר' אהרון זצ"ל והגאון הגדול הרב מפונובז זצ"ל שהם היו עמודי ובוני דורינו, וגם מהאשה הדגולה שרה שנירר ע"ה לחינוך הבנות, וביחד העמידו דור שלם מבני תורה ובנות יראה שמים וכל סיפוריו נשאבו ממקורות מוסמכים מאד. וודאי יצא מזה תועלת רב לאנשי דורינו אשר אנשים מקרוב ממש לדורינו למה הגיעו וא"כ למה נגרע!

והנני מברכו שחפץ ה' בידו יצליח לעורר לב בנ"י לגדלות בתורה ויראה ומפעלים גדולים למען ה' ותורתו.

החותם באהבה
המוקירו ומכבדו כערכו הרם
אלי' דב וכטפוגל

Acknowledgements

I take this opportunity to thank Reb Aharon Kotler's grandson, the Lakewood rosh yeshivah, Harav Malkiel Kotler, for reviewing sections of the manuscript. Another grandson of Reb Aharon Kotler also looked over the manuscript and provided invaluable corrections and insights. I likewise thank Harav Eliezer Kahaneman for examining part of the manuscript and offering his critical emendations.

Numerous other rabbis and experts gave of their time to read drafts of this book, and to provide critical feedback and editorial advice. Most noted among them is Rabbi MOSHE KOLODNY, renowned archivist at Agudath Israel headquarters and resident historical scholar. Special thanks to Rabbi Shmuel Bloom for having coordinated this arrangement. It would not have been possible to reproduce the pictures and artifacts in this volume without the Orthodox Jewish/Agudath Israel of America Archives in New York City.

Writing this book meant relying heavily upon earlier works by others. In every instance I have attempted properly to acknowledge my source, but, as books undergo an evolutionary process, I am aware that in the cutting and splicing some recognition might have accidentally been eliminated. I apologize in advance for any such inadvertent deletion.

Regarding Rabbi Aharon Kotler, the primary books I consulted were the fine works by Rabbis Alter Pekier, Amos Bunim, Shaul Kagan, Yitzchok Dershowitz, and Aaron Surasky. More about Rabbi Surasky soon. Leah Rotstein's prize-winning compilation about Rabbi Kotler was also a key resource.

As regards Reb Yosef Shlomo Kahaneman, I spent weeks in the Bais Yaakov archives in Jerusalem, as I had done regarding my other two protagonists, plowing through articles and essays about this ever-popular leader. But after all of my work, copious notes and reams of photocopies, *HaRav MiPonevezh* was published by Rabbi AARON SURASKY under the aegis of Rabbi Eliezer Kahaneman and the Institute of Jewish Life in Lithuania. There is no question that this three-volume set is the definitive work on the subject. For decades, Rabbi Surasky has established himself as the most eminent, reliable and stylistically graceful biographer* of our time — perhaps of all time. Any serious student of the Ponevizher

Rav should be required to read Rabbi Surasky's masterpiece.

Accordingly, in the section dealing with Rav Kahaneman, I do not refer to Rabbi Aaron Surasky's work as my source in order to avoid quoting his name several times per page. What I have written is neither a translation nor an adaptation of Rabbi Surasky's encyclopedic 900-page work, but it is virtually impossible to write anything about the Ponevizher Rav that cannot be found in *HaRav MiPonevezh.* I have weeks of research to corroborate this assertion. As always, in allowing others to quote his material Rabbi Surasky's generosity knows no bounds.

Pertaining to Frau Sarah Schenirer, primary sources were *Eim B'Yisrael* (Netzach), *Daughters of Destiny* compiled by Devora Rubin (a tasteful and moving anthology — assembled by highly competent high school students!), and *Rebbetzin Grunfeld* by Miriam Dansky (which I became aware of only after my book was in its final stages).

Initially I had planned to base my work entirely on what was already written. This would have enabled my project to be far less ambitious and presumptuous. Who am I to record the doings of Reb Aharon Kotler, etc.? But as I studied

---

*The footnotes alone prove that Rabbi Surasky is no less of a serious *talmid chacham* and erudite scholar.

the results of my original plan, even the printer seemed to be yawning. I feared that the oh-so-familiar rhapsodies that so many recognize would have been a drain on the patience of my readers. The decision was then made to interview individuals, and I extend my profoundest gratitude to those who granted me their time and their insights.

Yehudis Elkins and Vivien Orbach Smith expertly and graciously provided editorial assistance. FRIMY EISNER was an outstanding asset to this book; her keen eyes and felicity of style grace every page. Ruchi Koval did her usual masterful job of proofreading. Elcya Weiss is the best at what she does, and thank God, she does so much! I am saddened that illness has prevented Marsi Tabak from assisting me with this work, yet her years of wise, patient, and enlightening instruction continue to guide me.

As part of this book was written overseas, hardware accessories (read: printer) were often essential, and the magnanimous Rabbis Yosef Gelman and Yonason Karman of Masores Bais Yaakov graciously allowed me free access to their resources. It is high time to thank the devoted and tireless Feldheim staff in Monsey, New York, for their admirable distribution. More specifically, I gratefully acknowledge: Yitzchak Feldheim, Eli Meir Hollander, Judy Gruenbaum, Ilse Loeb, Devorah Slater, Alexander Rosenstock, Moshe

Grossman, Anshel Rosenberg and Ari Korn. Jeremy Staiman and team must be richly commended for their graphic prowess evident on this and earlier covers of mine.

This is a good place to acknowledge the assistance provided to me in matters other than book writing. Abe and Deborah Chames have taken me under their wing in a manner that I can barely fathom, let alone determine an apt way thank. For that matter, I have all but given up thanking the Paskesz Family for their non-stop accommodations and generosity. After all, how many times can you keep writing the same thing? Probably not enough.

I doff my hat to Rabbi and Rebbetzin Chaim Wakslak; their example leaves me in awe. Mrs. Aliza Grund is always there when I (and countless others) need her. Harry and Elkie Bram have rewritten the book on friendship, this latest version is a "must"! Reb Aaron Brand, I assume, would prefer that I not test his patience, but one would never know from his indulgent forbearance. One could never ask for more good-natured and generous friends than Paul and Haya Reisbord.

Not everyone is privileged to bring a book to press, and are hence denied, among other things (such as sleep, travel and expenditures), the ability to write "Acknowledgments." Therefore, on behalf of so many, allow me to be their spokesman in acknowledging our deep-felt appreciation to

Rabbi and Rebbetzin Yisrael Reisman for their lessons and example.

Getting more personal, I extend my profoundest gratitude to my aidel wife, and my loving family, up, down, and all around.

Thank you Hashem (trust me, I would use that as a title for a book if not for the marketing advice of my colleagues) for bestowing this honor upon me once again. I am grateful for everything else as well.

Lastly, at the risk of sounding corny — but it is my greatest conviction and deepest belief — I would not be who I am, where I am, and what I am were it not for the subjects of this book. To them all, my humblest appreciation.

Hanoch Teller
Jerusalem ת"ו
Erev Yom Kippur, 5761

לעי"נ
אציל הנפש
הבחור **יעקב מנחם** ז"ל
בן יבלחט"א הר"ר יחזקאל ישעיה פאנעטה

בימיו הקצרים היה דוגמא
ליראת ד' ולאהבת ישראל בצניעות מופלאה
ת.נ.צ.ב.ה.

Introduction

"TO CATCH A CHARACTER in trouble and to tell about it is the basis for almost any story." I'm quoting myself. "One small mistake, one tiny oversight," same source, "a minor impulse acted upon or resisted, can change the entire course of a man's life, crystallizing instantly into ineluctable fate. Someone once wrote about a hunter who misjudges the thickness of river ice and drowns as the ducks he had set out to kill circle in the air above him."

That was the introduction of a lesson in a class that I taught in a Jerusalem seminary years ago — in a class that had a surprise ending itself. I was trying to prove a point germane to the time that Yosef was lost when looking for his brothers and encountered a stranger. A discussion ensued about how, when you think you are headed one way, sometimes you are actually traveling in the opposite direction. Apparently this concept was the subject of many song lyrics of contemporary vintage, and before I knew it, the subject had devolved into a catalytic enzyme for "name that tune." These kids were experts, unspooling songs and artists in dizzying abandon. Only I did not recognize either the composers or their works.

Officially, I'm not such a fuddy duddy, and at the time I probably didn't have more than 12-14 years seniority over my students. And yet, and yet... there was a cultural divide in that classroom with the dimensions of a yawning chasm. That I was not au courant with the latest rock stars and their releases did not trouble me, but I was bothered because my students could marshal so much gray matter to absorb the biographies of these non-paragons of mankind, yet they were clueless about the luminaries of our People. And I said as much.

"Why is it that you've all heard of The Beatles, The Byrds, and The Skunks [I was just guessing on the last one], but you've never heard of Reb Shimon Shkop, or Reb Naftali Trop?"

Wide-eyed, gape-jawed wonder spread across the classroom as the girls lapsed into a long stretch of puzzled silence. Then one girl — I shall never forget that moment of apotheosis — raised her hand and said, "You're right. We don't know who they are. Why don't you teach us?"

I never did finish my point about Yosef, for from then on — and ever since — I have been teaching courses about *gedolei Yisrael* to seminary students that have had next to nil exposure to our spiritual giants. Even those students quasi-familiar with the names of *gedolim* didn't know if Kletzk is in Europe, or merely "out of town," the difference between Slobodka and Novhardok; or if the Vilna Gaon lived before or after the Maharam MiRottenberg.

Part of the ignorance — the part that was so troubling to me — was that there was no sense of gratitude for what these spiritual heroes had accomplished for us. We are here, I tried to stress, thanks to them.

Most specifically, in the last hundred years, the impact of three remarkable people — **not to detract from the wondrous and inestimable accomplishments of all of the others** — has significantly influenced who we are, the schools we attend and the lives we lead.

I call these three the "builders" for I can think of no other word that better captures the work that they did. From destruction that was physical and spiritual, emotional and material, they rebuilt upon the foundation of sanctity and tradition.

I have not attempted to write detailed biographies of these luminaries. My focus has been on how they built, but in almost every case it was necessary to provide background and framework material in order to better appreciative their accomplishments. This "background information" is not mere history; it is filled with timeless wisdom — as opposed to information. Because, while information may be easy to come by, wisdom still tends to play hard to get.

In relating the lives of these leaders it was important — for a change — to separate fact from fantasy. I realize that at this point readers of some of my earlier works may find their eyebrows creeping upward in surprise at this declaration. I therefore wish to clarify that the stories that I write are always *true* (though not always sticklers for fact), with multiple layers of meanings and implication in the subtle twists and turns of the telling. There seems to be an unwritten rule that truth will endure a little decorative writing, perhaps.

Having said all that, I know that it will not wash in this book. Writing about people of truth — whose every thought and action was unadulterated *emmes* — does not permit any license in the descriptive-liberty department. The greatest care and most meticulous precision were employed to ensure that the facts recorded are thoroughly faithful to what occurred. The downside of all this is that some preconceptions may be shattered by the information in the forthcoming pages, for like zucchini, myth has a long growing season in the lore of *gedolim*. Lastly, and this is important, writing about these three great people does *not* mean that they are all in the same rubric. Reb Aharon Kotler was unequivocally the *gadol hador*; Reb Yosef Shlomo Kahaneman, a rosh yeshivah with phenomenal vision and responsibility. Frau Sara Schenirer was not in that realm and not in that sphere. Her challenge was *chinuch* and she heroically and successfully undertook a mission for Jewish education that had never been tackled before.

Just as there is no attempt in the book to compare one with the other, the reader should also refrain from correlations and contrasts between the protagonists. What they share, as I endeavored to explain in the seminary course described earlier, is that we are here thanks to them, all of them.

There are still people alive who can recount the extraordinary respect the Ponevizher Rav afforded Reb Aharon, and how it was reciprocated. The perspective that these two *gedolim* had towards Sarah Schenirer is public record. The gist of what they acknowledged is that there would not be yeshivos today without the movement that she started.

It is my fervent hope that the lives of these "builders" will inspire further construction. They shall forever remain the foremen.

Author's Note

FAR BE IT FROM YOU, my brothers and sisters, to suffer the difficulty in writing a book like this. All of my laborious-work can appear marred because of seeming inconsistencies, capricious italicizing and spelling irregularities. I know how much these things would bother me, and accordingly I wish to detail the system to which I adhered.

Manuals of writing style maintain that foreign words are italicized only if they do *not* appear in the dictionary. In recent years, words such as mitzvah, Seder, Shabbos, yeshivah, etc. have found their way into Webster's. I have extended this liberty a tad further and not italicized words that appear consistently throughout the book. Rosh yeshivah is one example. As it is practically on every page, I left it in Roman.

Regarding transliteration I have adopted the policy of adding an "h" to any word that ends with a "*heh.*" And what if there are two ways to the same thing? Is the name of the organization Agudath Israel or Agudas Yisrael? In this particular instance the organization's stationery reads, "Agudath Israel," yet in colloquial parlance it is known as Agudas Yisrael. To refer to the organization as both would appear to be highly inconsistent, but as Einstein suggested, everything is relative. A representative of Agudath Israel testified before Congress, but Agudas Yisrael was popular among the *bochurim* of Krakow.

Beth Medrash Govoha is the chosen spelling for name of the Lakewood yeshivah, and I have naturally adopted their spelling although I would have preferred Beis Midrash Govohah. Theoretically, Torah Vodaath is no less correct than Torah Vodaas, or Torah Voda'as.

Uppers and lowers vacillate, pun intended. The word rabbi or rosh yeshivah will remain in lower case unless that title is commonly substituted for his name. For example: To the Rosh Yeshivah, the rabbi was wasting his time; he hadn't joined the Rabbi's group, like the other rabbi from out of town.

The point of this excursus is to inform the reader that stylistic policies were not adapted and abandoned whimsically and arbitrarily. *Smooth* is not the word that comes to mind when describing the inconsistencies that had to be employed to make this book consistent. I thank you in advance for your indulgence.

Rabbi Aharon Kotler

Rabbi Yosef Shlomo Kahaneman

Rabbi Aharon Kotler

One

ANY roads lead to yeshivah, yet many more lead away.

Some students enroll in a yeshivah because their family structure makes it the natural thing to do. Their fathers learned in yeshivah, and their fathers' fathers learned in yeshivah — and even if maintaining a son in yeshivah presents economic difficulties or results in ridicule from neighbors, the path of Torah learning would be followed nonetheless. Others, defying their families' concerted efforts to force an alternate education on them, attend yeshivah nonetheless.

Ironically, Rabbi Aharon Kotler belongs to both categories.

Born into an illustrious rabbinic family and endowed with a piercingly analytical mind, he was clearly on the fast track to Talmudic erudition and world renown. However, the so-called Enlightenists* who heard of this genius realized that he was a treasure that they could not forego. They set their sights on this little boy, confident that he was easy prey.

Orphaned at a very early age, and thrust into the stifling world of religious indoctrination, a keen mind like his must crave exposure to broad edification and secular fulfillment. Or so they thought. They even enlisted Araleh's sister in their plot to free him from the "clutches" of his overly protective uncle, Reb Yitzchak Pinnes in Minsk, who was raising and educating the prodigy.

The tenacity of the so-called Enlightenists knew no bounds; although their goal was to attain *every* Jewish soul, their primary targets were the bright and the gifted. In all of White Russia, there was no

---

* The Enlightenment, or Haskalah movement, denigrated Jewish tradition and embraced secular literature and wisdom as a means to assimilate into and be accepted by non-Jewish society.

one who qualified as richly as Araleh Kotler. Before reaching adolescence, he had memorized the entire *Tanach*, while his accomplishments in *Torah she-be'al peh* were no less impressive. Significantly, prior to bar mitzvah, he had completed the tractates *Kiddushin* and *Kesubos* with all of the *Tosafos*, a feat little short of amazing.

In light of these prodigious accomplishments, the Enlightenists did a little Talmudic reasoning of their own: If this is what the child could accomplish in archaic religious studies, imagine what he could contribute to contemporary wisdom!

The battle for this child's soul would be waged in earnest — at that time, similar conflicts occurred in many venues. But in this particular case everyone perceived that the stakes were unusually high. The *Alter* of Slobodka intercepted a letter that Araleh's sister had sent him, advising him to "leave the stale yeshivah benches" and to join her in the "hallowed halls of the university." The *Alter* had no doubts regarding the consequences such a letter might have on little Aharon, and promptly destroyed it.

But the *Alter*, the master pedagogue — taking the responsibility that only a giant of his stature could accept — saw to it that a forged reply was sent. The gist of that letter was: "As long as this is your agenda, don't bother writing again. Araleh."

Although this attempt by the Enlightenists failed, they never gave up. The teachers in Araleh's yeshivah concluded that Minsk was not a safe location for him. In those environs he was susceptible to the influences from which they wished to shield him, and vulnerable to the well-meaning but misguided influence of his sibling. And his teachers acted not a minute too soon.

Enlightenist agents had enrolled Aharon in a Minsk *gymnasium* and had his academic year carefully planned. The *Alter* of Slobodka intervened and had the boy brought to an appropriate venue, the Slobodka Yeshivah. In the *Alter*'s opinion, it was worth cultivating this famous yeshivah of over 500 students just to matriculate Aharon Kotler.

Aharon attended a *shiur* of boys significantly his senior, a *shiur* delivered by the rosh yeshivah, Reb Moshe Mordechai Epstein. In addition, he also attended the *shiur* of Reb Baruch Ber Leibowitz in the Knesses Bais Yitzchak yeshivah. There was no question that this boy truly excelled in Torah learning, and his prodigious accomplishments were brought to the attention of the *gedolei hador*.

As Aharon's knowledge broadened, so did his fame. Before the age of 16, the boy had already encountered Reb Chaim Soloveitchik and Reb Meir Simchah of Dvinsk and these two *gedolim* walked away from their meeting extremely impressed. Year by year, his reputation increased; it spread as far as Slutzk, where Reb Isser Zalman Meltzer, a *gaon* of the Volozhin yeshivah, was the rav and rosh yeshivah. Reb Isser Zalman duly noted the information that a genius was being polished in the yeshivah, and planned to access it in the most practical manner.

At the time, Reb Isser Zalman's daughter was still too young to commence the matrimonial process, but it was never too early to scout out a prospective candidate! Reb Isser Zalman prudently decided to keep this boy's brilliance under wraps, so that when the time came, he would be able to make his offer unimpeded by other contestants. But the day that he heard a report about a "shining diamond" glowing in the Slobodka yeshivah, he knew that the time had come to act.

And act he did, departing that very day for Slobodka. Fortunately for all, his mission was successful, and *tenaim* were drafted between Aharon and Chana Perel.

Subsequent to the engagement, the young man, just 22, was added to the teaching staff of the Slutzker Yeshivah. Reb Aharon's *shiurim* were presented on a very high level and the students had to extend themselves intellectually in order to comprehend them. In no time, he joined the administration as well, assisting his father-in-law in every aspect of the yeshivah, even in matters pertaining to Slutzk's Jewish community.

Reb Isser Zalman, obviously pleased with Reb Aharon's contribution to the yeshivah, modestly boasted, "I know only the page of *gemarah* that I am currently learning, whereas my son-in-law is well versed in *every* aspect of Torah."

After a *shiur* that Reb Aharon delivered in Slutzk, Reb Isser Zalman posed a question/refutation. Reb Aharon stated, "I know the answer to this question," with his usual intensity, but before he had a chance to articulate his thought, Reb Isser Zalman commented wryly, "I know you know. That is why I selected you for a son-in-law..."

A woman, days after her wedding, came to Reb Isser Zalman and complained that she had been defrauded by her husband. The man wore elevator shoes with inserts to make him seem taller. Only after the wedding did she discover that he was shorter than she had imagined.

Reb Isser Zalman pondered the issue and told her that he disagreed with the charge of fraud. "The drawback of a short husband," he explained "is that his shortness could be a source of embarrassment when the couple is viewed together. However, this embarrassment can readily be avoided by his wearing the elevator shoes which he already owns."

Reb Aharon was present when his father-in-law rendered his decision, and objected, claiming that fraud had indeed been perpetrated.

Those in the house at the time were accustomed to hearing Reb Aharon challenge his father-in-law in matters of learning, and the debates were always scholarly disputes that only the erudite could follow. But this time, they had no idea what issue Rabbi Kotler could have with such solid and logical reasoning.

It is a *mekach ta'os*, Reb Aharon argued, as she might have wed with the intention of having him put on elevator shoes once they were married. She now sees that this is no longer a possibility, since he has already enhanced his height....

As usual, Reb Isser Zalman beamed with parental pride at his son-in-law's incisive mind.

Two

AFTER the conclusion of World War I, the Communists applied quasi-religious zeal in their eradication of religious practice. Rabbis and roshei yeshivah were deemed the nemeses of the proletariat and the antithesis of those who wished to bask in the splendor of the "Worker's Paradise." Accordingly, the Communist regime declared all-out war against "subversive activity centers" (read: yeshivos) and anyone involved in fostering the dreaded "opiate of the masses."

Thus, the Slutzk Yeshivah was in the direct crosshairs of the trigger-happy Bolsheviks. Reb Isser Zalman was arrested numerous times, leaving Reb Aharon in charge of the yeshivah. Such a position was very risky, and Reb Aharon shouldered the obligation with sobriety and responsibility.

Reb Aharon was not spared the special attention the Soviets awarded religious leaders. He was subjected to countless interrogations, yet, despite the very real threat that the teachers and students would be transferred to Siberia, the Slutzk yeshivah continued its learning without interruption for four years. Their courage, with that of other yeshivah students at that time who were willing to risk their safety and freedom and not capitulate to the Russian regime, deserves a special chapter in the annals of our People's bravery.

It was axiomatic that Torah learning would continue unabated in the yeshivah, no matter what. But as Reb Aharon pointed out to his father-in-law, there had to be a better way. Across the border, in Poland, it was *not* forbidden to study Torah. And whereas the border between Russia and Poland shifted all the time, Reb Aharon assessed that the border city of Slutzk would remain forever in Soviet hands.

As a result of his geographic analysis, he

wasted no time in sending his two-and-a-half-year-old son, Shneur, to the town of Kletzk, on the Polish side of the border. For just as government-dictated closure of the yeshivah was a certain eventuality, the identical fate awaited the *chadorim*. But whereas Reb Aharon was able to implement a contingency on behalf of his son, he did not have this liberty regarding the yeshivah. Yet.

Rabbi Baruch Ber Leibowitz, Reb Aharon Kotler and his son Shneur.

Eventually, Reb Aharon convinced his father-in-law to relocate the yeshivah, and plans were set into motion. It really wasn't far, but there was an entire Russian army posted to prevent the escape of those discontent with Paradise, and a Polish army on guard to prevent entry by those fleeing from Supreme Bliss.

The state of relations between Russia and Poland was very tense. Fighting between the two had just ceased, and their mutual suspicions were reflected in tough measures on both sides of the border. Trying to escape from the Fatherland was adequate reason to be shot and attempted infiltration on the other side was deserving of the same response.

Furthermore, the flight to Poland was not only fraught with danger, but tinged with sadness. The students understood that even if they survived the escape, they would probably never see their families again.

In addition to being the rosh yeshivah, Reb Isser Zalman was also the rav of the town of Slutzk and, as such, he refused to join the flight to safety. Reb Aharon was aware that a shepherd may not abandon his flock, but he maintained that his father-in-law was a "wanted" man, so that remaining behind would also result —

under far more tragic circumstances — in the town being left without a rav. Still, Reb Isser Zalman stayed put.

Reb Aharon and fifty students managed to spirit themselves across Russian lines and set up camp in Kletzk, just six kilometers from the frontier. It was hoped that the border location of the yeshivah would provide refuge for any yeshivah student on the run, and enable him to resume his studies with ease.

But even in the new land, all was not safe. Although the Polish regime was not focused on the destruction of religion, it was — de facto — bent on the destruction of the Jews. To the hostile natives, rabid anti-Semitism was perfectly natural — a national pastime, as it were. Somehow or another, a way would be found to accuse and persecute the Jews. In this instance nothing could have been more uncontrived, as the students had arrived, and were remaining, illegally.

The Jewish community in Kletzk was only too happy to have a yeshivah grace its town. The townsmen vied for the honor of housing yeshivah students and provided whatever humble assistance they could afford to their guests.

Reb Aharon became Kletzk's rosh yeshivah at the age of 27, but thanks to the Bolsheviks, he was already experienced at the job. Rabbi Kotler placed all of his energy into his new responsibility and the yeshivah expanded and flourished. One visitor to Reb Aharon's humble, sparsely furnished home in Kletzk described it as a "Torah market" where students bought and sold, argued and disputed Talmudic wares.

With Reb Aharon at the helm, the yeshivah naturally attracted the brightest students, and the level of learning was on par with the finest well-established yeshivos in the world. A young dynamo named Reb Eliezer Menachem Shach, the son-in-law of Reb Isser Zalman's sister, joined the yeshivah there, and he was a great asset to its ranks. In a short time, Kletzk became one of the largest yeshivos in Poland, second only to the Mir.

The success of the new yeshivah, hailed throughout the Torah world, was less enthusiastically received by the local Poles. Anti-Semitic flare-ups occurred with alarming frequency, culminating on the second day of Shavous, 5685 (1925). This was no spontaneous eruption of Polish animosity toward the foreigner. Oh, no. It was a well-planned and deviously conceived attack, masterminded by none other than the foremost Jew-hater in the region, the local police chief.

This bully, together with a significant contingent of his gendarmes, arrived at Reb

Aharon's house as the boys were engaged in a festive *ne'ilas ha-chag* involving singing and dancing. Not until it was too late did they notice the thugs descending upon the premises. Without sparing any physical force, the officers shunted the defenseless students into one room and commanded them to present their papers. Few were able to comply with this order. Nothing could have given the policemen greater pleasure.

Unwarranted physical abuse was once again applied to the "criminals," sixty in number, and they were carted off and locked in the fetid horse stables. As soon as word spread of the arrest and humiliation, a delegation of local Jews approached the police chief and appealed for his mercy. "We hear screams from the horse stables and cries of agony — clearly some of the prisoners require medical attention!"

The police chief found this humorous and the smile of a drunken pirate spread across his face. But his amusement did not last long: "Get out of here!" he barked, "Or *you'll* be arrested and then you can inspect their conditions from close range."

Simultaneously, a different group of Jews traveled to Niesvizh, the regional capitol, where they met with the district chief administrator. Their mission proved to be far more successful, and the students' release was secured.

In spite of these setbacks, the Kletzker yeshivah thrived. It was natural for serious students to gravitate to Reb Aharon's *shiurim*, famous for their *hekef* — seemingly limitless scope. The standard *shiur* focuses upon one particular point and analyzes it methodically, or else provides a purview of the entire *sugya*. Reb Aharon would do both simultaneously. His *shiurim* focused on pinpoint analyses joined with broad comprehension, leaving the listener awed and intellectually stimulated.

Reb Aharon's *shiurim* were a reflection of his learning methodology. His engagement in Torah study cannot be portrayed simply as an intellectual pursuit, but rather as a subjugation to Torah wisdom. Reb Aharon never attempted to bolster or fortify an original idea by seeking corroboration from the texts. His own conceptions had to comply with what the Torah delineated. Thus, he would thoroughly study the texts until he was certain that he had grasped the Torah's intent, and then formulate his own reasoning accordingly. The result was, as Rabbi Shaul Kagan pointed out, not that Reb Aharon taught a *shiur*, but that the Torah talked through him.

Because of the difficulty involved in comprehending Reb Aharon's *shiurim,* the *beis midrash* was abuzz with interpretations, explanations and lively debates elucidating the Rosh Yeshivah's words. Reb Aharon was naturally party to the discussions, and he always made himself available to answer the students' questions. After davening, students would approach with their questions and difficulties, and the discussions lasted for hours!

Some students concluded that they were taking advantage of the Rosh Yeshivah and decided that they must allow him to eat his breakfast — sans interruptions. Reb Aharon would have none of this. He enjoyed talking in learning far more than any meal, and he was adamantly opposed to putting limitations on his accessibility. For this very reason, he would never permit a yeshivah administrator to allocate specific times when he was available for consultation.

REB AHARON could not forget the plight of his father-in-law, and constantly beseeched him to flee to Kletzk. Late one night, an assimilated Jew in Slutzk with strong connections with the Communist party barged into Reb Isser Zalman's house with a brief directive. He didn't say much, and that which he did say was whispered, but the message was clear: If the Rav wished to run for his life, the time left was negligible and rapidly diminishing.

When presented with such clear instructions, Reb Isser Zalman no longer debated where he belonged. Before sunrise, Rabbi and Rebbetzin Meltzer departed for Kletzk, to the yeshivah which was their home.

Reb Isser Zalman departed that same year to Jerusalem to become the rosh yeshivah of the Eitz Chaim yeshivah. His farewell was attended by all of Kletzker Jewry, who came to pay their homage to a giant who had founded their yeshivah in Slutzk. He could not have been leaving it in better hands.

Reb Aharon did not restrict his influence exclusively to the yeshivah, but took an active role in all affairs that affected Kletzk's Jewish community. He was intimately involved in the establishment of a *cheder* and Bais Yaakov school in town, and fought tenaciously against the plans to open a local secular school. Whenever Reb Aharon learned that a child had been transferred from the *cheder*, he did not rest until he could convince the parents to restore matters to their earlier state. He also personally made sure that the shops were closed on time on Friday afternoons — no matter what the weather.

Three

REB AHARON had a keen sense of his students' individual needs. For the boy of feeble constitution, he saw to it that a bottle of milk was provided every day. For the boy who could not afford a train ticket to visit his family, Reb Aharon made all the necessary arrangements. For the boy threatened with conscription into the Polish army, Reb Aharon not only secured emigration papers to Palestine, but arranged where the *bochur* would learn in Jerusalem. Reb Aharon's concern for every detail of the students' lives not only made a lasting impression upon them, but made them wish to be deserving of his love.

Most of Kletzk's first *talmidim* were severed from their families. Reb Aharon and his Rebbetzin showered these boys with love and concern. When students from Poland traveled home for Yom Tov, those from Russia were welcomed into the rosh yeshivah's house. Emotionally, spending the seder with Reb Aharon was second best to being at home, but as far as substance and meaning, it was second to none.

Little wonder that the Kletzk yeshivah's student population burgeoned. From its inception, the yeshivah's building — borrowed communal property which they had clearly outgrown — was never designed to be an academic institution.

The obvious solution was to construct a new building, an extremely ambitious plan for a yeshivah that could not adequately feed its students. Yet, thanks to Reb Aharon's tireless work, by 1927 adequate funds had been gathered to commence construction. In short order, the funds to continue the construction were depleted, and Kletzk was left with a partially erected structure and a permanently established debt. It was the worst possible scenario.

Someone — perhaps it was Reb Aharon himself — came up with the idea to proceed with the construction no matter how abysmal the debt, nor how much borrowing was yet to come. This seemingly foolhardy plan was deeply rooted in human psychology and sharp business acumen. The concept was that once the building was complete a gala *chanukas ha-bayis* could be held, and the enthusiasm generated would translate into funds that would cover the deficit.

The scheme was implemented, and after more than two years of construction a *chanukas ha-bayis* was held in the fall of 5689 (1929) in the presence of the rabbinic greats of Europe. One special guest came all the way from Jerusalem — none other than the former Slutzker rosh yeshivah, Reb Isser Zalman Meltzer. This beloved rosh yeshivah received a royal welcome, as befit a spiritual giant of his caliber.

Even the spacious new building could hardly contain the crowds, and the spill-over lined the surrounding streets and alleys. All of the religious schools were adjourned that day so that their students could also participate in the festivities. To top things off, the firefighter's band — that's right, the fire-chasers of Kletzk — managed to scratch out a few bars of *ashrei yoshvei vaisecha, v'tahair leebainu,* and *lulei Sorascha,* to the delight of the merry participants.

Reb Aharon's gamble more than paid off. The audience gave freely, many women removing the jewelry from their fingers and necks to help pay for Kletzk's new yeshivah. The contributions enabled the speedy completion of the final details of the building and the yeshivah finally moved into its own premises a few months later.

With this financial dilemma solved, another one came on its heels. Arranging another *chanukas ha-bayis* was certainly not an option, and the situation was so grave that the students were provided rations instead of full meals. Reb Aharon concluded that he had no recourse but to do that which was anathema to him: abandon the yeshivah in order to raise funds abroad.

Whenever this option had been aired earlier, he always rejected it out of hand, reasoning, "How good could a yeshivah be without a rosh yeshivah (on the premises)?" He then added tongue in cheek, "If I would be forced to travel abroad to collect for a yeshivah I would greatly prefer to represent one with an *active* rosh yeshivah..."

Reb Aharon set sail with the express purpose of establishing a financial infrastructure of steady

הגאון אהרן קאטלער קלעצקער ראש ישיבה קומט אן דינסטאג

ניו יארקער ארטאדאקסישע יו-
ם וועט דינסטאג קריגען א בע-
ון גאסט, איינעם פון די בע-
נסטע גאונים פון דער איצטי-
ט. דאס איז הגאון ר' אהרן
וועלכער האט זיך אזוי ווייט
ציכנט אין למדות נאך בעת
געווען א אינגעל, אז ווען ער
ט געווארען 22 יאהר איז ער
בעטרויט געווארען מיט דעם
ויבען אמט צו ווערען דער ראש
ה פון דער בערימטער סלוצ-
יבה, וועלכע האט שפעטער
צוזינען נאך קלעצק וואו די
פינט זיך איצט.

יכע גאון ר' אהרן קאטלער
עווען בערימט נאך אין
נע יאהרען אין סלאבאד-
אין בעקאנט געווען אלס
עלוי, וועלכער האט
שיבה מיט זיין חריפות.
נסקער גאון ר' מאיר
האט איהם דערזעהן
איהם איבערראשט
ט זיך אויסגעדריקט
: "איך האב זיך
לאבאדקער עלוי,
אז עלוי אפילו
עקיבא איגער".
עלוי איז מיט יעדען
געוואקסען און געוואקסען

קלעצקער ראש ישיבה אין וואשינגטאן ד. ס.

אין וואשינגטאן ד. ס. איז מאנטאג
פארנאכט אנגעקומען פון באלטימאר,
קלעצקער ראש ישיבה דער בערימטער
וועלט גאון ר' אהרן קאטלער שליט"א
אין בעגלייטונג פון מנהל הישיבה
הרב ר' שמעון גאדער. די געסט האבען
בעו ביים אנקומען געקראגען
גרויסארטיגע קבלת פנים. דעלעגא-
ציעס פון וואשינגטאנער אידען
פון שוהלען און אזוי ראבינאט,
הובבי תורה האבען מאסען מענשען
געבט בי זייער אנקומען אויף דעם
סטיישאן, און ענטהוזיאסטיש בע-
גריסט.

דער ראש ישיבה וועט פערבלייבען
אין וואשינגטאן שבת פ' ... ד און פון
דארט קומען צוריק נאך ניו יארק וואו
גרויסארטיגע קבלת פנים'ס ווערען צו-
געגרייט פאר דעם הישיבה'ן גאסט.

קלעצקער ראש הישיבה קומט היינט מיט דער מאדזשעסטיק

היינט קומט אן דער קלעצקער ראש-
הישיבה, הרב ר' אהרן קאטלער
שליט"א. די אגודת הרבנים האט
ארויסגעלאזט אן אויפרוף צו אלע
רבנים, און מוקירי והובבי תורה זיי
זאלען קומען צום שיף מקבל-פנים זיין
דעם גאסט.

הרב קאטין שליט"א פרעזידענט
פון אגודת הרבנים, האט צוגעשיקט
א לעטער אין וועלכען ער בעט איי-
נצולאדען איהם אין דעם קבלת-
פנים קאמיטעט פאר הגאון קאטלער.
די שיף "מאדזשעסטיק" קומט
אריין אין פיער 54 וועסט 14טע סט.
אומגעפעהר דריי אזייגער נאכמיטאג.

MONDAY, SEPTEMB

ראש-ישיבה פון
צקער ישיבה קומט
ארגעו, דינסטאג

אהרן קאטלער, דער ראש-ישיבה
לעצקער ישיבה, קומט קיין נ
מארגען, דינסטאג, 10טען סעפ
ע, מיט דער שיף „מאדזשעס
הרב קאטלער איז איינער פון
יכטיגסטע ראשי-ישיבה. צו 22

קלעצקער ראש ישיבה
וועט זאגען שיעור א
ישיבת ר׳ יצחק אל

דער בערימטער גאון, הרב
קאטלער, דער ראש הישיבה
בעריהמטער קלעצקער ישיבה
בעזואכט צו גאסט אין אמ
איז איצט שיעור דינסטא
זאגען א סעפטעמבער),
(הויזן עד ישיבת ר
טאג, אין
אמסטערדאם עוועני
רבנים און בעלי
נען געבעטן.

א חשוב׳ער ג
היינט, דינסטא
30
וועט
קבל
אין דער רוסישער שוהל, לאמבארד סטריט
פון אלע רבנים אין באלטימאר
פאר דעם גרויסען גאסט, פאר דעם שר התורה
הגאון האדיר מוה״ר
ר׳ אהרן קאטלער שליט״א
ראש הישיבה פון קלעצק
אין דער באגלייטונג פון דעם
מנהל הישיבה, הרה״ג שמעון גארע שליט״א
לע רבנים וועלען אנוועזענד זיין — בעלי בתים לומדים ווערען
בעטען צו קומען היינט אווענט און אפגעבען כבוד התורה צום שר
תורה און נהנה צו זיין פון די פערלדיגע דברי תורה וואס דער גאסט
עט זאגען.

supporters. His prolonged excursion to America in the winter of 1935 was somewhat successful as he managed to establish a small network of steady backers. His greatest success, however, lay in other areas.

Wherever Reb Aharon traveled he was an ambassador for the promotion of Torah study and *Torah lishmah.* He was dismayed by the low level of learning that he encountered in America, and blamed it on the absence of an exclusive Torah-learning environment. He shared his thoughts with the preeminent *mechanech* of America, Reb Shraga Feivel Mendlowitz, *menahel* of Yeshivah Torah Vodaas. Reb Shraga Feivel grasped the validity of Reb Aharon's claim; their discussion resulted in the inception of Bais Midrash Elyon in Spring Valley, New York, a forerunner of Torah excellence which has become standard in America today.

Reb Aharon's excursion lasted eleven months, an agonizingly long time, but in retrospect just the right period to establish the lay of the land and to acquaint himself with a country and its people with whom he would be doing the most important work of his life. Although no one knew it at the time, that trip sowed the seeds for the replanting of Torah in America.

Even after the trip, finances in Kletzk remained

a problem. During one of the yeshivah's more severe budget crises, Reb Aharon could not even provide the students' meals. The boys, realizing how difficult the times were for the yeshivah, and how much anguish the austerity caused the Rosh Yeshivah, refrained from making requests.

One *talmid*, however, was unable to adhere to this policy. His feet hurt and his toes were sore, so he turned to the Rosh Yeshivah. Reb Aharon did not conduct an investigation to determine how genuine the need was, or what provisionary arrangements could be adopted. In fact, he said nothing, handed the boy his own pair of shoes, and resumed learning.

REB AHARON'S influence was felt even beyond the municipal boundaries of Kletzk. He was among the youngest members of the Vaad Ha-yeshivos, but one of its greatest activists. Reb Chaim Ozer came to rely heavily upon Reb Aharon's advice regarding all matters of consequence to world Jewry. Other *gedolim* such as the Chofetz Chaim and Reb Elchonen Wasserman, both decades his senior, treated him like a colleague. Reb Aharon also assumed major responsibility in the leadership of Agudas Yisrael, and was a prominent participant in the *Knessiah Gedolah* in 1929, despite his relative youth. During that period he was not absent from a single meeting of consequence conducted by Agudah in either Poland or Lithuania, displaying a remarkable acumen for perceiving the problems of the time and advancing solutions for them.

Reb Aharon's strong affiliation with Agudas Yisrael was not a boon to his yeshivah's coffers. Zionist factions in Kletzk were less than enthused by Reb Aharon's Agudah connection, and were furious that he involved the yeshivah's students in such matters. These individuals were hardly passive in their opposition, and duly warned Rabbi Kotler that his activities were not without consequence, and would cost the yeshivah contributions. They also hinted — at first — that his outspoken anti-Zionistic declarations would imperil his safety.

The largest youth group in Kletzk was Zeirei Zion, a division of Poel Hazair. Reb Aharon fought vociferously against this movement and against a local "cultural school" that taught secular subjects under the pretense of religious studies. Rabbi Kotler announced from the pulpit that the education offered in this school was heretical; he thereby inflamed tender nerves not only in the nationalist camp, but even among the religious.

No one bothered to request clarification of this description, and a lynch mob arose to eliminate their nemesis. The malcontents reported to the Polish authorities the illegal status of the yeshivah students, and included the information that Reb Aharon was a wanted man and a draft evader.

Passions were becoming explosive and the powder keg was the shul where a nationalist speaker was invited to speak on Shabbos. The Kletzker Yeshivah was housed on the same premises, and the students had different plans for that time slot. They did not deliberately intend to interrupt or antagonize — they simply intended to go about their business of intensely (and noisily) engaging in Torah study.

Kletzk's foremost Zionist, an entrepreneur who owned a flour mill, called for quiet, but the *talmidim* continued to learn aloud. The mill owner screamed, yelled and clamored for silence, yet the *talmidim* dauntlessly continued their holy studies. The Zionist crossed the point of exasperation and began ripping *siddurim*. "Whoever tears holy books," Reb Aharon announced oracularly, "shall be torn himself."

In a fit of rage the man stormed out of the shul and entered his mill to oversee his Shabbos production. There, atop the grain chute, he lost his balance and slid down the shaft, where his feet were crushed by the grinding stones.

Reb Aharon was keenly aware of the consequence to those who earned his wrath. Half a world away and nearly three decades after this incident in Kletzk, a neighbor of the Beis Medrash Govoha yeshivah in Lakewood, New Jersey provided Rabbi Kotler and his students with significant anguish. This fellow claimed that the yeshivah was unduly noisy and, to accommodate his sensitive nature, Reb Aharon had the windows of the yeshivah closed during davening. Even in the summers, even in the hot sultry summers, even in the humid Lakewood summers before air conditioning had been installed.

One day a trouble-maker in the yeshivah deliberately opened one of the windows during davening, and this resulted in the neighbor opening up a floodgate of protest and invective. The fellow's unwarranted vilification was too much for the Rosh Yeshivah to bear and Reb Aharon had a few choice words in response.

Later that day, someone related to the Rosh Yeshivah that the attack had not been unprovoked, as a window had been opened during davening. Suddenly Reb Aharon turned very pale and somber and repeated numerous times, *"Ich nem zurick, ich nem zurick* (I take it back)!"

Four

THE FEEBLE resistance of the Polish army in the opening days of World War II enabled the Germans to conquer all of Poland in just two weeks. Kletzk, located in the eastern extreme of the country, was removed from the battlefront, but not from the new reality. The eastern sectors of Poland, in accord with the German and Russian alliance, were Soviet spoils. Only in comparison to the Germans, could the Russian conquest be considered an improvement.

The Russian goal of cleansing any vestige of religion was not curtailed by their sweep into

Poland, and the NKVD was an integral part of the occupying force. Just as before, the roshei yeshivah and yeshivah students were primary targets for the Bolsheviks.

With the outbreak of hostilities, yeshivah students left for home in a gut-wrenching exodus. Each departure disrupted the yeshivah and caused Reb Aharon great heartache. The Kletzker yeshivah had existed for nineteen years of relative calm, and the bonds of love and admiration between the students and the faculty were solid as granite.

Each farewell depressed their spirits further, and the uncertainty of the future filled them with gloom. Add to this the daily reports of atrocities, and the result was an atmosphere staunchly unfavorable to learning. Yet Reb Aharon weathered it all.

The Rosh Yeshivah made it very clear that marauding armies and secret police would not dictate when Jews may or may not learn Torah. In the midst of the turmoil, he called upon his students to strengthen their commitment to learning, for this was the ultimate test of one's commitment to serving Hashem. Reb Aharon's call was heeded and became a rallying cry for the remaining students as well as for numerous residents of Kletzk.

Meanwhile, connections with the world at large were severed, and income and resources could not reach the yeshivah. The residents of Kletzk stood by their rosh yeshivah and smuggled foodstuffs to him and his students, and provided other means of assistance. The shopkeepers sold their products to Reb Aharon on credit, in the hope that he would eventually repay them.*

The yeshivah maintained its full learning schedule for two weeks unfettered by the Soviets, until Sukkos 5699 (1939). The students, together with Reb Aharon, celebrated Simchas Torah just as in previous years, as each tried to make the most of what he knew could be their last Yom Tov together — perhaps their last Yom Tov alive.

All prepared contingency plans, yet none of them seemed especially safe or secure. Reb Aharon was terrified that the Communists would discover that he had been involved with the illegal yeshivah in Slutzk. It would not be the Bolsheviks' way to leave their account with him unsettled, and the way that they concluded matters always had a ring of finality to it.

Reb Aharon set off in pursuit of a safe haven,

---

*Via relatives of the local merchants, Reb Aharon repaid his debts when he arrived in America.

encountering Reb Elchonon Wasserman in Baranovitch. Reb Elchonon apprised Reb Aharon of the rumor that the Soviets intended to cede Vilna and the surrounding districts to independent Lithuanian jurisdiction. Escape could be plotted from neutral Lithuania to safer destinations.

Rabbis Elchonon Wasserman, Aharon Kotler, Moshe Blau

Reb Aharon continued on to Vilna, where many other roshei yeshivah had gathered to consult with Reb Chaim Ozer. The *gadol hador's* opinion was that all of the students must escape to Vilna. At once.

Reb Aharon conveyed instructions, and that night Kletzk's older students scattered into the fields to unearth the potatoes that would be their sustenance during their flight to Lithuania. Everything had to be done surreptitiously in order to avoid the suspicions of the Communists, who would never wish the yeshivah community to escape their clutches and the special cool reception prepared for them in the north...

Late the next night, without a word to a soul, Kletzk's remaining one hundred and fifty students divided into smaller groups that departed via horse-drawn wagons. When dawn broke, hysteria erupted throughout the town. The Jewish residents were beside themselves because the students had departed and their beloved yeshivah was abandoned. The Communists were furious because their plan to arrest and deport the incorrigible religionists had been foiled.

It was Friday morning when the Kletzker *talmidim*, careful not to leave a trail, arrived in Baranovitch. The distraught boys heard that Vilna was so teeming with refugees that it was pointless to attempt to squeeze in. Perhaps Reb Aharon, they reasoned, was not au courant with the situation, or perhaps it had changed since he had supplied them with their initial instructions. They were at an impasse until the rosh yeshivah's telegram arrived. He wrote that they must leave immediately and travel to Vilna by rail on Friday night. The implication of that ruling spoke volumes as to the gravity of the situation.

Reb Aharon's reunion with his yeshivah was bittersweet: They were together again, but Vilna was still not safe territory. They had fled under the assumption that Vilna would be returned to Lithuania under Russian protection, but this event had yet to occur. And if it didn't, they would have engaged in one of the most futile flights of the century.

Their prayers were answered on October 10, 1939 when the "mutual defense treaty" brought about Vilna's return to Lithuania. Thanks to the foresight of Reb Chaim Ozer and other roshei yeshivah, 2500 students — comprising numerous yeshivos — were able to resume their learning in Vilna and simultaneously plot their escape to safer shores.

Reb Aharon assumed the responsibility for his students' welfare. He knew that their safety in Lithuania was ephemeral. The Vilna time bomb would eventually explode with either a Nazi invasion or a Soviet annexation. Either way the future was bleak and a way to escape had to be found. Reb Aharon had already received entrance permits to Palestine for his family, but he refused to depart until he could acquire the same documentation for all of his students.

In a poignantly ironic twist, Reb Isser Zalman begged to differ with his son-in-law. Just as Reb Aharon could not convince his father-in-law to leave Slutzk, despite the personal risk he confronted, Reb Isser Zalman now could not persuade his son-in-law to depart Vilna as long as his students were still trapped. On one occasion Reb Isser Zalman wrote Reb Aharon that he was "sitting upon a volcano that would imminently erupt."

Reb Aharon did not need any analogies or similes to underscore the gravity of the situation, but he would not — at that stage — alter his policy. He sent telegrams to any person that he thought could be of help and dispatched a barrage of letters begging for documentation that would enable his students to travel abroad.

For the time being — for safety's sake and in the interest of securing a location better suited for learning — Reb Aharon moved his yeshivah out of bustling Vilna to the nearby village of Yanova. It was in the foreign environment of the Lithuanian countryside that the relationship between Reb Aharon and his *talmidim* became deeper and tighter than before. They were all "in the trenches" together, and Torah study was their sole ammunition.

The inevitable occurred in June, 1940, when the Soviets annexed the autonomous territory.

Reb Aharon greatly feared for the lives of his students and himself. They had escaped the Bolsheviks from Slutzk to Kletzk and then from Kletzk to Vilna. They were unlikely to avoid evasion a third time. Accordingly, Reb Aharon implemented the policy of Yaakov *avinu* and divided the yeshivah into three separate camps. The risk to the student body was now lessened threefold, but his personal security was proportionally increased as he regularly visited each outpost and delivered *shiurim,* despite the danger and the bedlam on the roads.

The Soviet annexation resulted in a massive deterioration of living conditions and an atmosphere of constant fear and terror. Material provisions all but disappeared, and Reb Aharon understood that it was time to reassess his policy of remaining until all of his students could also leave. Despite his incessant efforts, he had still not acquired the necessary documents for his *talmidim,* and every day his own chances of escape were dwindling. Perhaps, once he was free he would be able to accomplish more to secure their liberation.

It was a theory worth considering, but an encounter one Friday night rendered his dilemma academic. Reb Aharon was summoned for interrogation by the NKVD because of a document they found in the home of the suspect. They had discovered a page of Reb Aharon's notes on *hilchus avdus.* What greater crime could there be than promulgating revolutionary literature designed to upset the socialistic order of perfection for the proletariat?

Reb Aharon claimed in his defense that he was merely engaged in Torah research which far predated the Communist Manifesto. This presumptuous reply generated a barrage of ridicule about Judaism and its Torah. Even as a prisoner of boorish Communist thugs — NKVD officers no less — Reb Aharon could not remain silent when the Torah's honor was slurred. He declared that according to Stalin's 1936 declaration, as echoed in the Soviet Constitution, freedom of thought and belief were ensured. This defense was also a source of amusement to interrogators not renowned for their platonic pursuits or keen sense of justice. But Reb Aharon's tone of conviction and resolute mien gave them pause, and the officers decided to release the rabbi.

Reb Aharon had little doubt that his reprieve was only temporary, and he departed for Kovna, the fulcrum for all documentation and escape activity. As soon as it was learned that Reb Aharon was stranded in Kovno, associates in America pulled every string right up to the Oval Office to ensure that permission to emigrate was issued forthwith for the Kotler family.

Five

THE DAY of the Kotler family departure, the Vilna train station was filled to capacity with Jews who had come to bid Reb Aharon farewell and simultaneously to encourage his success in securing their release. Reb Aharon needed every blessing he received, as his trip was fraught with danger.

En route from Vilna to Vladivostock — a journey which crossed twelve time zones and the vast tundra of Siberia — the train made a scheduled stop in Moscow. The escaping Jewish passengers on board gladly waived this opportunity to stretch their legs and catch a momentary glimpse of Russia's impressive capitol. They would not do anything that might jeopardize their flight to freedom or draw attention to themselves.

Reb Aharon saw this stop as an opportunity to reach out to any Jew who had been isolated from his or her Judaism since the Bolsheviks came to power. He thus detrained, and as Rabbi Alter Pekier records, right there in the terminal Reb Aharon met Reb Zalman Leib Instulin, a *talmid chacham* of note who had been denied all access to Torah and the company of scholars for close to twenty years.

Reb Aharon re-exposed this gentleman to the sweetness of a serious Torah discussion, temporarily erasing the nightmare of abuse and persecution that he had suffered. When it came time to reboard the train, the two scholars tearfully embraced. Reb Aharon shed his coat and offered it to Reb Zalman Leib, who had only tatters to cover his weakened body.

REB AHARON possessed the proper documentation to continue on to America, but once he arrived in Japan he was in no rush to leave. A free man, he assiduously set about fulfilling his pledge to save his students. This entailed placing international phone calls to anyone who had visa connections, as well as visiting the consulates located in Kobe, Japan. Reb Aharon also encouraged the Europeans settled in Japan to depart for Shanghai, as the living conditions there were the same, and their departure would open the roster of the Japanese quota, thus allowing the immigration of additional Jewish refugees.

His efforts brought about a modicum of success, and several people owe their lives to Reb Aharon's intervention. The bulk of his efforts, however, were rendered worthless when the Soviets reneged on their commitment to allow emigration, even for those holding valid visas.

ONE DAY while in transit in Japan, Reb Aharon asked a young *talmid* of his from Kletzk, Reb Moshe Cohen, to escort him to a bank in Kobe. The two were already on line when a special alarm sounded, announcing that the Imperial ruler Hirohito was traveling through the streets. In those non-democratic days, during the very thick of World War II, the emperor was not merely the symbolic head of state. He was believed to be a direct descendent of the sun-goddess, hence supernatural, hence the object of elaborate pageantry and incredible homage. His public movements were carefully regulated and under no circumstances was a subject allowed to gaze upon him as he passed.

Thus the alarm was the signal for everyone to fall to the floor in an act of obeisance appropriate for those in the presence of a being akin to a god. Alas, Reb Moshe Cohen did not know the theology surrounding the tocsin and did as everyone else. It was not all that illogical to drop to the ground when you heard a siren during a war. Reb Aharon, however, like Mordechai *ha-Yehudi*, would neither neither bow nor bend.

Reb Aharon pulled off quite an act of insurrection and those in the bank knew just how to deal with it. From all sides servants of the emperor lunged at the infidel, knocking him — as inappropriate as the term sounds in this context — senseless. For days Reb Aharon lay in bed recuperating, but he felt no remorse for his actions.

IT WAS now time for Reb Aharon to continue his journey and he was impaled on the horns of a dilemma. His father-in-law, Reb Isser Zalman Meltzer, insisted that he travel to Palestine, while Reb Moshe Feinstein (according to the apocryphal legend) contended that he must travel to the *midbar* of America. It is reputed that Rabbi

Feinstein felt (according to the same dubious source) that only the well of Reb Aharon's learning was deep enough to water the desert of America and bring it to life with widespread Torah learning.

Reb Aharon could not resolve whose advice to accept. Would it be Jerusalem or would it be New York? He resorted to the *goral ha-Gra*, the method taught by the Vilna Gaon, in which one finds a Scriptural verse that indicates which direction to follow in a quandary. The *goral ha-Gra* fell on the following verse... "And God said to Aharon, go to Moshe in the *midbar* — desert" (Shemos 4:27).

Reb Aharon did as he was directed — as the Torah instructed him — and embarked to water the *midbar* of America.

Six

WHEN Reb Aharon came to America he looked as if he were still escaping for his life. Thoroughly indefatigable, he didn't lapse from his mission for a moment. After disembarking in San Francisco, he was on the phone with influential individuals in New York and Chicago. He departed for New York at his first opportunity because influential contacts were more readily accessible on the East Coast.

His arrival at Pennsylvania Station in New York City in April 1941 was nothing like his departure from Vilna's train terminal. Few in America had ever heard the name "Aharon Kotler" before, and a select delegation of those who were aware of his reputation assembled on the concrete platform. This skeletal welcoming committee consisted of individuals from the Agudas Harabbanim and Agudath Israel.

As the train rumbled closer, a tingle of excitement surged through the men. The great Kletzker rosh yeshivah, who had barely escaped with his life, would now settle in their midst. What an honor! Surely the *gaon* would turn his arrival into a festive occasion by pronouncing his sincere thanks at the welcome awarded him and offer some humble tribute stating his desire to be worthy of the hospitality afforded. Perhaps he would even use the opportunity to relate a simple Torah thought that the lay leaders, who had taken off time from their work to join in the welcome, would be able to appreciate. Other, similar conjectures were also aired.

Rabbi Eliezer Silver of Cincinnati, who had accompanied Reb Aharon on the last leg of his journey, was the first to step out of the car. Rabbi Silver, who was justly noted for his poise and enviable stage presence, lived up to his reputation. "I heartily introduce," boomed Rabbi Silver in his theatrical baritone, "my dear friend, the great *gaon*, who is the greatest Torah teacher of our generation. Rabbi Aharon Kotler and his family have succeeded in leaving the continent of blood and reaching our country. I am certain that he will raise the level of Torah in America. We will now be able to educate great Torah scholars here. May his coming be for peace and success."

The tiny assemblage, already pressed tightly together, took a mini-step closer to hear the expected boiler plate acknowledgment formalities. Reb Aharon looked at his audience — make that stared — and got straight to the point. To a man, the committee was left slack-jawed by his unexpected words: "European Jewry is being consumed in fire," he said in rapid, staccato Yiddish, "and the yeshivos have been destroyed. There is not much time left. Only you, the Jews of America, can save them!" Reb Aharon's piercing blue eyes stung the assembled. "*Now*, there isn't second to waste. *Save them*!"

The very next day Reb Aharon was on the phone asking those that he had met on the train platform what they had done. Every one understood that this was to be the first in a series of many phone calls to come…

Reb Aharon and his family had been saved through the efforts of the Vaad Hatzalah (emergency rescue committee) which had been formed by Rabbi Eliezer Silver at the behest of Reb Chaim Ozer Grodzinsky. Rabbi Kotler joined the Vaad and became its driving force.

Up until that point, American Jewish organizations had not made rescue work a priority, and even sections of the Orthodox community were tragically apathetic. Consider: At what was supposed to be a major fund-raiser for Vaad Hatzalah's efforts in early 1940, at the home of the reknowned philanthropist Joseph Shapiro, one of the most aristocratic members of America's Orthodoxy — featuring a guest speaker no less prestigious than Rabbi Joseph B. Soloveitchik — not a single soul showed up!

Reb Aharon infused the Vaad with the impetus that it needed. He insisted that the Orthodox groups stop their internecine fights and work together for the common goal of rescue. In other words, there could be only one umbrella group for all Orthodox relief and rescue efforts, mandating the fusion of Mizrachi, Young Israel, Agudath Israel, Union of Orthodox Jewish Congregations and the Agudas Harabbanim. The result would net greater resources and political clout for the coalition.

But even with this added muscle, the Vaad had great difficulty in courting the assistance of the established Jewish organizations: the Joint Distribution Committee and the American Jewish Congress. Relations between these organizations were in a steady state of deterioration because of a host of ideological reasons and antithetical modes of operation.

The Joint would act only within the law. As Aaron Rakefet details in *The Silver Era*, their policy was that as an American organization they were required to uphold the guidelines of the American government. In other words, sending desperately needed aid to the refugee scholars trapped in Shanghai would, in due time, become a reprehensible violation of the "Trading with the Enemy Act."

Although the Vaad leadership was loathe to violate the letter of American law, their primary allegiance was to Torah law, which mandated that everything must be done to save a life. As the future of the Jewish people, its Torah and its scholars were at stake, they believed that any and every effort to save the victims from the Nazi inferno were justified and legitimate.

The leader of acculturated American Jewry at the time, and certainly the most powerful figure in the established organizations, was Rabbi Stephen S. Wise, who had intimate connections with President Roosevelt and numerous cabinet secretaries. He was the quintessential Reform rabbi, with polished speaking skills and a liberal agenda that was foreign to traditional Judaism.

Rabbi Aharon Kotler, on the other hand, did not speak English and, as Amos Bunim points out in his father's biography,* was known by only a handful of Orthodox Jews. According to the criteria by which the majority of American Jewry gauged a rabbi at that time — oratorical abilities, stage presence, high-powered connections, political savvy — and not Torah scholarship — Wise was a natural leader. Rabbi Kotler seemed to be a relic of the shtetl, fitting into the prevalent stereotype of meek and otherworldly Torah scholars, devoted to studying irrelevant, arcane texts and incompetent to relate to the contemporary world or to enlightened man.

Although rabbis such as Rabbi Kotler were known to be at home with Jewish law, they were assumed to be at sea concerning matters of political consequence. Hence in their attempts to exert political influence and impact upon the Jewish community they were at a decided disadvantage. It was therefore in the Vaad's interest to work with the well-oiled establishment Jewish organizations in order to effect relief services and

*_A Fire in his Soul,_ the story of Irving Bunim (1901-1980)

lobby for the relaxation of immigration laws. More often than not, these organizations did not consider it in *their* own interest to cooperate with each other.

Reb Aharon maintained that the pitiful tokenism accomplished by these organizations in the realm of rescue was felonious. What the Rabbi could not have understood at the time was that their stand was a matter of policy. Wise and his colleagues supported FDR's exclusionist approach, which translated into unspeakable torture and murder for untold numbers of European Jews. Wise's primary concern was anti-Semitism on the home front, which, although a legitimate issue, made him shun any activity that could hint at dual loyalty. As a result, he was an apologist for FDR and his cabinet's policies, some of which were blatantly anti-Semitic.

Reb Aharon not only opposed the approach of acculturated American Jewry; he attacked its very foundation. Torah scholarship alone dominated every facet of Jewish life, from the kitchen to the political arena. Torah law dictated the parameters of rescue work even if it contradicted conventional reasoning and the law.

The Jewish establishment contended that the Vaad had no right to violate the British blockade of German-occupied territories, and they formed the Jewish Boycott Council. Efforts to help the sick and the starving were hampered by these groups which contended that British policy had precedence over humanitarian concerns. They even went so far as to picket the offices of Agudath Israel for sending food packages in 1941. Strife and animosity mounted daily between the Jewish establishment and the Vaad, but Reb Aharon could not be deterred from pursuing Torah directives that mandated that all must be done to save European Jewry.

To reach this goal he had no compunction against joining forces with any organization — even with Rabbi Wise on the few opportunities that this was possible — as long as it advanced relief work. Reb Aharon encountered criticism for these alliances, but he rejoined, "I would work with the Pope if it would save the fingernail of one Jewish child!"

Rabbi Kotler understood very well that the small, undermanned and underfunded Vaad would be more effective if it worked with other organizations. Ideology was not a factor when the real issue was saving lives. Nothing was a deterring factor if it could improve the dismal situation. Reb Aharon therefore saw to it that American dollars were sent to Torah scholars stranded in Siberia, despite the Soviet exchange policy that left no more than 20 cents to the dollar.

According to Bunim, Rabbi Kotler was challenged regarding the wisdom of this policy. He replied that minimum relief from maximum aid is better than no relief at all. Reb Aharon was later vindicated when survivors recounted how the meager amount that arrived meant the difference between life and death.

In late 1944, Yitzchak Sternbuch informed Reb Aharon from Switzerland that the Nazis intended to separate American Jewish POWs from the others. Their purpose was no mystery and Reb Aharon called his trusted assistant, Mr. Irving Bunim, to accompany him to Washington at once. Bunim rushed to the Rabbi's house, only to discover that he was too ill to travel. Bunim tried every creative means to convince the rosh yeshivah not to go — to no avail; Jewish lives were at stake, and every second was precious.

On the train to Washington, Bunim composed a memorandum on the POW issue which Reb Aharon adjusted, tweaked and eventually approved. To the great astonishment of this lay leader, Reb Aharon saw little point in having the paper delivered to the President. Although American Jewry was intoxicated with FDR, and considered him their genuine friend, Reb Aharon understood otherwise.

Accordingly, the memorandum was delivered to the President's Jewish assistant, David Niles, Jr., who conveyed it to the Supreme Allied Commander of the European Theater of War. General Dwight Eisenhower was so incensed by the insidious plan regarding the POWs that he employed his not-insignificant leverage to ensure Nazi noncompliance with Hitler's directive.

IN WHAT would have been the most important rescue effort of the war, known as the Musy Negotiations, 600,000 Jews were to have been freed by the Nazis in exchange for one million dollars. The Vaad had no way to raise such an amount and turned to the Joint Distribution Committee.

The Joint, of course, would have nothing to do with a plan involving trading with the enemy, which was a gross violation of federal law. As Amos Bunim records, the Vaad and the Joint nonetheless agreed to a meeting. Despite opposing agendas, an arrangement was finally worked out whereby the Joint would agree to forward the figure, provided the Vaad acquired a license from the United States government allowing the Vaad to transfer the money to Switzerland, whence it would be delivered into Nazi hands. The Joint was certain that this plan would never come to fruition.

There was but one man in the United States of America who would be able to sanction such a controversial plan, but based on his record, FDR was really the longest long shot imaginable. And yet, nothing could prevent Reb Aharon from trying, and a Vaad delegation set off for Washington. An audience with the President was not forthcoming.

The Rabbi's group was referred to the Secretary of the Treasury, hyper-assimilated Henry Morgenthau, Jr. Mr. Morgenthau had come a long way since his initial refusal to be of help to the Vaad, yet what the committee was currently seeking was way, way out of his league and he flatly refused. Reb Aharon ordered Irving Bunim, who served as his translator, "Tell him that if he cannot help rescue his fellow Jews at this time, then he is worth nothing, and his job is worth nothing, because one Jewish life is worth more than all the positions in Washington!"

As Amos Bunim records, his father hesitated, then said something that only vaguely resembled what Reb Aharon had dictated. Morgenthau looked relieved, convincing Reb Aharon that his precise message had not been translated. Reb Aharon then instructed that his *exact* message be translated, word for word. Bunim paused for breath and did as he was instructed.

Morgenthau's composure sank as he faced Reb Aharon's fiery stare. An awkward silence filled the room and the secretary placed his head down on the desk for what seemed like an eternity. He then sat up and dictated for Bunim to translate, "Tell the Rabbi that I am a Jew, and that I am willing to give up my life, not only my position, for my People." Morgenthau was as good as his word, but the deal was eventually scuttled due to Jewish intervention.

Seven

REB AHARON'S professed goal was to reestablish in America what had been lost in Europe. This dream remained in abeyance during the first part of the war when all of his attention was focused on rescue work via the Vaad Hatzalah. But when an opportunity arose in this direction he did not hesitate, despite any advice to the contrary.

Reb Aharon was invited to direct America's first *kollel*, located in White Plains, New York. From the time he took over it was clear that Reb Aharon intended to replant Kletzk and Slutzk in America and, given the local mindset, the idea seemed absurd and highly unrealistic. No one believed that a yeshivah whose goal was *Torah lishmah*, i.e., learning for its own sake, not for the sake of becoming a rabbi or a Talmud teacher, would work in America in the 1940s.

Reb Aharon countered that the current yeshivah system in America, where boys learned a few hours of gemarah for just a few years, *would* never and *could* never produce Torah scholars capable of plumbing the depths of the Torah. Consequently, America would be unable to maintain the *mesorah* and produce *gedolim*.

Reb Aharon's bleak prognosis did not resonate as a disaster to American Jewry. A groundswell of support did not suddenly materialize to confess "guilty as charged." As a matter of fact, the "So?" response to Reb Aharon's accusation was almost audible.

The mindset at the time was to "get ahead," regardless of whether this impacted negatively on one's Torah accomplishments or mitzvah observance. Parents understood that a handsome livelihood entailed sacrifices, but at least their children would not have to undergo the hardships that they had experienced making it in the New Land. This was a high-falutin' way of saying "college education" which took precedence over all other pursuits.

Reb Aharon's approach flew in the face of everything they had believed. There was hardly *a* supporter or contributor to Reb Aharon's yeshivah who believed that the Kotlerian sans-secular approach would last. Financial betterment was always associated with long-term secular education; thus, if any yeshivah intended to maintain its student body and parental loyalty, it had to conform to this reality.

Reb Aharon was implacable, and his approach did not even entail a polite "nothing doing." His yeshivah would not veer from the European model; and to better enable this goal, he sought a location away from the tumult of the City. Establishing the concept of *Torah lishmah* in America was going to be an uphill battle; doing it in New York City would be nearly impossible. A search for an "out of town" property was undertaken, resulting in the acquisition of two adjacent homes in Lakewood, New Jersey. One would serve as a *beis midrash,* the other as a dormitory.

Despite Reb Aharon's promulgated policy on the matter, some of the yeshivah's early supporters once again recommended that secular studies be introduced into the yeshivah, as was customary in other yeshivos in America. Reb Aharon did not allow them even an additional nanosecond to articulate their idea. "I shall not be at the helm," he declared emphatically, "or even employed by a yeshivah that has secular studies. I would prefer to be a wretched *shamash* in a deserted shul, and if such a job is not available then I shall call out to my Father to take my soul for I have no place in America." Lest anyone misinterpret his short speech as melodramatic histrionics, he then fainted, making his point gravely clear.

Reb Aharon's fierce opposition to secular studies was a matter of deep-seated ideology. He considered such study an unjustifiable waste of time whereby one trades Godly knowledge for temporal wisdom. Its pursuit could only be harmful to Torah learning, as it would fill up the mind with non-vital information. He also deemed it an insult to the Almighty, as it implied a preference of man-conceived ideas over those of Hashem. And, just maybe, Reb Aharon was aware of the fact that had his sister had her way and introduced him to secular studies in Minsk, he might have ended up "Professor Kotler," instead of the rosh yeshivah revered by the entire Torah world.

Regardless, the social conditions in America were not in Rabbi Kotler's favor. The cities were populated by a multitude of immigrants and by masses of wage earners, most of them at the bottom of the social ladder, struggling to better their economic and social position. In *Progress and Poverty*, Henry George complains about the materialistic appetites and prevalent lust for wealth, "Get money — honestly if you can — but at any rate get money! This is the lesson that society is daily and hourly dinning into the ears of its members."

Such a mindset was not exactly a fertile breeding ground for a corps of Torah learners, nor did the inheritance left by the earlier wave of immigrants ease Reb Aharon's mission. *Chillul Shabbos* was rampant, and a generation was being raised without a Jewish education. Nature abhors a vacuum, and the well-organized and adequately budgeted Reform Movement jumped into the breach feet first. The challenge that religious leadership could offer was pitiful, until Rabbi Kotler commenced his revolution.

The White Plains Kollel provided 12 students, and Beth Medrash Govoha was in business. A board of directors assumed the financial responsibilities of the school, enabling Reb Aharon to devote himself exclusively to the spiritual dimensions of his position. This arrangement did not last long, however, thanks to Reb Aharon's own undoing of the system.

Reb Aharon could never retreat from the needs of world Jewry to the seclusion of his *beis midrash* in Lakewood. He was intimately involved with Hatzalah work, and later with many other projects including Torah Umesorah, Moetzes Gedolei HaTorah, Chinuch Atzmai and spear-heading the opposition to plans and undertak-ings detrimental to the primacy of Torah in America and overseas. What all of these causes shared in common was a priority of Jewish con-tinuance, and a desperate need for funds.

As the *manhig hador*, Reb Aharon was inci-sively aware of all Jewish needs and he never made his own yeshivah a priority over a more pressing cause. He therefore felt no compunction in turning to the supporters of Beth Medrash Govoha to solicit funding for a different neces-sity, effectively denying Lakewood access to these contributors.

Reb Aharon's policy was that other yeshivos were not competitors, but partners in *Torah lishmah*. This admittedly noble approach was self-defeating in terms of fund-raising. It eroded the initial arrangement whereby he was not to be involved in the yeshivah's finances, for, under the conditions that Reb Aharon had created, the board of directors could not raise the capital that they had envisioned.

Thus, Reb Aharon had to assume the role of Lakewood's chief fundraiser. This entailed, among other things, spending four days a week in his apartment in New York and the balance — without his family — in the yeshivah where he lived in the dormitory with everyone else.

When Reb Aharon would depart to his home in New York from Lakewood, he would be handed some fruit for the journey. Reb Aharon instructed his Rebbetzin to make a precise accounting of what fruit was *not* eaten, and to compensate the yeshivah accordingly. That which was eaten en route, he reasoned, was *tzeidah la-derech*, but the rest was personal gain, an expense that should not be borne by the yeshivah.

Along these very same lines, the Rebbetzin assumed that food that was supplied to her by the yeshivah was meant to be consumed only within Lakewood city limits. Therefore, whenever Rebbetzin Kotler traveled to New York* she would calculate exactly how much food to bring along for the journey.

As a matter of course, she purchased only inferior fruit and vegetables for her own family so

---

* Originally the Kotlers lived in Lakewood; this NY-NJ arrangement was later adopted.

as not to overtax the yeshivah budget. Stale bread from the yeshivah's dining room reappeared in her own to complement the yeshivah's leftovers, which the Kotlers ate six days a week.

The same woman who would never throw out food provided by charity funds would also never accept a check from the yeshivah until she had depleted all her cash resources.

Rabbi and Rebbetzin Kotler celebrated the marriage of their son at Beth Medrash Govoha. Reb Aharon kept a careful account of every cup or plate broken, as well as other minor expenses incurred during the *simchah,* so that he could later reimburse the yeshivah.

Because he often stretched out to rest during his commutes from Lakewood to New York, occupying two seats on the bus, Reb Aharon would insist on paying double fares.

Reb Aharon's son, Reb Shneur, who succeeded his father as rosh yeshivah, carried on the family tradition. Once a California millionaire with no relatives signed a check to the Lakewood Yeshivah after Reb Shneur had visited him and encouraged him to increase his yearly donation of one hundred dollars. The very same day, the rosh yeshivah received a call from the tycoon's aide, informing him that the benefactor had passed away before he could fill in the amount on the check. "Rabbi," the aide asked, "tell me how large a check you'd like. There are millions of dollars sitting in the bank and no heirs to collect them. It's either Sacramento or Lakewood."

Reluctant to take more money than the donor might have intended to give, Reb Shneur promptly responded, "One hundred dollars, like every year."

And, as Reb Aharon taught so well through example, integrity often entailed more than just money. He had completed a fund-raising mission to Montreal and was headed home, totally unaware that his close friend, the Satmar Rebbe, would also be departing Quebec on the very same train.

A party about thirty strong escorted the Rosh Yeshivah to the train station to bid him farewell. As soon as they arrived they found a far larger contingent gathered to send off the Satmar Rebbe. Reb Aharon asked the gentleman in charge of the logistics of his journey if it would be possible to board the train without passing through the crowd assembled in the terminal.

Not familiar with alternate routes, his guide turned to a railroad employee and posed the question. The man pondered the request, and after he was handed $10 came up with a solution. *"Après moi,"* he instructed.

The group followed the conductor out of the terminal and onto the tracks. Soon they were abreast of the New York-bound train, but did not board the platform. The sleeper accommodations were in the lead car and the procession continued — single file — passing perilously close to a train departing to Ottawa, until the trainman announced that they had reached their destination. Their collective sigh of relief could have been heard in the caboose.

As the party escorting the Rosh Yeshivah issued their final goodbyes, one of them had the temerity to inquire what the strange routing was all about. Reb Aharon explained that had they gone the conventional way through the terminal, people might have mistakenly concluded that he was the intended recipient of the honor arranged for the Satmar Rebbe. Ten dollars and a circuitous detour was well worth not misleading others or detracting from someone else's honor.

Eight

BECAUSE REB AHARON was in charge of the yeshivah's finances, significant sums of money passed through his hands, none of which ever ended up in the Kotler home. His family was sustained by a very modest salary, and his personal needs and wants were negligible. When the yeshivah administration decided unilaterally to raise the Rosh Yeshivah's salary, he blocked the idea and banished the notion. When his family switched apartments in Brooklyn, wealthy supporters seized upon the opportunity to secretly furnish the new abode with tasteful furniture. Reb Aharon and his rebbetzin were most vehemently opposed to this plan and refused to enter their new quarters until the fancy furniture was removed and the old "spare parts" were restored.

The poverty in the Kotler home was so extreme that the notebooks that the Rebbetzin maintained read like a farcical spoof on the Depression Era: *I borrowed 3¢ from my neighbor; owe the store 2¢* etc. Even necessities were at a premium, and in Reb Aharon's case this meant there was a dearth of *sefarim*. Any entry-level yeshivah student had several-fold more *sefarim* than this *gadol hador*. Basically, he owned a *shas*, and everything else was borrowed from neighbors.

The neighbors were only too happy to lend their *sefarim* to Reb Aharon; aside from being a great honor, the books that otherwise would have remained gathering dust on the shelves, achieved a scholarly, well-used, heavily worn look. Family members were given the task of fetching *sefarim* from neighbors, and they were assisted by Marvin Schick, then a student at City College, who lived nearby and always made himself available for favors.

Every year Reb Aharon would deliver the *Shabbos Ha-gadol drasha* in the Agudah on 14th Avenue. One year, in preparation for the *shiur*,

Rabbi Kotler asked Marvin to borrow a *Minchas Chinuch* from the (well-stocked) Agudah library. A few days later the Agudah librarian asked the young man to return the books that he had borrowed, as he had taken them out under his own name.

Marvin Schick did not have the gumption to ask Reb Aharon to return the *sefarim* so he bought a *Minchas Chinuch* and presented it to Reb Aharon with a cumbersome and elaborate excuse of how he had "received" an anonymous gift for the Rosh Yeshivah. While he was there delivering the "gift," he "remembered" that he had to return the library's *Minchas Chinuch*.

The next day Reb Shneur visited Marvin Shick with a message from his father. The gist of the communication, delivered with the ultimate in urbanity and tact, was that even performing a favor for the Rosh Yeshivah cannot warrant veering from veracity.

As far as Rabbi Kotler was concerned, he was nothing less than a millionaire. Rabbi Shaul Kagan relates an address Reb Aharon delivered to the students at the conclusion of Yom Tov. They were all gathered in the yeshivah's dining room singing a familiar tune to the words of the Psalmist, "Were it not for Your Torah being my delight,

I would have succumbed to my poverty."

Reb Aharon stood up and called a halt to the singing. "Listen to what you are saying!" he implored. "*Tanach* attests to the fact that Dovid *Hamelech* was one of the richest men in history. And yet he felt himself thoroughly impoverished and bereft of possessions aside from the Torah." And with that cameo interpretation of a common song, Reb Aharon succinctly expressed why *he* lacked not a thing in the world.

In the early days of the Lakewood yeshivah, the chairs in the dining room were selected (it appeared randomly) from stores that had closed down. This contributed to the overall ambience of the bare bones simplicity that pervaded every aspect of the yeshivah and Rabbi Aharon Kotler's life. The meals were quite plain, and on Shabbos Reb Aharon would join the *bochurim* in the dining room. His first matter of business was always to enter the kitchen and wish the employees a "*gut Shabbos*." He would then engage the *talmidim* in a lively discussion of Torah content.

It was through learning that Reb Aharon established a bond with his *talmidim*. As Marvin Schick points out, despite the considerable age difference between the Rosh Yeshivah and the students, and despite the even greater cultural gap — they were, by and large, typical American boys — he was able to relate to them and to earn their respect and devotion. Admittedly, many of the students could not grasp Reb Aharon's brilliant *shiurim* and a good number could not even comprehend his rapid-fire Yiddish. The boys spoke Americanized Yiddish that was different in vocabulary and diction from the Rosh Yeshivah's European speech. Yet what communication could not establish, warmth and love achieved.

The *talmidim* were intimidated by Reb Aharon's intensity and towering brilliance. But

it was the same fire that burned within him and made them tremble, that also warmed their hearts and assured them that they were heading down the proper path. Reb Aharon used the opportunity afforded by the yeshivah's communal meals to strengthen the boys in their resolve. He would occasionally relate stories about *gedolim* of pre-Churban Europe and also join the singing of *zemiros*. This was always a near-hilarious scene as Reb Aharon, the *Litvishe* rosh yeshivah, would instruct a student to *"**zug** (say) a niggun."*

When the cholent was served it was not nearly as flaming as Reb Aharon, who was heatedly relating intricate concepts. Alas, Reb Aharon could maintain his heat far longer than the dish, and when the students finally did manage to eat their meal it was usually no longer warm. Rabbi Yitzchok Dershowitz, who has recorded valuable biographical and anecdotal information about Rabbi Kotler, attests that the newcomers to the yeshivah deemed it inconsiderate for the Rosh Yeshivah to talk to the boys at that time — until they comprehended that he was teaching them a nourishing lesson in *ahavas ha-Torah.* In short order they ingested that in the presence of Reb Aharon Kotler the least important aspect of the Shabbos meal was the food.

Just about the only time he was not talking

to the *talmidim* in learning was when he was unable to, such as when he had washed his hands for bread. But he was certainly absorbed in learning even during those moments. One Shabbos Reb Aharon cut the challah and was *motzei* the yeshivah in *lechem mishneh.* In the process of slicing the bread, he inflicted a deep incision on himself, cutting into one of his fingers. The Rosh Yeshivah was thoroughly unaware of what he had done until he saw a puddle of blood on the table and then traced it to his hand.

Be it in the yeshivah, at home or on the road, Reb Aharon never focused on the food that he was eating but rather on the discussion that he was conducting. He brought the *beis midrash* with him to the table, only occasionally allowing the fork to fulfill its function — invariably on auto-pilot. Rebbetzin Kotler attests that Reb Aharon never ate without an open *sefer* adjacent to his plate. Other witnesses corroborate that he left over a sizeable amount of what he was served, in fulfillment of *ta'anis ha-Ra'avad* which stipulates that refraining from becoming satiated reminds diners of their spiritual purpose and they can achieve atonement. It was not uncommon for Reb Aharon to forget to eat altogether.

Nine

IF SOMEONE would discuss, argue or challenge Reb Aharon in learning by quoting an unfamiliar source, the Rosh Yeshivah would immediately incorporate this knowledge, and reason in accordance. Rabbi Kotler's uncanny ability to immediately assimilate information never ceased to amaze his disputants. They had studied and mastered the esoteric opinion, and Reb Aharon had just heard it for the first time, yet he mastered it at once!

Whenever they challenged him, questioning how he could employ a source that he not yet learned, he would reply, *"Ich hob yetz gelernt* — I just learned it now!" To this scholar, hearing information was absorbing wisdom, and its application was immediate.

It is hard to imagine any greater fulfillment of the talmudic dictums, "One should always be as soft as a reed..."(*Ta'anis* 20) and "A *talmid chacham* that boils over, it is the Torah [not the person] which is agitated" (*Taanis* 4) than Rabbi Aharon Kotler. His dealings with people were soft and pleasant; he would stroke children on the cheek and exude fatherliness to total strangers. But once the discussion moved into the arena of Torah learning, there were no holds barred. It was not uncommon for him to flare into a rage and shout, exactly as the Talmud says, "boiling over."

An ancillary explanation that attempted to explain Reb Aharon's conduct would probably be along the lines of trying to convince someone that nighttime was day; make that arguing that night was day while the speaker is explaining something of paramount importance. Reb Aharon's Torah concepts were well calculated with impeccable logic and air-tight substantiation. To dispute them made as much sense as to posit that the sun rises at night.

Those who asked the "nighttime during the day" variety of question would be shot down at once. Once a *talmid* decided to elicit a predictable reaction by posing a question from the non-clever medley in order to provoke an outburst from the Rosh Yehsivah. Reb Aharon, with his discerning brilliance, looked up for just a second, ascertained the motivation behind the query, smiled, and calmly continued the *shiur* without responding to the question.

Most were wise enough not to challenge Reb Aharon during a *shiur*, but there were a few lion-hearted who had the umbrage to frequently enter into *hari kari* discussions. Reb Moshe Eisemann, one of the yeshivah's prize *talmidim*, was among those who had the gumption to challenge and question Reb Aharon's positions in learning. Eisemann's questions were always the catalyst for stormy debates that included raised decibels and elevated blood pressure.

On one occasion, Rabbi Eisemann raised an objection which triggered the usual thunder, but he didn't back down. Suddenly the weather forecast darkened substantially and the thunder erupted into an electrical storm which caused everyone to tremble, but still Rabbi Eisemann held his ground. By this point the fire within Reb Aharon could neither be contained nor harnessed, and lightning struck all around, thunder following almost without pause.

Finally (and understandably), Rabbi Eisemann gave up and — in keeping with the overall climatic conditions — stormed out of the room. Yet, Reb Aharon was still not done with him. The esteemed rosh yeshivah finally finished his tirade with the instructions, "*Varf em arois* – throw him out." One of the students present apprised Rabbi Kotler that Moshe Eisemann was no longer there. Reb Aharon's comment was, "*Breng em arein, und varf em arois* — bring him in, and throw him out!"

Since Torah was his life, Reb Aharon took it very, very seriously. In this regard his passion was contagious and he could inflame even the most sedate individuals. On one visit to the home of Reb Shmuel Greineman, he paid his respects to the sage's nephew, the Chazon Ish. This scholar was clearly one of the most calm and dignified men to ever walk this planet. Still, their Torah discussion sparked into a vociferous argument. Suddenly the Chazon Ish, "Rabbi Composed" and the persona of quintessential serene tranquility, joined Reb Aharon in the fray. Rebbetzin Shoshana Eidelman, who had lived in that house for decades, had never seen anything like it; in fact she couldn't believe her eyes. She ran to Rebbetzin Greineman at a loss if she should call the police or the ambulance, for she was certain the two *gedolim* were about to come to blows.

And yet the Talmud also states that one must be as soft as a reed. No contradiction: A meeting of roshei yeshivah was taking place in the Kotler home and Reb Aharon excused himself. His grandson Yaakov Eliezer was crying and that evening the Rosh Yeshivah was in charge of that domain as well. Rabbi Kotler begged everyone's apologies and went to tackle the problem.

How would the famous rosh yeshivah — with a house full of prestigious guests — deal with the issue? After all, how much of an asset is it to be one of the generation's greatest minds and the most outstanding *talmid chacham* when a toddler is bawling?

Those gathered around the table did not have long to wonder as they heard the lightning-fast *gaon* utter in nursery sing-song, "*Hakoneis zoan l'deer* – one who enters a *ziggeleh,* a white little *ziggele* with fluffy wool all over..." and thus the Rosh Yeshivah continued lullabying the *mishnah* until... the crying stopped. To the disappointment of the captivated audience it took but one *mishnah* to do the trick.

RABBI PAYSACH KROHN (*In the Footsteps of the Maggid*) relates how, during World War II, Reb

Yankel Kviat wished to escape annexed Lithuania on the basis of a letter from the already defunct British Embassy. Kviat's plan was to take a train from Kovno to the port of Memel in the hope that there he would be issued a visa based on the all-but-worthless letter he possessed. Reb Aharon felt that the plan was foolhardy and that attempting to leave Soviet territory would surely earn Reb Yankel a one-way ticket to Siberia. Yet Yankel was adamant, and set off from Yanova to catch a train.

A few hours later a telegram arrived, stating that a visa would indeed be issued at the port. Reb Aharon departed for Kovna at once. The train station was thoroughly mobbed and bedlam reigned. Reb Aharon began calling out, "Yankel, Yankel Kviat!" Even at the top of his lungs the Rosh Yeshivah could barely be heard over the din. He darted back and forth, scanning the swarms of people for his *talmid*.

Reb Aharon then climbed onto the platform and tried to get the attention of the passengers on the train, all the time calling out, "Yankel, Yankel Kviat!" From car to car the Rosh Yeshivah searched, banging on the windows, trying to locate a single individual among the thousands of refugees, passengers and escorts. Rabbi Kviat might have already departed, have booked a later train, or have abandoned his plan. Still, Reb Aharon kept up his feverish search.

Finally, in the last car of the train, Yankel heard the banging on the window and saw his rosh yeshivah. "What's the matter?" he called from within, all fear and trepidation.

"Yankel, don't worry!" Reb Aharon reassured with a sigh. He held up the telegram to show that everything was arranged. "You can travel without fear, *l'chaim ul'shalom*!"

Ten

REB AHARON'S schedule in New York did not allow respite, and it was rare that he found time even to eat a modest meal in his apartment late at night. The few fleeting minutes that he allocated to dinner were inevitably interrupted by visitors and phone calls. The Kotler family believed that after such a hectic and fast-paced day it would be wiser and more healthful if their father's post-midnight meal were to be eaten in peace.

Reb Aharon begged to differ. According to Rabbi Alter Pekier's recording of events: "Do you think," he glowered, "that people come to me for their enjoyment? They come in the hope that I will be able to help them with the problems that burden them."

Not all of the family members found this reasoning compelling, and surreptitiously took the phone off the hook during mealtime. But once Reb Aharon caught on, this policy was abolished.

Managing a burgeoning yeshivah, tending to the needs of *klal Yisrael* and being available for countless personal queries, meant that the Rabbi simply did not have time to eat, certainly not in a steady manner. Rabbi Yitzchok Dershowitz relates how one student who was assigned to drive Reb Aharon around New York noticed Rebbetzin Kotler placing a wrapped piece of cake into her husband's jacket. "Maybe, maybe," she explained, "he'll feel something bulky in his pocket, and maybe, maybe he'll insert his hand to discover what it is, and maybe, maybe he'll open it up, and maybe, maybe he'll actually eat it. Otherwise he won't eat a thing all day long!"

The whole world seemed to rest upon Reb Aharon's broad shoulders, but somehow there was room up there for solitary individuals and their petty little problems too...

It was Friday afternoon when one youthful Mr. Epstein came to visit his friend Mr. Levy who was learning in Lakewood. The two rehashed old times until it came up in conversation that Epstein was owed five dollars by Camp Agudah. Apparently this debt was a source of significant anguish to Epstein, and once he got on the subject, he couldn't abandon it.

His friend Levy had the perfect solution.

Why, Rabbi Aharon Kotler was the head of the Moetzes Gedolei HaTorah, which was connected somehow to Agudah. "Everyone knows," Levy assured, "that the Rabbi has a lot of pull in the organization." Therefore, Levy plotted, "Tonight when you go around to say *'gut Shabbos,'* tell the Rosh Yeshivah how Camp Agudah stiffed you five dollars."

Admittedly, this story would be far more plausible had it occurred in the Lakewood Cheder, but honest and true, it took place in Beth Medrash Govoha, in the year 1959. And do you think that Epstein, the 17-year-old visitor, had any compunction approaching the Lakewood rosh yeshivah and *gadol hador* on Shabbos about his five dollar dispute? No way.

Here was the classic elephant gun let loose on a flea, nay, the bazooka being used on a mosquito. But Levy was quick to remind his friend that he had a legitimate claim, and that Reb Aharon was always the first to bring about justice.

Thus, Friday night, as Epstein wished Reb Aharon *"gut Shabbos,"* he also apprised him of Camp Agudah's long-standing, four-month-old debt. *"Gut Shabbos,"* replied the Rosh Yeshivah.

A few days later Epstein received five dollars in the mail. A year later he returned to Lakewood for Shabbos. When his turn came to wish the Rosh Yeshivah *"gut Shabbos"* Reb Aharon usurped the initiative by asking, *"Hut ehr shoin kegruggen?"* (Did you receive it?)

Bein ha-zemanim – yeshivah intersession — was approaching and Reb Moshe Carlebach, a *talmid* in the yeshivah, came across a "drive-away" scheme that would get him to his home in Detroit for a fraction of the regular cost and in significantly less time. The only catch was that in order to cash in on this deal he would have to leave yeshivah two days before *rosh chodesh* Nissan to drive the sponsor's car to Detroit.

Reb Moshe approached the Rosh Yeshivah and explained his thorny predicament. It was

Reb Aharon's position that two more days in yeshivah were worth more than all of the savings in both time and money.

Two days later, on *rosh chodesh*, Reb Moshe approached Reb Aharon once again, this time in parting. Instead of reciprocating by putting out *his* hand, Reb Aharon reached for his wallet and asked, "How much do I owe you?"

When a different student wished to leave the yeshivah a few days prior to intersession to land a job so that he could afford a new pair of pants, Reb Aharon again vetoed the plan. Rabbi Kotler realized that there were extenuating circumstances, the boy being an orphan, but why should he have to suffer more because of his tragedy and leave the yeshivah prematurely? Without any hesitation Reb arranged for a new suit of clothing to be delivered.

When this very same *talmid* wished to leave Lakewood in order to acquire rabbinic ordination (an honor not bestowed at Beth Medrash Govoha), he approached Reb Aharon to part good-bye. As a rule, leaving the yeshivah for the purpose of *semichah* was something that Rabbi Kotler did not approve of, but the Rosh Yeshivah realized that this case was different. As an orphan, the boy was understandably concerned about his source of income. The Rosh Yeshivah therefore — contravening his standard policy — told him to remain put and *personally* issued him rabbinic ordination.

BETH MEDRASH GOVOHA'S administrators were embarrassed by the paltry salary Reb Aharon agreed to accept, but nothing they could do could convince him to accept a raise. He was not open to negotiation — he would not even allow his grandchildren to attend the yeshivah tuition-free.

The Rosh Yeshivah's wardrobe was the sparse minimum. He was clean and neat, but never would he buy a new hat, jacket or any other item of apparel unless he was thoroughly convinced that he could no longer wear what he already possessed.

The Kotler apartment was furnished with old, unmatched chairs, and a worn-out couch. Well-meaning *baalei battim* sought, on numerous occasions, to better furnish and enhance his home, but he would not hear of it — claiming that it was a pity to squander Jewish money.

And they weren't the only ones who tried to better the situation. After rendering a decision in a significant *din Torah*, both parties paid Reb

Aharon a substantial fee for services rendered — stipulating that the money was earmarked for personal expenses in his home. Reb Aharon, whose policy on this matter was well-known, accepted the check. He then handed it over to the yeshivah's coffers, explaining with a twinkle in his eye, "There is no doubt that the yeshivah is my home..."

Beth Medrash Govoha before and today

Eleven

REB AHARON'S devotion to Torah learning defies description. Despite physical weakness, he never languished in his learning. He once explained his approach in light of the Rambam's words (*hilchos Talmud Torah*): "One who wishes to acquire the crown of Torah should be careful not to squander his nights eating or sleeping, discussing or the like, but should engage exclusively in *talmud Torah* and the words of wisdom." The value of a crown, explained Reb Aharon, is assessed by the composite of all of the jewels which comprise it.

A flawed crown is of insignificant value — even though the individual stones may be very precious. Accordingly, there is but one way to acquire the "*kesser Torah*" and that is through an "entire" process. Forfeiting just one night of Torah learning results in an imperfect, flawed crown.

To adorn himself with this crown, Reb Aharon treasured and utilized every moment. He never walked at a leisurely pace — for speed-walking was a more time-efficient way to arrive at a destination. While plotting his escape from Poland, he and his associates would listen to the military news on the radio and between dispatches, during pauses in the broadcast, or when static made the news momentarily undecipherable, Reb Aharon would consult his gemara as if he was listening to a *shiur*. During his train ride across Communist Russia, where mortal danger lurked along every inch of the way, he conducted himself as if he was sitting at a *shtender* in a Vilna *beis midrash*.

Twenty years later, nothing had changed. Rabbi Avraham Stefansky, a Lakewood student, drove Reb Aharon to an Agudah convention and they arrived as delegates and guests milled about in the lobby. If those present had blinked, they would have missed their fleeting glimpse of the rosh yeshivah. In his typical style, Reb Aharon zoomed inside, passing Reb Moshe Feinstein and other prominent *gedolim*, and was off to his room.

Rabbi Stefansky made great strides — literally and figuratively — to keep up with the Rosh Yeshivah and this was no facile endeavor. Rabbi Stefansky opened the door for his mentor and Reb Aharon noticed to his horror that the room was not equipped with a table and chair. The escort understood at once what his mission was.

When he returned to the room a few minutes later with the minimal furniture, he found Reb Aharon lying on the bed writing his *chiddushim*. Despite the absence of the proper facilities, not a second had been lost.

Avraham Stefansky noticed, on numerous occasions, that the Rosh Yeshivah would open his ever-present notebook and begin writing exactly where he had left off, without ever referring backward or pausing to gather his thoughts, even if he hadn't made an entry in hours — or days!

One student from the yeshivah who was assigned to drive Reb Aharon was astounded by the amount of learning the Rosh Yeshivah managed before, after — and presumably during — meetings, as well as on and off the road. The boy had picked up Rabbi Kotler directly after breakfast, and there wasn't a single let-up or slowdown the entire day. Each hour was crammed with meetings, solicitation visits, interviews — enough to make an average person yearn for a vacation and a less stressful occupation.

Throughout the day, Reb Aharon's sole nourishment was a small apple. It was close to midnight when the two finally arrived at the Kotler home. Reb Aharon entered the apartment, emitted a painful *krechzt*, and hurried into the living room. "I've not yet learned today!" he moaned, looking as though he had just become aware of a terminal condition. In fact, he held a *sefer* in his hands throughout the day and constantly consulted it, unless he was "talking in learning" with the driver.

Reb Aharon reached for a gemara and sat down with great haste. When the Rebbetzin brought out a bowl of soup, the Rosh Yeshivah declined the meal and requested that it be given to the exhausted driver. After a day like this outside of the *beis midrash*, Reb Aharon had no time to eat.

Because Rabbi Kotler was so astute, he often figured out the end of the story long before the narrator had completed his rendition. Thus, after grasping the point during a recitation, Reb Aharon would offer his opinion or comment. He wanted to assist, but he did not want to waste his time...

Basically, his conduct was unwavering and predictable. Reb Aharon carried a *Mishnah Berurah* wherever he went, and it is hard to find a snapshot of the Rosh Yeshivah without locating that *sefer* within the frame. Even when dealing with matters of life and death — the kind of issues that could make the lionhearted tremble — he still invested every free second in studying the *sefer* that was always in front of him. Even between dialing a number and the onset of the ringing, he would immerse himself in learning.

Countless witnesses recall the familiar pose of Reb Aharon holding the phone in one hand and a *sefer* in the other. Rabbi Kotler once noticed that a *bochur* was thoroughly agog at how the rosh yeshivah managed to squeeze so much learning into a phone call (unbeknownst to the yeshivah benefactor on the other side of the line). "You see," Reb Aharon said to the boy, "you must learn when you are young [and have time]!"

Invariably, Reb Aharon followed the same practice every time he entered his home: He would rush over to the bookcase, remove a gemara, and get straight to work. The urgency in his stride was manifest, the economy of his motions measured. Only after he had accomplished what he had set out to in this sphere, was his mind at ease so that he could proceed with the other obligations that weighed on his shoulders. No matter what it was that he did next, it was never without a *sefer* within arm's reach.

Rabbi Kotler informed his wife about the ten or more calls that had to be made, and she eagerly fulfilled her part of the partnership. The Rebbitzen would dial the numbers and hand the Rosh Yeshivah the phone only when the party was already on the line. She managed to reduce his *bittul Torah* to a fraction of a second. As soon as he finished the call he would place the receiver down — the very handset that he had just held in his hand — as if it wasn't there. The Rebbitzen would then replace it on the cradle and begin the next assignment. She would have it no other way.

Long before Reb Leib Heiman became the rav of the Bayit Vegan neighborhood of Jerusalem, he was a young student in the Lakewood yeshivah. He was once visiting the Kotler home and Reb Aharon, of course, was sitting with an open gemara. The Rabbi's appointment book was on the table and he asked Reb Leib to read to him the phone number of an individual that he had to call. Alas, Reb Aharon's personal phone book was not a masterpiece of order, and names and numbers were scribbled down in haphazard abandon. Reb Leib managed to find the name of the man that was supposed to be called, but he could not find a phone number, juxtaposed, in proximity or even in the greater area of that page.

Rabbi Heiman expressed his difficulty, and the Rosh Yeshivah thought for a long second until he remembered the phone number that he had heard once, days earlier. A flash of a smile adorned Reb Aharon's face over this achievement, and it was not missed by the Rebbetzin who had just entered the room. She immediately grasped what had happened, and commented under her breath, "What a pity that such a head is being used for *narishkeit*." Reb Aharon's smile, which had long since disappeared, was replaced with a deep blush.

Just a few minutes later, Reb Leib opened up the curtain off the living room in the Kotler home to bid farewell to the Rosh Yeshivah and he saw a scene that was not intended for his eyes: the Rebbitzen was begging *mechilah* for what she had said. Thus was the conduct of those two spiritual giants disguised as flesh and blood.

Twelve

GENERALLY, even before Reb Aharon returned home at night, the house would fill up with people who sought his advice. When Reb Aharon finally arrived — whenever that would be — he followed his usual routine, making a beeline for a gemara, and in many ways he looked no more at home than anyone else who was there. He would afford his attention to everyone who had come to see him, but it was hardly at the expense of his learning.

Hard to imagine and equally difficult to describe, he somehow managed to do both simultaneously. On one particular night the house was brimming with so many people that the din was similar to a market. Rebbetzin Kotler was concerned that the Rosh Yeshivah, engrossed in his gemara, was not following all that was being asked and said.

She therefore approached her husband, but before she could even express what was on her mind Reb Aharon reassured, "*Ich hob altz gehert* (I heard everything)," and then to prove the point he repeated what had been said that evening, as if he was reading from a stenographer's text.

Reb Aharon's frequent travels to and from Israel were made without any fanfare. Customarily, his first stop from the airport in Lod would be at the home of Rabbi Mordechai Shulman, his relative and the Slobodka rosh yeshivah in Bnei Brak. One witness related how he saw Reb Aharon step out of the taxi, haul his suitcase out of the trunk and then personally drag it up the stairs.

Reb Aharon was let into the apartment and then, as usual, he went straight to work. Once Rabbi Shulman realized who had entered he sent word to the yeshivah that Reb Aharon had just arrived and a delegation should come immediately in order to wish "Shalom Aleichem." Rabbi Kotler appreciated the gesture — probably — but it was hard to tell as he was so engrossed in his gemara (*Menachos, daf 12,* no less!).

A contingent about twenty strong arrived in the apartment, and each one timidly walked over and wished "Shalom Aleichem." As each boy went by, Reb Aharon tilted his head partially out of the gemara to acknowledge the politesse, and quickly returned it to its proper venue.

Reb Shraga Feivel Mendlowitz was overwhelmed by Reb Aharon's efficient employment of time. He related how the two of them once strode hurriedly toward the elevator on their way from an important meeting — a forum which gravely discussed a matter of the greatest importance to the Jewish nation — when Reb Aharon muttered, "Now Rabbi Akiva Eiger's *kasha* is resolved."

A word of explanation is indicated here: Reb Akiva Eiger's *kashas* are the benchmark of ultimate erudition in the world of Torah scholarship. Comprehending one of these queries requires significant aptitude and thorough immersion in the subject. To resolve such a question surpasses the ability of many of the greatest minds of the yeshivah elite. And yet Rabbi Aharon Kotler, who undoubtedly was fully involved in the issue being discussed, was able to switch gears in a manner so quantum that it defies comprehension.

His mental capabilities were so unsurpassed that he cried because he had never experienced the *tza'ar* of not comprehending the gemara. The difficulty that, well, we all have with translating words and comprehending the simple intention of the gemara was a phenomenon that Reb Aharon had never experienced. He bemoaned the fact that he lost out on an aspect of learning that everyone else shares.

At a meeting of roshei yeshivah, Reb Yitzchok Hutner, the famed Chaim Berlin rosh yeshivah, related a story about a Torah scholar who had not been blessed with an especially good head who nevertheless managed to overcome this disability with his incredible diligence. After this fellow became engaged, his prospective father-in-law began to wonder how much the groom would excel in learning.

He brought his dilemma before one of the Torah giants of the day, Reb Yehoshua Leib Diskin, who assured him that there was nothing to worry about. "כל המקיימה מעוני סופה לקיימה מעושר" "Engaging in Torah study with only meager means, will ensure — ultimately — a rich reward." The absence of intellect would be more than compensated for by his son-in-law's dedication and devotion and result in riches. And sure enough, the couple lived a happily married life, and this *masmid* developed into a reknowned *adam gadol*.

No sooner had Rav Hutner finished his account,

then Reb Aharon stepped out of the room. Rav Hutner was afraid that there was a connection between what he had said and Reb Aharon's exit, and he therefore followed on his heels.

There in the hallway, face against the wall, he found the Lakewood rosh yeshivah, silently sobbing. "What have I said?" queried Rav Hutner all concern and apprehension. Fighting back the tears Reb Aharon found his voice and wept, "I never acquired these riches..."

The fact that a student, even without a superior intellect, could achieve productive contentment in Torah through extensive effort was something foreign to Reb Aharon, and it moved him to tears. He was envious of the man whose diligence alone could get him so far, and cognizant that the riches promised to those who "fulfilled in poverty" were something that he would not acquire.

Rabbi Shaul Kagan attributed Reb Aharon's legendary diligence *not* to intellectual pleasure or to a sense of duty, but rather as the consequence of the deep fulfillment that Torah learning provided him. Every additional word that he mastered contributed to a fuller dimension of life. Rabbi Kotler said as much when interpreting the gemara (*Sukkah* 46): "The ways of God differ from the ways of man." Unlike mortal man, God may add to a vessel that is already full. It is possible to inject Torah non-stop into the soul without fear that it will swell beyond capacity. Just as a child's height and weight increase as he grows, so does man's soul. The more Torah learning, the richer and the more expansive the soul.

When Rabbi Shlomo Heiman, the rosh yeshivah of Torah Vodaas, passed away, Reb Shraga Feivel Mendlowitz invited Reb Aharon to take over the *shiur*. Reb Aharon complied, and Reb Shraga Feivel realized that he had gotten far more than he had bargained for. Until then he had not fully fathomed how brilliant Reb Aharon truly was. Without any hesitation, he requested Reb Aharon to become Torah Vodaas's new rosh yeshivah. Rabbi Kotler replied that he was flattered, but he had his own yeshivah. He had accepted this interim position only in order to minimize *bittul Torah* in Torah Vodaas during the transition period.

IN ORDER to rectify the dearth of proper educational facilities in America, the *gedolim* and roshei yeshivah created an umbrella network which they called Torah Umesorah. The director and visionary behind Torah Umesorah was Reb Shraga Feivel Mendlowitz, or, as he referred to himself, Mr. Mendlowitz. Although an accomplished scholar himself, Reb Shraga Feivel ensured that all of Torah Umesorah's decisions and policies be administered by a board of Torah leaders, and Reb Aharon was appointed as the head.

Reb Aharon would never allow his involvement with an organization to be merely symbolic or titular, and he played a seminal and dominant role in Torah Umesorah. The questions that he dealt with ran the gamut of Jewish life in America. Some of the questions that arose included issues of co-education, the involvement of non-Orthodox elements, and the like, dilemmas that rarely surfaced in Slobodka, Slutzk or Kletzk.

Reb Aharon, who had spent his entire life in the *beis midrash*, was still savvy about the problems of the day, displaying a remarkable comprehension of the nuances of American Jewish life. He understood very well what could and what could not be accomplished in the United States, and his criteria regarding schools focused upon whether the educational institution in question was sincere and serious in its goal of elevating its students to higher Torah knowledge and observance.

As Marvin Schick points out, if the above criteria were fulfilled, then there was room to countenance practices that would not be acceptable in other settings. Such decisions, however, could only be taken by an individual who was immersed in the organization.

Gedolei Torah have always been involved in a number of organizations and it is presumed that their guidance and leadership direct and instruct all policy decisions. This assumption mandates reflection.

All great rabbis have overwhelming responsibilities to study and to teach, to write and counsel, and to lead their disciples, among countless other demands. All of these obligations are taxing and overwhelmingly time-consuming — without the additional burdens of organizational life. A *gadol* is thus faced with the following questions as he embarks upon organizational life: Should he become involved in a limited way — perhaps just peripherally — in which case his influence, let alone control, would be limited; or should he take the helm of the organization in question, as a result of which he becomes even busier and more burdened? Such a decision is hardly whimsical; the consequences will seriously affect the rest of the man's life.

As Marvin Schick has highlighted, with the possible exception of Reb Chaim Ozer, no other *gadol* in recent generations has matched Reb Aharon's involvement in organizational life, consistently assuming the position of leader. No matter what he was involved in, he was always the pre-eminent influence. The only accurate English title would be "general." Even when he consulted with his colleagues he would politely inquire as to their opinion, and then dogmatically assert, "This is what we are going to do," whether they were in agreement or not.

For Rabbi Kotler, being the head of an organization did not mean simply making decisions. It meant carrying them out. If this entailed — and it always did — making countless phone calls, enduring lengthy car rides, raising colossal funds, convening last-minute meetings, lobbying politicians and businessmen, estranging supporters

Rabbis Reuven Grozovsky, Yaakov Kaminetsky and Aharon Kotler

of his own yeshivah — so be it.

Largely as a result of Reb Aharon's influence, by the 1950s the roshei yeshivah emerged as the dominant authority in Orthodox life in America. The prominence that these scholars achieved was inevitably at the expense of pulpit rabbis, and not all of these rabbis took kindly to the reduction of their influence. They claimed that their sway had been usurped and the prestige of their position had been undercut. Furthermore, they alleged that the roshei yeshivah responsible for this deterioration also discouraged their students from entering the rabbinate and respecting synagogue life.

As the leading rosh yeshivah of that period, Reb Aharon, although not singled out by name, was the focus of their invective. The accusation was not only inaccurate, but reflected a total ignorance of Rabbi Kotler's modus operandi. He was not in the least a negative person and would never engage in disparaging remarks about others. *Petty* is the last description that would fit him, and as Marvin Schick — who had so much interaction with Reb Aharon in public matters — points out, Rabbi Kotler was generally warm and friendly toward synagogue rabbis, even when their views did not coincide.

Thirteen

REB AHARON'S principles were rooted in his unswerving commitment to *emmes*. No matter what the issue — even acquiring the desperately needed funding for Beth Medrash Govoha — his *emmes* could never be compromised.

For example, the yeshivah's ever-deficient operating budget paled next to the funds required for construction of its new building. Fund recruitment was in high gear and every single lead in this regard was assiduously pursued — until the yeshivah's executive director was sure that he had hit the jackpot! Two affluent brothers agreed to donate $75,000 to the building fund — provided that a different party would contribute $5,000 toward the same goal.

Albeit the stipulation was a bit, well, bizarre; the yeshivah's executive committee was nonetheless confident that since this particular individual was a consistent supporter of Beth Medrash Govoha, everything would work out. Their optimism, however, was misplaced, as the man was incensed and highly insulted that others dared to dictate how he should donate his charity. Accordingly, the deal — this critically vital, save-the-yeshivah-in-the-eleventh-hour deal — was off.

Then one of the ingenious members of the executive committee came up with the innovative idea that if this man were to solicit $5,000 for the yeshivah from his friends , then the money could legitimately be labeled "his donation," enabling the yeshivah to collect the highly-craved $75,000 pledge. Reb Aharon, however, would have no part of this conspiracy. To his mind the stratagem amounted to *g'neivas da'as* (deception) and was therefore forbidden.

Likewise, Reb Aharon forbade the publication of a brochure that included the architect's sketch for the building under construction. The artwork depicted greenery that did not (yet) exist, and therefore was misleading and untruthful.

Reb Aharon once visited a wealthy individual — object: fund solicitation for Lakewood — but his mission was unsuccessful. He did not give up immediately and tried several different approaches in an effort to elicit a positive response. This all came to an end when he discovered that this potential contributor had helped fund the construction of Heichal Shlomo, the seat of the Israeli Chief Rabbinate.

Heichal Shlomo was otherwise entitled the "World Spiritual Center of Judaism" which, to Reb Aharon, and many other *gedolim,* smacked of halachic revisionism — an august authority, as it were, that could add or detract to Torah observance. The fact that the Israeli government supported the establishment of Heichal Shlomo was a worrisome sign that the institution would be subject to political influence.

Reb Aharon switched gears and focused exclusively upon the mistake of contributing to Heichal Shlomo. It was a violation, he maintained, of the commandment to heed the counsel of the Sages. Once Reb Aharon saw that his words were having an effect, he abandoned the original purpose of his meeting, confident that his visit was a success after all.

Men who accompanied Reb Aharon to the offices of rich businessmen were left slack-jawed and aghast by the reproofs he awarded the very same people from whom he wished to solicit funds for his yeshivah. Reb Aharon was simply unable to avoid pointing out the error of their ways — no matter who they were. His escorts couldn't see the business sense of this policy; they considered it injudicious and highly unproductive. Reb Aharon replied that Lakewood can fall, but *daas Torah* cannot be altered!

Countless times Reb Aharon risked, if not in fact relinquished, financial support for his yeshivah because he would not remain silent when *kavod ha-Torah* or *da'as Torah* was at stake. An American entrepreneur donated a significant sum to Lakewood and humbly asked in return that the Rosh Yeshivah bless him as he was about to depart to attend the *chanukas ha-bayis* of Heichal Shlomo in Jerusalem.

Reb Aharon placed the check on the table and it was rebuke, *not* a blessing, that he offered. Further, Reb Aharon stated that it was forbidden for the man to attend the ceremony! The philanthropist politely explained that his father-in-law was being honored at the event, and his absence would be an egregious insult. Reb Aharon viewed the matter differently and would not relent. Needless to say, the unsolicited censure cost this benefactor's future support, but money could never influence Reb Aharon to compromise Torah ideology. Never.

Reb Aharon solicited a large contribution from a fabulously wealthy man who related that he prayed in a Conservative Temple. The Rosh Yeshivah did not respond so as not to embarrass his host, but when this fellow asserted that the Conservative Movement was building Judaism in America he crossed, trespassed, invaded and assaulted Reb Aharon's red line. Reb Aharon wished to set the record straight, "The Conservative Movement is *not* building Judaism, but destroying it!" the Rosh Yeshivah stated most firmly. "Their anti-halachic declarations and conduct are as productive as cancer to the body."

The millionaire let it be known that Lakewood should look elsewhere for financial support, now and forever more. Rabbi Aharon Kotler had no regrets.

One *talmid* who was privy to the daily hardships Reb Aharon underwent as he collected funds for the yeshivah once asked him if the strain and inconvenience weren't too much to bear. Reb

Aharon explained that he gladly accepted the lot that the Lord had given him. He then added, "Since you are aware of all that *I* must do, then it behooves *you* to apply yourself even more to learning!"

Reb Aharon never forgot to acknowledge the fortunate few who appreciated the value of Torah study and afforded it their full support. Thus, when he prepared to take a two-hour taxi-ride to Long Island to attend a wedding on a sweltering summer day, everyone tried to dissuade him. "It's far too hot to travel," concluded one of those present. "Think of the time you'll waste," argued a second. "Some of the guests will undoubtedly be immodestly dressed," offered yet a third.

None of this reasoning had any impact on Reb Aharon, who retorted, "The bride's father supports Torah, and he must therefore be accorded all due recognition." Likewise, at the funeral of Samuel Kaufman, one of the original supporters of Beth Medrash Govoha, Reb Aharon eulogized him even though it was Chanukah, when eulogies are forbidden for everyone but Torah scholars. Reb Aharon set the public record straight, stating that a Torah supporter is equal to a Torah scholar.

On Manhattan's Upper West Side, religious Jews of every stripe attended a parlor meeting for the Lakewood yeshivah. Reb Aharon related to the potential donors the Chofetz Chaim's interpretation of the verse in Proverbs: [The Torah] is a tree of life for those who grasp it, and its supporters are praiseworthy. "In the World to Come," explained the sage, "everyone will be engaged in Torah study. The greatest scholars of all time will be delivering lectures, the Rashba, the Ritva — but what possible enjoyment could a *baal ha-bayis* derive from *shiurim* that will be way above his comprehension. This hardly seems to be a praiseworthy situation!

"But this is precisely what this verse is teaching: In the World to Come the supporters of Torah — in merit of their dedication and sacrifice — will be taught and know just as much as the most erudite roshei yeshivah."

Therefore, continued Reb Aharon, supporting Torah not only ensures the World to Come, but it is also the means to become a *talmid chacham* in the Next World.

Present in the audience was a layman, a staunch supporter of Beth Medrash Govoha, who was friendly with Reb Aharon from the time they had been together in Slobodka. This fellow, barely able to contain the note of cynicism in his voice, questioned the Rosh Yeshivah, "Come on. Do you mean to say that in the World to Come I will be as big a *lamdan* as the Rosh Yeshivah? How could I possibly attain the very same level?"

"*Kimt eich,*" replied Rabbi Kotler. "You deserve it. *S'kimt eich,* it is truly coming to you."

"But how," this flabbergasted *baal ha-bayis* persisted, "could this be? How could my donations to a yeshivah ever make me deserving to be as great a *lamdan* as the *gadol hador*?"

Reb Aharon, without a second's hesitation, explained, "For you have given up this world, while we who engage in Torah study all day long merit to have both the World to Come *and* this world!"

There, on Manhattan's Upper West Side, time stood still for a moment as the assembled pondered the Rosh Yeshivah's words. He allowed them into his ken and the purview was revolutionarily ingenious. It was an apotheosis of a kind. To the Rosh Yeshivah, that is, according to Torah ideology, the pitiful *baal ha-bayis* was wasting his time — but would yet be rewarded for the sacrifice he made to enable others to utilize *their* time. Regrettably, the *baal ha-bayis* had never experienced the joy of comprehending a Rashba and for that enjoyment he had to substitute such trivial pleasures as a comfortable home, a steady pay check and elaborate vacations. *Nebach.*

GRATITUDE was also a factor Reb Aharon never neglected when it came to Torah supporters. Late one night he raced into the dormitory and woke a student with the instructions that he gather a *minyan* to pray for Rabbi Emanuel Laderman of Denver who had taken ill.

The groggy student hesitated, suggesting that perhaps the *tefillos* could wait until the morning, for he did not think that the other students would appreciate being awakened at that hour. That was not an option for Reb Aharon.

"This is not a matter of convenience," Rabbi Kotler explained with unmistakable clarity. "It is a matter of gratitude, and therefore it is urgent and cannot be delayed or postponed. During the emergency campaign to rescue Jews during the War, I cabled all of the rabbis, stating that not a second could be wasted. Rabbi Laderman, at three o'clock in the morning, was the first to respond. It is only right that we use this opportunity to reciprocate."

When the incumbent Indiana Senator, Homer

Capehart, sought reelection against liberal Democratic challenger Birch Bayh, the former trailed in the polls. When Reb Aharon learned about this, he instructed every Orthodox rabbi in Indiana to lobby for Capehart, as the senator linked funding for Chinuch Atzmai to then-Secretary of State Dulles' foreign-aid package for Israel.

Amos Bunim was given this mission, but was not especially successful. Each rabbi he called explained that he was a liberal, and intended to vote for Bayh. Reb Aharon was very distressed by Bunim's report. "I see that I must personally teach them a lesson in gratitude regarding one who has labored for *klal Yisrael,*" Rabbi Kotler concluded. "Amos, you know the numbers, get them on the phone for me!" Over and over, Reb Aharon explained to these rabbis Torah law in the matter of gratitude.

Reb Aharon was consistently grateful to those who labored for Torah causes, and created a warm and loving relationship between himself and numerous lay leaders who were not especially learned and invariably modern in their orientation. This never stopped Reb Aharon from genuinely respecting these lay leaders and affording them and their families deserved appreciation.

Fourteen

BUILDING the infrastructure for *Torah lishmah* and simultaneously bankrolling it entailed perpetual rejection and scorn. Yet these hardships never depressed Reb Aharon; they caused him to apply himself even more. As recorded in Irving Bunim's biography, Rabbi Kotler used to say, "We have to do this and the *Ribbono Shel Olam* will help us. If we freely give of ourselves with *mesiras nefesh,* He will do the rest."

Others not only found it hard to subscribe to this perspective, but found the corroboration a tad wanting. There are many such examples, including the time Reb Aharon devoted his entire day to fund soliciting and all he had to show for his exhausting efforts were five dollars! Reb Aharon swore his driver to secrecy for fear that such information might discourage anyone from ever aspiring to become a rosh yeshivah.

Reb Aharon certainly had a point, the driver thought, but he was still beside himself as to why this had become the sorry lot of the roshei yeshivah. Reb Aharon explained that running around from city to city attempting to collect money is akin to "exile" — the punishment meted out to one who kills accidentally. Since many roshei yeshivah have hurt their students' feelings — albeit inadvertently — they must pay a price to atone for the anguish they have caused. The rabbinic approach is that hurting feelings, even unintentionally, is tantamount to killing. One who kills accidentally must be banished to a city of exile; therefore, they had to undergo this hardship.

When Beth Medrash Govoha's cash reserves sank to a pitifully low level, a wealthy New York businessman offered to donate a significant amount to the yeshivah provided that an affair be conducted where he would be photographed with the Rosh Yeshivah. Thus far, his request — while not an approach Reb Aharon would have encouraged — was within the realm a major contributor was entitled to request. But when this benefactor further insisted that these photos be published in the two Yiddish dailies, *Der Tag* and *Der Forvitz*, Reb Aharon could no longer agree. These two newspapers were *m'challel Shabbos* and for this reason Lakewood never used their services.

Reb Aharon's intransigent policy was heartbreaking to the deprived students, but he mollified them by assuring, "God will yet provide and we shall not suffer. A *chillul Hashem* is a route that we may not follow." The wealthy patron finally rescinded his condition when he saw that Rav Aharon could not be swayed, and donated generously without imposing any conditions.

Once Irving Bunim and his son Amos accompanied Reb Aharon to seek a donation from a tycoon in the building trade. After being forced to wait in the outer office for three-quarters of an hour, Amos could not contain his irritation over the degradation Reb Aharon was suffering. The Rosh Yeshivah's time could have been so much more productively invested in working for *klal Yisrael*, delivering a class, or talking with his *talmidim*.

Reb Aharon attempted to console his livid friend by relating, "Remember this all your life:

From the time that Moshe Rabbeinu had to break the tablets of the Ten Commandments, anything connected with genuine Torah must be accompanied by hardship and humiliation. If activity for the sake of Torah does not entail difficulty, then you must be concerned about the authenticity of the Torah connection. Not everyone merits to support Torah study and is afforded this privilege."

On one occasion Amos Bunim accompanied Reb Aharon to seek support from a wealthy man who had only insult but no funds to offer Rabbi Kotler. Bunim was infuriated at the affront to *kavod ha-Torah*, and was quick to stand up for Reb Aharon's honor. Again Reb Aharon corrected him and explained that Amos was sorry for the wrong man. According to the Bunim biography, Reb Aharon clarified, "I forgive any personal insults, but you should really pity this man who does not have a share in supporting Torah learning."

The Rosh Yeshivah was once scheduled to depart for Cleveland on a fundraising trip for Beth Medrash Govoha. He refused to leave, however, until he received a guarantee that his mission would not be harmful to the Telshe Yeshivah, located in a suburb of Cleveland. He was assured that the Telsher roshei yeshivah were eagerly awaiting his arrival, and had even arranged a meeting between Rabbi Kotler and a wealthy, not-yet-religious businessman, who had donated handsomely to Telshe.

Apparently this gentleman was not similarly inclined toward Lakewood. Au contraire. He launched into a rabid and interminable tirade against the yeshivos and nothing Reb Aharon could do or say could stop the venom. When the man finally finished his vitriolic excursus, the Rosh Yeshivah was instructed to leave though a side door that fed into the warehouse — the corporate version of the "back of the bus." Weaving around forklifts and skirting workers loading racks, a secretary caught the rabbi's attention with the trusty ol' index-finger-and-thumb-depressing-the-tongue shrill whistle and wrote him — in accordance with her instructions — a paltry check.

The insult upon insult was too much for Reb Aharon's escort to bear, and he insisted that the miserly check be refused. Reb Aharon feared that such a course might end up being detrimental to Telshe, which had coordinated the appointment. As long as the insult was "only" personal, Reb Aharon accepted it with equanimity and incredible self-restraint.

Fifteen

WHEN THOUSANDS of Jews fled to France from Algeria in the wake of that country's independence, they were easy prey for missionaries who knew just how to take advantage of those lacking food and shelter. Reb Aharon was determined to counteract their aggressive proselytizing, and convened a meeting of prominent roshei yeshivah including Rabbis Moshe Feinstein, Yaakov Kaminentsky, Yaakov Ruderman, Yitzchak Hutner, Avraham Kalmanowitz, and Gedaliah Shorr with the head of the fund-allocation division of the Joint Distribution Committee, Mr. Willie Jordan. Also present was youthful, clean-shaven, Shmuel Klein who was Rabbi Kotler's assigned driver for the day. On the agenda was the creation of yeshivos and religious schools to serve as an alternative to the missionaries' attractive offer.

As host, Jordan, a Yiddish speaker, chaired the meeting and opened with, "Gentlemen, in which language should we conduct out meeting?" The unanimous reply was, "Yiddish."

Although the politesse was offered, it was hardly intended, and Jordan continued, "It suits me to conduct the discussion in English." This should have augured decisively as to where this meeting was headed, but when the lives and souls of so many Jews were at stake, the goal was all that mattered to Rabbi Kotler.

Rabbi Kalmanowitz was appointed the spokesman for the roshei yeshivah, as his command of English was the best. Still, it was not lost on Willie Jordan that Reb Aharon was in charge of the visiting delegation. The JDC official was skeptical — as a matter of fact, downright scornful — of the proposed plan, and he did not attempt to couch his disapproval in anything less than insult-ridden invective directed squarely at Rabbi Kotler.

The roshei yeshivah were outraged at the

insults hurled at the *gadol hador*, yet Reb Aharon was thoroughly oblivious to the affront and remained focused on the purpose of his arrival at the Joint office. His personal honor was meaningless to him; the plight of these hapless Jews meant everything to him.

Rabbi Kalmanowitz introduced each of the roshei yeshivah, but Jordan wanted to know who the young man was and what he was doing there. Albeit Rabbi Kalmanowitz was Rabbi Kotler's spokesman that afternoon, now that someone else's honor was compromised, Reb Aharon quickly took the floor. "Duss iz Rabbi Klein," the Lakewood rosh yeshivah shot back.

It was then back to business and Reb Aharon instructed his translator to relate that there was an opportunity to save Jews from *shmad* — forced conversion, and they had a holy obligation to do everything within their power to prevent this catastrophe. Jordan didn't buy it. "Have you ever been to Marseille?" the official wanted to know.

Reb Aharon admitted that he had not, but he was nonetheless familiar with the situation. Jordan countered that he had personally been to Marseille six times and was in a far better position to judge the situation. Reb Aharon started getting very emotional, and dispensed with the use of a translator. "Sephardic Jewry used to be the pride of our People," Reb Aharon declared. "The giants of our nation were of Sepharadic origin, but for centuries they have been in the backwater, allowed to seep through the cracks. Here is a critical historic opportunity to reach out to those who have been so denied, to those who are so defenseless — "

Mr. Jordan cut him off by informing him that Joint policy was not to distribute funds without documented proof. As long as the rabbi could only offer rhetoric without documentation — neither he nor the JDC was in a position to help.

Off the record, Willie Jordan wanted to know why a group of Ashkenazim was getting so worked up about Sepharadim. Reb Aharon, who up until that point had been ardently impassioned, could no longer contain himself. The dam broke and the Rabbi's love of his brethren that knew no bounds spilled out as he cried that there was absolutely no difference between an Ashkenazic and a Sephardic Jew. We are all brothers and our responsibility to each other surpasses origin and custom.

Obviously the appeal had some impact, as Jordan — although he was not about to violate JDC policy — related that he would soon be in

Switzerland and if someone could meet him there with definitive proof of the situation he would lend an attentive ear.

The meeting adjourned and the gedolim assembled to figure out who was the right man to carry out this mission. Reb Aharon was convinced that the pious and remarkable Isaac Shalom who ran the Otzar Ha-Torah organization in Iran was the perfect candidate. Reb Aharon knew that Shalom was currently in Teheran, but would be returning to America via Europe.

Now the question was, who would be the right emissary to enlist Shalom? One of the gedolim suggested that Shmuel Klein would be an excellent agent as he was present at the meeting and understood what would satisfy the Joint.

Reb Aharon vetoed the plan. "*Zuhl ehr nit gain, zein makom iz in yeshivah* — He cannot travel, for a single young man belongs in yeshivah." With the chilling accuracy of a heat-seeking missile locked onto a target, Reb Aharon never veered from Torah directives. Whether the matter was trivial, or of earth-shattering importance, he always understood which path was the proper direction.

Reb Aharon was always able to focus on his

mission to the exclusion of *everything* else. Ego and self were never a factor. One *gadol* commented, "Reb Aharon did not know what *kavod* is." This assessment was corroborated by his Rebbetzin. "In fifty years, he never once spoke about himself."

Most modest people make it their business to remain in the background. Reb Aharon's humility is a seminal lesson in the nature of Torah leadership. An *adam gadol* must counsel and instruct, direct and command. By definition this means being in the limelight, no matter how contrary this is to his desire for anonymity. No matter what, he may not abdicate his responsibility.

Marvin Schick writes, "No one understood or exemplified better than Reb Aharon the affinity of exalted leadership and exalted modesty. He was the most modest of men, for while he asked nothing for himself — neither deference nor honor — he was insistent on *kavod ha-Torah.*"

Further proof comes from Reb Nosson Wachtfogel, the sainted *mashgiach* of the Lakewood yeshivah until his passing in 5758, who worked together with Reb Aharon for three decades. Rabbi Wachtfogel pointed out that from the day Reb Aharon landed in America he never mentioned the Kletzk yeshivah. There is no doubt that Rabbi

Kotler loved and cherished the yeshivah that he personally had fashioned, and yearned for his dear *talmidim* who had perished. Yet once he reached America, his job was to build for the future, and he could afford no distraction from that goal.

One last example: Reb Isser Zalman wished Reb Aharon to succeed him as the rosh yeshivah of the Eitz Chaim Yeshivah in Jerusalem.* Even though accepting this position would conflict with his responsibilities to Beth Medrash Govoha, Reb Aharon nevertheless could not decline his father-in-law's request. This entailed traveling to Jerusalem — without his wife so as not to burden Eitz Chaim with an extra expense — almost every year and remaining for an extended period.

During one of these excursions, in the late 1950s, an Eitz Chaim student asked Reb Aharon to officiate at his marriage. The wedding was held

---

* On one of Reb Aharon's trips to Israel, he was walking with Reb Isser Zalman when he spotted a poor man. He told his father-in-law that several years earlier he had distributed charity to a group of indigents, but had run out of coins when he came to this man. Reb Aharon therefore had decided that if he ever saw this man again he would make it up to him. And that is precisely what he did. Reb Isser Zalman commented that this anecdote refects not only upon Reb Aharon's phenomenal memory, but also on his pure and deep fear of Heaven.

in the Meah Shearim neighborhood which, at the time, was the border between Israel and Jordan. In the midst of the celebration, Jordanian soldiers began shooting into the hall, causing everyone to dive under the tables and take cover. All the people in the room feared for their lives, and with very good cause. A wedding guest huddled next to Reb Aharon heard the great sage pray, "Father, sweet Father in Heaven, don't take me yet. I have yet a mission to complete!"

Sixteen

IN 1952 the Israeli government considered legislation compelling women's conscription into either the army or a national welfare service (*sheirut leumi*). The *gedolim* in Israel maintained that for a woman to participate in either option would be a cardinal sin, threatening the traditional parental control over the life-style instilled in Jewish girls from religious families. Reb Aharon therefore lobbied against the amendment, which meant contacting the Mizrachi party that leaned toward support of the bill.

Rabbi Kotler and the famous Torah leader

Dayan Yechezkel Abramsky went to see Israel's Chief Rabbi, Isaac Herzog, to solicit his support. Rabbi Herzog, a scholar of the highest caliber, had great respect for his esteemed guests and summoned the heads of the Mizrachi party, Moshe Shapiro and Zerach Warhaftig, so that the issue could be aired.

These two gentlemen, who were also government ministers, contended that fighting against *sheirut leumi* was a very unwise idea that could result in the drafting of yeshivah students (whose exemption was unchallenged). This argument did nothing to dissuade Reb Aharon, who claimed that the Mizrachi was using this issue as a ploy to achieve their own agenda. To drive home the point he offered the following analogy:

A Polish *poritz* (landowner) acquired some rare and expensive champagne and offered some to his neighbor Moshe. Moshe explained that Jewish law forbids drinking non-kosher wine except under the threat of death. The *poritz* understood Moshe's drift, unholstered his pistol and ordered "Drink!" The *poritz* then asked his neighbor if he enjoyed the beverage. "Would you mind," asked Moshe, all hope and anticipation, "pointing your pistol again...?"

A demonstration to protest women's conscription was planned in New York and Mizrachi attempted to prevent it from taking place. Part of their campaign was a series of advertisements that accused the *gedolei Torah* of being *"sonai Zion"* (haters of Zion). The crusade was quite effective and supporters of Beis Medrash Govoha threatened to curtail their contributions. Reb Aharon, as always, could not be intimidated on a matter of Torah ideology and thundered, "Let Lakewood be erased and let the yeshivah be destroyed, but I shan't alter my *da'as Torah."*

Reb Aharon took great offense to and was deeply hurt by the title, *"sonai Zion"* for who could possibly love Zion and the Jewish People more than the esteemed *gedolim* who opposed women's conscription? These spiritual giants conducted lives of austerity in the Holy Land and devoted to their people their every waking moment without personal agendas. Furthermore, 30,000 residents of Jerusalem, who cherished their homeland, also protested the proposed amendment. Reb Aharon sadly concluded that the promoters staging the anti-protest campaign had tragically confused the Lovers of Zion with its Haters.

One day, as all of this turmoil was brewing, a Lakewood student saw Reb Aharon dashing through the streets of Manhattan. True, Reb Aharon valued time and it was not uncommon to see him rushing wherever he went; yet this sight was truly out of character. Something was definitely wrong, and the *talmid* exerted himself to his fullest to catch up with the rosh yeshivah and find out what the haste was all about. Reb Aharon had no time to stop and explain himself, but he did gesticulate to the exhausted boy to join him.

The student barely had the cardio-vascular stamina to comply, but fortunately it wasn't far to the destination. Reb Aharon raced into the office of the Agudas Harabbanim with this boy huffing and puffing at his heels. The Rosh Yeshivah continued down the hallway at his usual Olympic sprinter's pace, explaining as he progressed that just that morning he had received a letter from his father-in-law declaring that the matter of women's conscription was an issue so cardinal that the law of *yehareig v'al ya'avor* applied.

"If so much sacrifice is required from women," Reb Aharon questioned rhetorically, "then shouldn't I act with equal *mesiras nefesh* on this matter? That is what brought me here now."

Witnesses confirm that Reb Aharon had been eating breakfast at the time the letter arrived. As soon as his eyes glanced across the page, he commenced *bentching* — without completing his meal — and then rushed out of the house to convene a meeting of the Agudas Harabbanim. Rabbi Kotler claimed that the issue of women's conscription into the army brought about the premature deaths of the Chazon Ish and Reb Isser Zalman Meltzer.

This was not the only time that Reb Aharon voiced opposition to Israeli government policy and encouraged public protest: Yemenite immigrants to Israel were deliberately uprooted from their religious practices and background. Reb Aharon felt that it would be wise to alert the world to what was being perpetrated, but many people — even of religious persuasion — felt that it was inappropriate to launch demonstrations against the Israeli government. At the time it was unheard of for Jews to criticize the State of Israel. Reb Aharon was pained by the prospect, but spiritual lives were at stake and he persevered. As a result of his foresight, a number of Yemenite Jews were freed from environments antithetical to their upbringing.

Seventeen

REB AHARON'S support of Agudas Yisrael was consistent and absolute. Since Agudah was the vehicle to implement the decisions of the Moetzes Gedolei HaTorah regarding the application of Torah Law, compliance was mandatory. When asked why he didn't involve his students in Agudah activities, Reb Aharon replied that the raison d'être of Agudah is to enable yeshivah students to learn without interruption.

Here is a glimpse of Reb Aharon's clarity of

vision. For his students to participate actively in the organization's activities, as he did, would have contradicted the very purpose of the Agudah.

When Reb Aharon assumed the mantle of leadership of the Moetzes Gedolei HaTorah, he brought about a shift in its agenda. Until that point, the Moetzes served as the arbiter for any matter brought to its attention. Reb Aharon shifted the focus from "arbiter" to pro-active "supervisor" regarding any matter that affected or impacted upon religious Jewry — whether or not the body had been consulted.

Prior to Reb Aharon's ascension to leadership, Agudas Yisrael was a small organization with a modest scope. There were a limited number of rabbis in America at the time, and the majority of them were affiliated with Mizrachi. In order to make Agudah a viable alternative — even an organization worthy of contention — it was critical for it to become more involved in Jewish life. Reb Aharon pursued this course aggressively.

A critical collaborator of Rabbi Kotler's in this regard was Rabbi Moshe Sherer, president of Agudath Israel of America. Rabbi Sherer maintained that for over thirteen years a day did not go by (with the exception of when Reb Aharon was overseas) that he did not speak with the Rosh

Yeshivah at least once a day. Their discussions, of course, concerned guiding policy for an organization that mushroomed and assumed political clout far more significant than other organizations with significantly greater constituents.

Moshe Sherer, who is credited with being the genius behind Agudah's unprecedented growth and influence, was always quick to direct the credit to where it belonged. The main wall of his sukkah was adorned with photographs of the luminaries of the Torah world — past and present. The display of these portraits — as one can imagine regarding an individual who headed an organization representing every facet of Orthodox Jewry — was politically correct. Misnagdic and chassidic, Ashkenazic and Sephardic rabbis were all displayed with careful thought regarding geography, topography, neighbors and any other innuendo one could read into where a particular gadol was positioned.

With all of this thought and planning, dominantly front and center were the photos of Rabbis Elchonon Wasserman* and Aharon Kotler, the two *gedolim* that had the most dominant influence upon Rabbi Sherer, or as he put it, "The two that developed me."

The relationship between Reb Aharon and

Sherer had ramifications that extended past the ambit of Agudath Israel. For example, the Kennedy administration placed significant importance upon raising the level and the standard of the American school system. The movement that was generated to improve education spread to parochial schools, and for the very first time a window of opportunity was opened to secure government aid for private school students. Twelve leaders from different denominations were invited to the White House to testify before the Chief Executive regarding aid to non-public schools. Moshe Sherer was one of those selected.

An issue of such vital importance was going to require more than just the standard phone call to Reb Aharon. Rabbi Sherer went to meet the Rosh Yeshivah and was treated to an intensive lesson in constitutional law, public relations and

---

* In 1938 Reb Elchonon Wasserman traveled to America to raise money for his yeshivah in Lithuania. A stranger in a very foreign land, he needed someone to accompany him on his mission and Rabbis Shraga Feivel Mendlowitz and Shlomo Heiman from the Torah Vodaas yeshivah — in an act of either piercing insight or remarkable clairvoyance — selected Moshe Sherer for the job. Although there were numerous boys in the yeshivah who were older and seemingly more qualified, these two educators (must have) suspected that Sherer — and consequently the entire Jewish People — would only benefit from this match.

ethnic pride. Needless to say, Sherer took accurate notes of what he was instructed, and his diligence would bring handsome rewards.

Lots were drawn regarding the order of speakers and Sherer was slated to be the very last. Sherer's lot ended up making him even more nervous about the imposing task that lay before him. Everyone was issued the same amount of time to make their presentation, and, the President stipulated, "we will not dwell on any one speech, but offer general comments at the conclusion."

An extremely nervous Moshe Sherer was handed the podium. Aside from the august location and the importance of the attendees, riding upon Sherer's narrow shoulders was the potential millions of dollars in assistance to middle- and low-income yeshivah and day school families. Influential Leo Pfeffer from the American Jewish Committee had preceded Moshe Sherer and argued against government subsidies to parochial school students and aid to the general studies programs of these schools. After eleven back-to-back addresses, the Oval Office had all the excitement of a mausoleum on a slow day. Extreme, almost pained boredom was in the air.

With a quick intake of breath like someone about to plunge into icy water, Rabbi Sherer cleared his throat and drew courage from the fact that his speech was written by the *gadol hador*. When he concluded, JFK violated his ground rules by stating, "Although I said that we will not dwell on any one particular speech, after hearing the rabbi, I have changed my mind..."

The rest is history. Moshe Sherer was placed at the forefront of parochial aid and countless yeshivah and day school students — and their associates from other faiths — have all reaped the benefits of Rabbi Kotler's speech.

REB AHARON saw to it that his supervision of Agudas Yisrael was not restricted solely to the shores of America. He was in constant touch with Agudah offices and representatives across the globe, particularly in Eretz Yisrael. Agudah's Members of Knesset, whom Rabbi Kotler viewed and referred to as *shlucha d'rabban,* would not render a decision or voice an opinion on any matter of substance without first consulting with Reb Aharon.

Prior to the Knesset elections in 1961, Reb Aharon traveled to Israel to encourage voter support of the Agudah list. To Rabbi Aharon Kotler, this was far from a simple matter of political expediency.

"The Knesset elections," he said, "are nothing less than a referendum regarding who accepts the Kingdom of Heaven. The election results are public knowledge, and therefore failure to exercise this religious duty is a public desecration of the Almighty's Name. The transgressor will have to assume the responsibility for his action until the end of time, because the consequences of elections are reflected in countless decisions that im pact on the future."

One Friday, weeks before Israeli national elections, Reb Aharon walked by a billboard well-plastered with election posters, but a passerby would have been hard-pressed to locate a placard espousing the Agudah platform. Reb Aharon took due note of this, which is the same as saying that he would see to it that the situation would be rectified.

When Rabbi Menachem Porush, Agudah's Member of Knesset, was told that Rabbi Kotler was on the phone, he assumed, as usual, that he was about to receive policy guidelines and instructions regarding the weighty matters of the day. However, the Rosh Yeshivah had something else in mind: He related the precise city coordinates of the deficient billboard and instructed that the omission be rectified before the onset of Shabbos.

TO RABBI KOTLER's perspective, the creation of the State of Israel was an unprecedented educational opportunity to provide Torah instruction to countless immigrants and refugees. The Torah infrastructure that existed at the time was grossly inadequate for that purpose. Virtually every Israeli yeshivah was on the brink of financial ruination, meals could not be provided, and bills could not be paid. Yet Reb Aharon, in what appeared to be disregard for his own yeshivah, campaigned tirelessly to save the yeshivos in Israel. To those who questioned the wisdom of such a policy he responded to the effect, "We're all rooting for the same team."

Reb Aharon was appalled by the fact that there were only 5,000 Israeli children enrolled in Torah-oriented schools in 1950. With great urgency, he convened a meeting to deal with the matter, and he had no time for committees to debate and theorize regarding possible solutions. Early the next morning he was on the phone demanding to know what had been done since the night before. Reb Aharon's energy became contagious — and the fact that everyone would have to answer to him was in no small measure responsible for the meteoric rise in enrollment and the burgeoning of religious schools.

Israel's Ministry of Education maintained four autonomous educational tracks, but in 1952 the law was changed, rescinding autonomy. From then on, all school policies were required to be under strict governmental supervision; the Chazon Ish said that such scrutiny would be disastrous and was forbidden.

What alternatives were there? To create an independent, self-funded network would be nigh impossible, especially for the immigrants from North Africa and Arab countries who would be hard pressed and not necessarily willing to afford the tuition.

A more realistic plan would be to establish an independent school network — a *chinuch "atzmai"* — that would be subsidized by the government. The Chazon Ish passed away before the idea could be executed, leaving the entire project upon Reb Aharon's broad shoulders.

The government was willing to underwrite only 60% (later 85%) of Chinuch Atzmai's costs, leaving a colossal balance. Teachers were worried that they would not receive their salaries, suppliers were afraid to fill orders. Reb Aharon leaped into the breach and dispatched a sum large enough to enable the operation of Chinuch Atzmai without threat of bankruptcy.

Reb Aharon held that Chinuch Atzmai was a number one priority of Jewry worldwide. Every one was responsible for the education of Jewish children, especially for the new immigrants who would be sent to secular or missionary schools if there weren't a religious alternative available to educate them.

Wherever the classes did not meet the size requirements recognized by the government — such as in smaller communities — Chinuch Atzmai was required to pay the *entire* cost of the school's operation. No expense was too great for Reb Aharon when it came to Jewish education, even though meeting the budget inevitably meant turning to supporters of Beth Medrash Govoha.

Just when he did not have the funds to complete the construction of his own yeshivah, Reb Aharon unleashed a monumental campaign for Israeli schools, a large part of the donation consisting of a personal loan. Whoever has the means to support Chinuch Atzmai, he maintained, was enjoined by the Biblical injunction, "Do not stand by your brother's blood."

Reb Aharon approached a wealthy man on behalf of Chinuch Atzmai, but the potential contributor could not get hooked on the idea. However, as the esteemed rosh yeshivah had traveled all the way for a solicitation, he offered to donate to the Lakewood Yeshivah, so that Reb Aharon would not walk away empty-handed. Rabbi Kotler refused. He had come on behalf of Chinuch Atzmai, and neither Lakewood nor any other worthy cause could collect the spoils of that visit. The man was so impressed by Reb Aharon's integrity that from that day on he became a staunch supporter of Chinuch Atzmai.

Reb Aharon's involvement with Chinuch Atzmai surpassed merely raising its budget. His sleeves were rolled up all the way to assist with any matter that plagued the network, from organizational matters to hiring teachers. Nothing was too great or too small for his active participation.

Every morning Reb Aharon would call up (or be called by) the executive director of Chinuch Atzmai, Rabbi Henoch Cohen, to hear a report of what had transpired and then assign Rabbi Cohen tasks for the day. Intimately familiar with all that had to be done, he told Rabbi Cohen whom to call and whom to visit, where to go if this didn't work out and where to turn if that didn't work out.

Rabbi Alter Pekier noted that Reb Aharon's passion for Chinuch Atzmai was no different than his obsession to save lives from the Nazi inferno. To this Torah authority, spiritual destruction was no less nefarious than physical annihilation; the absence of 150 students was far more worrisome than a deficit of $150,000. He instructed Agudah's Members of Knesset to arrange for Chinuch Atzmai teachers to become entitled to the same benefits and pay scale as public school teachers.

The same effort Reb Aharon expended for Chinuch Atzmai, he devoted to the Tashbar network — a group of schools that dated back to the establishment of the religious *yishuv* in Jerusalem that did not receive — by choice — government subsidies. Patterned after the *chadorim* of Eastern Europe, these schools covered their budgets exclusively by tuition and outside donations. As the

amount of money they could hope to raise from impoverished parents was negligible, Reb Aharon's involvement was critical to Tashbar's success.

Rabbi Hillel Zaks once asked Reb Aharon if he should more profitably invest the one dollar he had for charity in Tashbar or Chinuch Atzmai. Reb Aharon sharply retorted, "You are concerned about your *one dollar* and would prefer that it go to Tashbar whose student body, curriculum, and teachers are above reproof... But I cannot shake from my conscience the responsibility of 40,000 children that Chinuch Atzmai is addressing."

Reb Aharon's exertions in regard to Chinuch Atzmai, the elections and Agudah matters in Israel is thoroughly remarkable considering the distance separating America and the Holy Land. Furthermore, there were ample *gedolim* in Israel who could rule on matters of substance, but Reb Aharon, realizing the comparative aloofness of these towering Torah luminaries regarding Agudah matters, stepped in. Over six thousand miles and clumsy, inefficient communication systems could not prevent him from taking charge and asserting decisive leadership.

Eighteen

REB AHARON deeply loved his *talmidim*. His Rebbetzin used to quip, "He loves his grandchildren *almost as much* as he loves his *talmidim*." This love was reflected in many ways. One evening he placed his own money in the pocket of a *talmid* who was leaving to visit his *kallah* and explained, "When you're with your *kallah*, you've got to be a sport..."

Rabbi Yechiel Perr once accompanied Reb Aharon on a flight from Chicago to New York. Reb Aharon's hostess had packed six pieces of strudel for the journey and three of those ended up on Rabbi Perr's tray-table. The latter dozed off at the beginning of the flight and when he opened his eyes and saw the pastries, he declared that he could never eat what had been intended for the Rosh Yeshivah.

Reb Aharon replied that he had already eaten (his share). "But the Rosh Yeshivah can eat the rest later," Rabbi Perr protested.

"Later we will be at our destination," Reb Aharon's tone changed from request to order. "Just take one piece! One."

Rabbi Perr complied, and then was told that he must eat a second piece, as it is questionable if one piece of strudel is an adequate amount to require an after-blessing. "You must therefore eat the second piece," Rabbi Kotler ruled. Once again Rabbi Perr had to comply.

"You know," Reb Aharon ruminated with a sheepish grin and a twinkle in his eye, "Even after two pieces, a doubt still remains..."

AT a *sheva brachos* a *chassidishe* fellow approached the Rosh Yeshivah and asked, "*Avu shtait mir darf*

trinken a l'chaim — where does it say that we must drink a *l'chaim*?"

Without hesitation, the Rosh Yeshivah made a clever pun in Yiddish on the word for substantiation by replying, "***Shtait** offen tish.*"

Imbued with a sense of humor, he never failed to see the light side. One day, as he entered the *beis midrash* to deliver his *shiur,* he noticed that a little girl, unbeknownst to her father, had climbed onto the Rosh Yeshivah's chair. By the time the father located his daughter, Reb Aharon was only a few paces away and closing in fast.

"Come here right away!" the father ordered. "That's the Rosh Yeshivah's chair."

"I was here first," the girl responded with smug assuredness. Reb Aharon was already in earshot and the father gesticulated madly for his daughter to climb down.

The father was mortified and died somewhere near a thousand deaths, but Reb Aharon found the situation very amusing and began to laugh. With a broad smile, he finally said, "Let her stay," and commenced his *shiur*.

The Rosh Yeshivah's jocular approach could

open many doors: He would often get frustrated when his young grandchildren would not eat. Holding a spoon laden with food he would chase after the toddlers and attempt to reason with them, "*Kinderlach,* there is but one mitzvah you have..." It was his favorite approach to score a deposit.

ONCE Irving Bunim found Reb Aharon playing chess with a middle-aged gentleman. It was an incredible sight that seemed thoroughly out of character. Reb Aharon's schedule didn't allow for a square meal — how could he possibly squander time in a chess game!

Bunim later learned that Rabbi Kotler's chess partner had lost his family in the Holocaust and was in a deep depression. Reb Aharon hit upon the right therapy — in daily installments — that enabled this fellow to take charge of himself, remarry and start all over again.

Rabbi Kotler's concern for others was constant. He was available to anyone who needed him, night or day, and had neither a secretary nor anyone empowered to shield him from the masses.

He would begin his phone calls, "This is Kotler

calling," or "This is Kotler from Lakewood." Never did he refer to himself as *Rabbi* or by any other title. His stationery said merely, "Aharon Kotler."

When traveling on the Garden State Parkway, he instructed the driver to head to the toll collector and avoid the toll machine. Respect for a human behooves preference over a machine — even if it will cost a little more time.

This anecdote gives one cause to ponder: One might imagine that if the toll collector stands to make more money based on the number of cars that are serviced, that might be a reason to prefer a person over a more expeditious machine. Furthermore, if the toll collector is reputed to be an especially moral person or a fellow Jew — this too would be reason to opt for this preference.

Yet none of the above is applicable, and Rabbi Kotler still issued this directive. And this precisely is what he was trying to teach; *kavod ha-briyos* mandates that human beings always receive preference — no matter who they are or how little they have accomplished.

Reb Aharon used to instruct his drivers to stop for hitchhikers on the road. In one instance (*l'halachah aval lo l'maaseh*) it had just started to rain and Reb Aharon spotted two burly gentiles with their thumbs protruding. He immediately instructed the driver to pull over, but the man at the wheel had enough sense to keep on driving. He pretended that he had not heard the Rosh Yeshivah, but Reb Aharon repeated himself so loudly and clearly that the hitchhikers probably heard him.

"But I've long passed them," the driver offered in justification, merrily continuing along. Reb Aharon had to remind the boy *who* was in the (figurative) driver's seat in that car and instructed him to exit right away and circle around to pick them up. "It's raining outside," the Rosh Yeshivah added to avoid further protests.

Rabbi Aharon Kotler, noted for his incisive mind and instantaneous grasp of a situation, was suddenly talking like someone out of touch — way out of reach — with reality. The driver could not believe his ears. "We don't know who they are, where they're from, or what they've drunk. All we know is that they are big and robust. It's risky."

"We're three, and they are two," Reb Aharon countered and pointed to the exit ahead.

Once again some commentary is indicated. The possibility that a Lithuanian rosh yeshivah and two meek yeshivah students could overpower two strapping gentiles was a bit, well... remote, yet Reb Aharon's Torah perspective governed his every move. When it came to Torah intuition, the man was definitely in touch.

ONE day, as Reb Aharon was already on the way to Lakewood, he remembered with a start that he had forgotten something. With a meek and an apologetic smile, he turned to the boy who was assigned to drive him that day and related his dilemma. This student, eager to assist and at the same time impress the Rosh Yeshivah, showed that he could deftly employ some Talmudic reasoning of his own. "I know someone leaving Brooklyn later this afternoon..." he began, all hope and confidence. Reb Aharon held up his hand to quash the idea, but there was no silencing this student. "If this doesn't work out, I can call my grandmother's neighbor, this lady — trust me, Rosh Yeshivah — she knows everything. I'm sure she knows where we're going right now. This will be a cinch for her — "

Again Reb Aharon held up his hand, but there still was no stopping the helpful young man. "I know. No problem whatsoever! Barry Stein, he's 'the man.' He lives in Borough Park and works out on Route 9 just twenty minutes from the yeshivah. I'll call him right now, and no matter what it is that the Rosh Yeshivah forgot he can handle it. He's got this big, real big station wagon. If he can't bring the thing to the yeshivah, I'll swing over and get it...."

There was a brief hiatus in the driver's recitation, but apparently he was merely pausing to catch his breath. Reb Aharon tried to seize the opportunity, but before he could get out a word, the Rosh Yeshivah learned more about what an asset Barry Stein would be for him. And from "Barry" the conversation — make that monologue — drifted to other ideas all aimed at preventing Reb Aharon from shlepping back to the City. Reb Aharon finally had no recourse but to employ extraordinary measures to prevent this fellow from sharing any more ideas of how he would save the day. "I'm afraid," the Rosh Yeshivah said forcefully, "that this is something that I must see to myself."

"Let me just think about this a second," the driver said, unwilling to give up. "I'm sure there is a way that — "

"Like I said," Reb Aharon stopped him in mid-sentence. "I must attend to this myself."

"At least I tried," the driver consoled himself as he made his way back to the congested streets of Brooklyn. Upon arrival at the Kotler home he politely offered to run up and retrieve whatever it was that was forgotten, but Reb Aharon once again explained that the matter was something that he had to see to himself. With no further explanation Reb Aharon bounded up the steps and personally said to his wife what he had neglected to wish her earlier: *"A gutten tug*, have a good day," and was on his way.

Nineteen

REB AHARON'S thoughts and statements were all governed by the Torah. This meant that sometimes he took stands that did not conform with the politically correct thinking of the time. One such position, taken with ten other roshei yeshivah, was the prohibition forbidding Orthodox rabbis from joining organizations with Reform and Conservative clergy, such as The Synagogue Council of America and the New York Board of Rabbis. Reb Aharon maintained that belonging to such an organization afforded legitimization to those that he labeled the "forgers of Torah."

This ruling was courageous and visionary — and highly controversial. Courageous in that it was a slight to the all-powerful (at the time) Reform and Conservative movements; and visionary in that it foresaw an Orthodoxy that would be able to chart its own course in the future. Controversial insofar as it introduced the concept of *emunas chachamim* and *da'as Torah*. Those who abided by the *psak* felt compelled to heed *da'as Torah* and those who ignored it were adherents of an Orthodoxy that did not have *gedolei Torah* at its center.

Amos Bunim records that a second contentious event occurred in 1961, when Rabbi Kotler supported federal aid for parochial schools. This was considered a blatant violation of the (sacred at the time) principle of separation of church and state. Up until that time Orthodoxy, like every other division of Judaism, attempted to maintain a low profile. Reb Aharon could see neither a Torah or a legal violation in accepting federal funding, only benefit. In both subjects, Reb Aharon demonstrated convincingly how much he was ahead of his times.

REB AHARON had no difficulty distinguishing between people and their ideals. If a person's opinion was incorrect, it did not mean that the individual was at fault. For example, Reb Aharon opposed the Mizrachi movement because of its endorsement of programs that he considered diametrically opposed to Torah ideology. Yet he maintained a long and cherished friendship with Israel's Chief Rabbi, a spiritual head of Mizrachi. Reb Aharon was present in Israel when Chief Rabbi Herzog passed away, and he attended the funeral and eulogized the great scholar.

There was no shortage of criticism hurled at Reb Aharon for honoring a man whose beliefs contravened his own. Yet, Reb Aharon countered that he was honoring the man's Torah knowledge, not his politics.

Likewise, Reb Aharon was opposed to Rabbi

Rabbi Joseph Baer Soloveitchik, Rabbi Aharon Kotler, Mr. Irving Bunim

Joseph Baer Soloveitchik's sanction of secular education and support of the State of Israel. Still, he approved the famous *gaon* as the honorary chairman of Chinuch Atzmai's first dinner. At that occasion each of the sages heaped lavish praise upon the other.

REB AHARON was frail, yet his energy never waned; an old man, yet somehow younger than anyone in his company. In the summer of 1962, the Rabbi's physical situation deteriorated noticeably. After Simchas Torah, Reb Aharon had departed the yeshivah to return home to Brooklyn when he asked the driver to return so that he could take his Shabbos clothes with him. It was the Rosh Yeshivah's inviolate policy that he always spent Shabbos in yeshivah, so the request was disconcerting.

As Rabbi Alter Pekier records in his biography of Rabbi Kotler, after the Rosh Yeshivah had gathered his clothing and returned to the car, he inexplicably returned a second time to make sure that everything was in order in the yeshivah. He still did not enter the car and returned yet a third time to verify that everything was to his satisfaction. Nothing could have been more atypical for the man whose every gesture was measured and finely calculated.

This was to be his last time in Lakewood, and a final farewell.

The next morning, during *Shacharis,* Rabbi Kotler collapsed. He regained consciousness quickly but it was important that he be evaluated in a hospital and an ambulance was summoned. In the interim, Reb Aharon received a phone call from someone seeking help in locating a job for a *talmid chacham*. The caller had no idea that Reb Aharon was not well, and Rabbi Kotler afforded him no clues regarding the situation.

Rebbetzin Kotler pleaded with her husband to postpone this discussion to a time when he was in better health. Reb Aharon would not hear of it. "A sick man is not absolved from the mitzvah of *chesed,*" he declared, before being whisked off to Columbia Presbyterian Hospital in Manhattan.

This episode repeated itself in the hospital when a woman called to speak with Reb Aharon while the ravages of stomach cancer were racking his body. Those present said that it was impossible for him to come to the phone, but when the rosh yeshivah overheard that he was needed, he insisted that he be handed the receiver. All marveled at what he was able to do in his condition and one doctor commented, "I don't have a medical explanation for how the Rabbi can do it. I don't think he is existing on anything but spiritual energy!"

At the most acute stage of Reb Aharon's illness he was allowed neither food nor drink. This resulted in a very parched mouth, significant pain and the inability to speak. His prayers were silent, yet when he came to *refa'einu*, suddenly an audible voice was found as he articulated the names of various *cholim*.

Desiccated lips, a dehydrated mouth and a baked tongue were given no reprieve until one Friday a nurse arrived at her shift and announced, "Today the Rabbi can have a lollipop," and produced the craved sweet from behind her back. The very thought brought an onset of relief. This was no mere treat, it was more valuable than a sumptuous feast. As such, Reb Aharon figured, it should be saved for Shabbos. With the same heroic discipline he displayed all his life, he put the lollipop aside for the onset of Shabbos.

Later that morning the Rebbetzin arrived and became suspicious when she saw the tantalizing candy and wished to clear it with the doctor. It was a good thing, and medically expedient that she located the doctor in the hospital, for the physician exploded. He looked and sounded like a man rocketing towards a coronary.

The Rebbetzin accurately deduced from this that Rabbi Kotler was *not* permitted to lick the lollipop under any circumstance, and the relief that it would have afforded him would have elicited an exorbitant price.

DURING one of the Rebbitzen's visits to the hospital she tried to lift Reb Aharon's spirits by assuring, "*Veit zein goot* — things will be good."

"*Chalilah,*" replied the Rosh Yeshivah. "*S'es shoin goot,* it is already good, for all that God does is for the good."

Reb Aharon, in excruciating pain, prayed for life — not for himself — but for *klal Yisrael,* the People that he wished to continue to serve. After a month, Reb Aharon succumbed to serious weakness, surgery, hemorrhaging, and a heart attack. He was summoned to the Heavenly Yeshivah on the second of Kislev 5723 (1962) and was afforded the largest funeral ever given to a Jewish leader in America till that time.

Harkness Pavilion Columbia Presbyterian Medical Center

THE PRESBYTERIAN HOSPITAL
IN THE CITY OF NEW YORK
AT
COLUMBIA-PRESBYTERIAN MEDICAL CENTER
CONTINUATION SHEET

Name [illegible] Age
Unit No.
Location

Rabbi Aaron Kotler, one of the world's foremost Jewish scholars and Torah authorities, passed away today (Thursday) ~~after~~ in the Columbia Presbyterian Medical Center, ~~after~~ at the age of 71. He was considered the spiritual head of orthodox Jewry, and played ~~an~~ a decisive role in Jewish affairs, in addition to his ~~[illegible]~~ activities as the dean of Beth Medrash Govoha in Lakewood, New Jersey, post-graduate school for higher Talmudic research.

Rabbi Kotler arrived in the United States in 1941, when he founded the Beth Medrash Govoha, whose student body consists of the most gifted graduates of rabbinical seminaries throughout the country. He was also the chairman of the Council of Torah Sages of the Agudath Israel World Organization, which has far reaching influence in policy-making for orthodox Jews in the throughout the world. As chairman of the Rabbinical Council of Torah Umesorah, national society of Jewish day schools, he ~~[illegible]~~ guided the expansion of [illegible] Jewish day school movement in the U.S.A.

Rabbi Kotler visited Israel regularly, where he was looked up to by broad masses of orthodox Jews for spiritual leadership. In Israel, he helped found the independent orthodox educational system "Chinuch Atzmai" and was the main driving force in expanding ~~the~~ school network to an enrollment of 40,000 children. [illegible]

* * *

Rabbi Kotler was born in Sislowitz, Poland, [illegible] ... Yeshiva ... of the most brilliant scholars of Poland in Europe. After his marriage he became the dean of the Yeshiva of Slutzk, Poland. In 1920, he transplanted the Yeshiva to Kletzk, Poland. In

Obituary submitted to media written by Rabbi Moshe Sherer at the hospital bedside.

המודיע
בטאון אגודת ישראל העולמית
ב"ה ירושלים יום ועש"ק פ' תולדות ג' כסלו תשכ"ג (30 בנובמבר 62) שנה י"ד גליון 4017
המחיר 25 אגורות

הגר"א קוטלר אינ

ניו יורק, יום ה' — הגאון מרן אהרן קוטלר, ראש גולת אריאל נתבקש היום לישיבה של מעלה, בשנת ה־71 לחייו.

ימיו האחרונים

...i Aaron Kotler Dead at 71; ...sey Rabbinical School Dean

...Aaron Kotler, a leading ...cholar and an authority ...orah, died yesterday at ...bia-Presbyterian Med...r. He was 71 years old.

...Kotler was dean of ...drash Govoha, a post-...school for higher rab...udy in Lakewood, N.J. ...a frequent visitor to ...here he helped found ...pendent Orthodox edu-...system.

...s born in Poland of a ...f rabbis. He studied in ...odka yeshiva (school) ...e became renowned in ...s one of the most bril-...olars in eastern Europe. ...came head of the Yesh-...lutzk in Poland. In 1939 ...his students fled from

...ron Kotler

...: a daughter, ...grandchildren. ...be held Sunday ...Synagogue, Pike ...Broadway. The ...vn to Israel for

...Rabbi Kotler's ...agner said yes-...deeply grieved ...of this great ...live on in the ...ts of all who

... the Sidewalks ...N. Y.—Grieving ...r Beloved Rabbi

...hadow of Manhat-...on the Lower East ...nts and sobs fil-...ugh a public ad-...m yesterday to a ...5,000 standing out-...atherbeaten syna-

...n, emotion-choked ...aimed in Yiddish: ...ve lost the crown ...ead . . . we are ... we have lost our

black coats, young boys with curly earlocks flowing beneath their skull caps, and others set to weeping and praying.

The object of their grief was Rabbi Aaron Kotler, 71, an internationally known Talmudic authority, who died Thursday and whose funeral was held yesterday at the Congregation Sons of Israel Kalwarier, 15 Pike St.

על הסתלקות אביר הרועים עמוד התורה והיראה
רבן של כל בני הגולה ומדברנא דאומתא

מרן רבי אהרן קוטלר זצוק"ל

מתאבלת מרה

הסתדרות צעירי אגודת ישראל
הנוער האגודתי בארץ ישראל

יחד עם כל בית ישראל מבכים אנו מרה הסתלקותו של גאון ישראל והדרו, שר התורה, אביר הרועים, רבן של כל בני הגולה

מרן רבי אהרן קוטלר זצוק"ל

אוי לה לספינה שאבדה קברניטה

...ר אראלים את המצוקים, שר התורה, אביר הרועים, ציס"ע, רשכבה"ג

...גאון מרן רבי אהרן קוטלר זצוק"ל

ראש מועצת גדולי התורה בארה"ב
ראש ישיבות קלצק בארה"ב ו"עץ־חיים" בירושלים

עלה בסערה השמימה

וכל בית ישראל יבכו את השריפה אשר שרף ה'

...סת' אגו"י העולמית — הועד־הפועל
הסת' אגו"י בא"י — המרכז הארצי

יתומים היינו ואין אב

גאון ישראל ופארו, שר התורה, אביר־הרועים, רשכבה"ג

מרן רבי אהרן קוטלר זצ"ל

מקים עולה של תורה ואביהם של תנוקות של בית־רבן

נתבקש לישיבה של מעלה

וכל בית ישראל יבכו את השריפה אשר שרף ה'

מרכז החנוך העצמאי
בארץ ישראל

...הגאון ר' אהרן קאטלער זצ"ל נפטר געווא...

אידישע וועלט אין טרויער; לוויה היינטיקן זונטאג

Epilogue

Among the throngs of teary-eyed mourners at the funeral, were the products of the Kotler legacy: Boys and girls who, thanks to Reb Aharon, were *not* enrolled in public schools and who would continue from day schools on to yeshivos and seminaries. *Baalei battim* who — although denied this world — would have their share in the World to Come thanks to Rabbi Kotler's involving them in the building of Torah institutions. Holocaust survivors who directly or indirectly owed their lives to the Rosh Yeshivah, who always made their plight the most important thing in the world. *Kollel* fellows and their wives who had not the slightest doubt as to who had enabled them to lead such a noble life. Visitors from Israel who owed their education to Reb Aharon's intervention. Roshei yeshivah and *gedolim* of America who had not only lost their leader, but a very part of themselves that would forever be missing.

The Ponevizher Rav, Reb Aharon's partner in rehabilitating the generation, was also there. So was the Satmar Rebbe, whose own honor was not diminished in the train station, to afford the final respect to the man about whom he applied Rashi's comment regarding Aharon the High Priest, "Aharon — *melameid shelo shinah* Aharon did not change." Rabbi Kotler was in America as he was in Vilna and in Vilna as he was in Kletzk. He did not change, but he changed the world.

The renaissance of the Orthodox community in America and the explosion of higher Torah education and consciousness was the result of many factors, but no one man had a greater influence on that rebirth than Rabbi Aharon Kotler. Born with a unique sense of obligation and limitless ability to sacrifice, giving of his prodigious talents was his very essence. His towering intellect was marshaled for this service so that the results were exceedingly successful.

Still, how did Reb Aharon do it? He didn't speak English, was unfamiliar with the American idiom, and even in Yiddish was not a gifted or charismatic orator. Perhaps his unparalleled zeal and burning passion for Torah enabled him to accomplish what others never dared. He was the unquestioned leader of religious Jewry, and while others may have differed with him, no one challenged his authority.

Or, perhaps, he was simply a gift from Heaven. A gift to a generation that had lost so much that it craved a shepherd. A gift to a generation that had conceived "scholar" to be a euphemism for "parasite." And a gift to a generation that had become rudderless and needed the Torah to steer it in the proper direction.

Against all odds, Reb Aharon achieved his goal, and there isn't a Jew alive who is not his beneficiary.

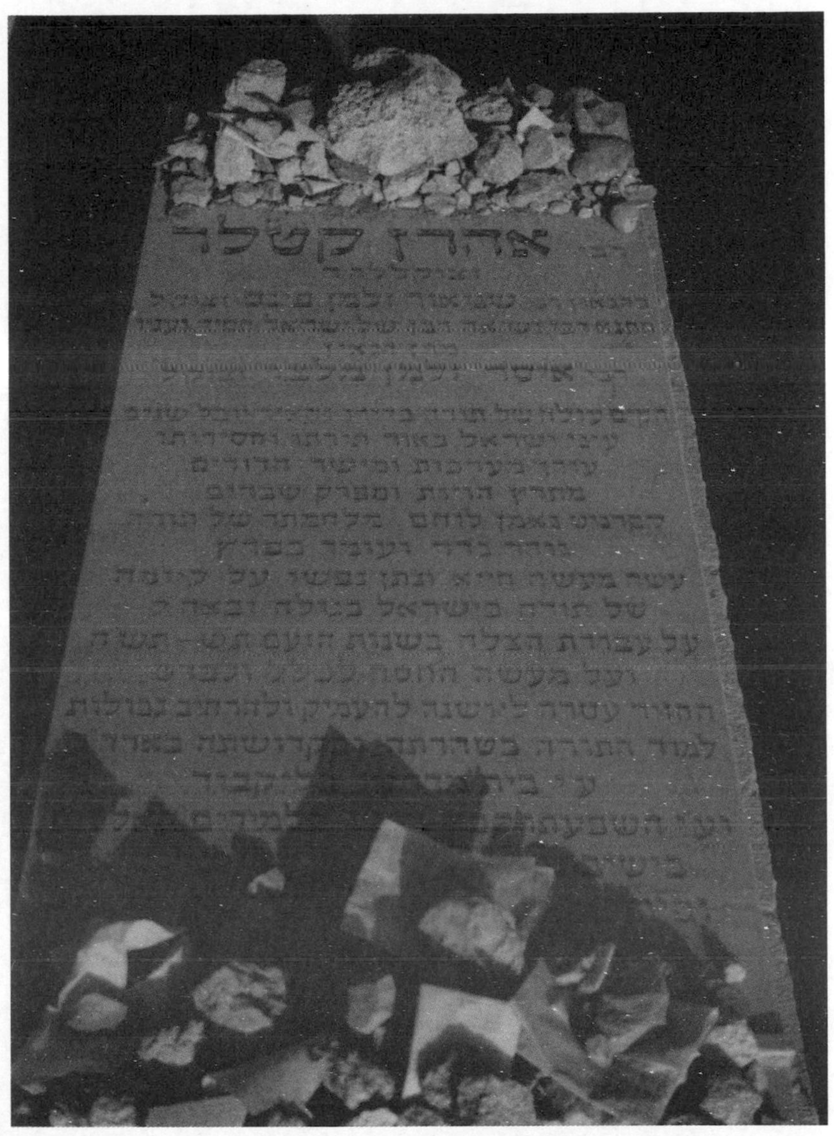
אהרן קטלר

Rabbi Yosef Shlomo Kahaneman

Twenty

THE LITHUANIAN WINTER. The temperature tenaciously persisted at double-digits-minus, climbing to zero only on rare occasions. Amidst that icy frigidity was a single bastion of warmth: the Kahaneman home in Kuhl. The poor itinerants who wandered from village to village — as the war of 1812 raged off America's shores, and Napolean began his retreat from Russia — knew this address well. It was there that they lodged, cozying up to the potbellied stove in an attempt to warm their freezing bones.

And as these indigents defrosted and hibernated, Fraidel Kahaneman would remove their "poorman's boots," the pitiful rags they wrapped around their feet as shields from snow and rain. These putrid rags were soaked with mud and other filth and their stench was abhorrent. Fraidel laundered the rags so that they were clean, odor-free — practically sanitary — and most importantly, they would be *dry* by morning.

This legacy of kindness and devotion to those in need was bequeathed by Fraidel Kahaneman to her son Yehudah Leib, and to *his* son Yosef Shlomo... the future Ponevizher Rav.

Indeed, the poor came with such frequency to Yehudah Leib Kahaneman's home that his wife, Itah Leah, would not permit her children to eat when they returned from yeshivah. She reasoned that the children had already consumed one meal that day, while the destitute had yet to taste their first morsel.

Notwithstanding their legendary generosity, the Kahanemans were themselves so poor that they only owned one pair of children's boots. Itah Leah would thus lead one child at a time to *cheder* in the snowy winter, remove his boots, and return home to embark upon another frigid excursion with the next child.

In Yehudah Leib's generation, as in his father's

time, the cold could not dispel the natural warmth of a happy household which cherished Torah study. Yehudah Leib arose at 4:00 every morning to learn, and when his wife awoke she often announced that she was in *gan eden,* despite rather compelling evidence to the contrary. To this deeply spiritual woman — whose material needs were so few — awakening to the names of the *tanaim* and *amoraim* liltingly sung in her husband's sweet mellifluous voice was the greatest pleasure she could imagine.

A man possessed of no ego, Yehudah Leib gladly assumed all of the menial, janitorial labors of the Kuhl shtetl. He was also the shul's *gabbai,* his only remuneration being first crack at hosting any guest who passed through the village.

It was not uncommon for indigent folk who traveled to Kuhl to attend the *"y'rid"* (the regional fair and market) to knock on the Kahaneman door very late at night to beg for a loan. These poor souls who had made the grueling trek to expend their few pennies, had discovered that they had forgotten their sorry satchel of coins at home. They apologized to Reb Yehudah Leib for robbing his sleep, but he was delighted by the disturbance. He put them at ease by saying with complete sincerity that had they not knocked he would not have been given the opportunity to perform a mitzvah at that hour.

Even tragedy could not dim the light of Yehudah Leib Kahaneman's soul. When his oldest son was threatened with induction into the Russian army, the youth fled the Slobodka yeshivah but contracted a fatal disease while in flight. Summoned for the burial, Yehudah Leib offered these words: "Master of the Universe, You know that I never interrupted my son's learning, nor did I ever take him away from the gemara. Yet if this is Your desire, I cannot question Your intentions. The Lord provides and the Lord takes, forever may His name be blessed."

YOSEF SHLOMO Kahaneman was undeniably a child prodigy, a local legend by the time of his bar mitzvah. He marked that occasion by completing Tractate Sanhedrin 15 times. In those days prior to yeshivah dormitories and dining rooms it was the custom for meals to be provided via the "*teg*" system, in which community members were expected to feed the hungry boys on a rotating basis. Many did not take kindly to the imposition foisted upon them, expressing their disdain by serving the boys rancid leftovers.

But in Yosef Shlomo's case, the *baalei battim*

vied for the honor of feeding the brilliant and charismatic boy. He used his favored status to "his advantage" by switching with a student who didn't enjoy such privileges. The result was that an otherwise deprived student would be able to receive a square meal at least once a week.

Notwithstanding his superior intellect and exceedingly kind nature, Yosef Shlomo was unable to gain admission to the academy of his dreams: the Telshe Yeshivah. According to the Telshe rules, he was too young to be considered, and was firmly told that the faculty made no exceptions. He was even denied the opportunity for an interview.

He had all but despaired of being accepted when he fortuitously encountered one of the most famous roshei yeshivah of Telshe, Reb Shimon Shkop, who, accompanied by numerous senior students, was vacationing in the resort town of Polangen. Yosef Shlomo approached Reb Shimon and asked permission to attend the *shiur* to be delivered during the upcoming Shabbos. "Why?" asked a puzzled Rabbi Shkop. A youngster requesting to attend his *shiur* was akin to a second grader asking to study calculus.

Yosef Shlomo confidently responded that he would be able to comprehend the lecture; as proof, he would relay it in its entirety on Sunday. Reb Shimon found this very hard to believe, but Yosef Shlomo persisted, begging and even crying, thereby convincing Reb Shimon to acquiesce.

On Sunday, Yosef Shlomo kept his word, recapitulating the entire *shiur*, detail for detail, displaying profound understanding. Reb Shimon was highly impressed. Realizing that he finally had the rosh yeshivah's attention, Yosef Shlomo articulated his desire to be admitted to Telshe. A few days later a letter of acceptance arrived in the mail. Reb Yosef Shlomo Kahaneman would always say that this was one of the happiest days of his life.

Thus began the questing youth's spiritual and intellectual apprenticeship to some of the greatest teachers and rabbinic minds of the day. In the Telshe yeshivah, Yosef Shlomo fell under the dynamic influence of the Telsher Rav, Reb Elazar Gordon. From there he traveled to the Novardhok yeshivah. Although he spent only an Elul there and a winter semester (far too little time, by his own admission), Reb Yosef Shlomo maintained that his ability to sacrifice himself for Torah was learned under the aegis of the *Alter fun Novardhok*, Reb Yoizel Hurvitz.

His next stop was fated to be the place most responsible for his development as a scholar and as a leader; a place where he learned *b'chevrusah* with Reb Elchonon Wasserman and declared that he was "spiritually reborn": the Chofetz Chaim's yeshivah in Radin.

Why did he leave Novardhok for Radin? Apparently, Reb Yosef Shlomo — like so many others at the time — was swept up in the enthusiasm for the Communist doctrine. The very idea of social justice and equality for all is something that deeply appealed to his giving and egalitarian nature.

Behind the scenes one rabbi knew better, and saw to it that this budding *talmid chacham* would go to a place where he would not entertain such perfidious thoughts.

Upon arriving in Radin, Yosef Shlomo naturally went to the Chofetz Chaim's house and quietly waited. The Rebbetzin eventually discovered him, and just as they were about to exchange pleasantries, a sharp wail rang through the house, terrifying the young visitor.

The plaintive sobs were those of the Chofetz Chaim. The Rebbetzin explained that her husband had just received word of a woman from a neighboring village who was having terrible trouble in childbirth. The cries of the Chofetz Chaim were so deep and emotion-charged that Yosef Shlomo made up his mind at that moment that he would not leave Radin. How could he leave a town where there was someone who could cry so sincerely for the suffering of a fellow Jew? He also concluded that Judaism — not Communism — was the source of true compassion and humanity.

A close and edifying relationship developed between Yosef Shlomo and the Chofetz Chaim, a relationship that would bear fruit for the entire Jewish People for generations to come. The Chofetz Chaim clearly recognized Yusha Kuhler's (as Yoseph Shlomo was called as he came from the town of Kuhl) leadership qualities and he allocated adequate time to nurturing and directing them. The Chofetz Chaim felt so connected to his protégé that he refered to Yosef Shlomo's students as "my *eineklach.*"

The Chofetz Chaim once asked Yosef Shlomo, "What is more important — to achieve one's personal maximum, or to facilitate the growth of *talmidim* at the expense of one's own personal growth?" Who could answer such a question? Who could ever know if learning with *talmidim* was preferable to self-growth and perfection?

Who but the Chofetz Chaim. The sage explained that the route to be followed is whatever will result in a greater amount of *kavod Shomayim*. These few words provided Yosef Shlomo with a signpost that would guide him for the rest of his life.

Twenty-one

WHEN the famous gaon, Reb (Aryeh) Leib (Rubin) Vilkomeer was looking for an appropriate match for his daughter Faigah, he stopped at the Chofetz Chaim's yeshivah to inquire about potential candidates. The visiting rabbi was informed that Yusha Kuhler was a *lamdan* and a great catch. Reb Leib, however, had been in yeshivos long enough to have heard that title bandied about quite freely without necessarily being accurate. This scholar, imbued with a cool Lithuanian rational approach, did not see a reason for excitement. There were plenty of *lamdanim* throughout the land.

The Chofetz Chaim, however, set the record straight: "This young man is not merely a *lamdan*, but also a fearer of Heaven, a *baal midos*, an orator with uncanny ability... in short, there is none like him all of Lithuania!"

According to an apocryphal tale, after hearing that all of the *talmidim* were exceptional, Reb Leib decided that the only way to find out for sure was to check himself. Accordingly, he delivered a *shiur* in the yeshivah followed by a difficult question posed to the students. Left unsaid was that the one who could answer the question would earn his daughter's hand in marriage. Silence, long silence, filled the room. No one in the hall crammed with supposed *lamdanim* could resolve the difficulty. It was therefore time for Reb Leib to depart and continue his search elsewhere.

Rabbi Rubin had already loaded his wagon and was clippity-clopping out of Radin when a panting student ran up and begged, "Rebbe, you asked a difficult question, but what is the answer?"

With that one dramatic act, which displayed his true thirst for learning, Yusha Kuhler had indeed answered his father-in-law's question.

Following his marriage, Reb Yosef Shlomo accepted an invitation to become the rabbi of

Vidz. The Chofetz Chaim had instructed that a rabbinic position should be accepted only in a town that hosts a yeshivah. The theory, presumably, was that the character and life of a city with a yeshivah is vastly superior to one without one. Yosef Shlomo naturally abided by his rebbe's dictates, but permitted himself an innovation: he moved into a town that lacked a yeshivah — until his entry.

As Reb Yosef Shlomo proceeded to build a new yeshivah, he did not neglect building his own "home in Israel", as the following anecdote illustrates. Very early in their marriage Faigah prepared a dish that her husband detested. But, aware of the trouble she had taken, he did not relate his dislike. Au contraire, he heaped compliments upon her culinary abilities, earning him — until her tragic murder at the hands of the Nazis, — frequent servings of this dish that, as she believed, he so liked.

The young and energetic Rav Kahaneman founded, opened and served as rosh yeshivah for the academy in Vidz. This entailed a host of arduous full-time responsibilities, such as delivering the *shiurim* and paying for the upkeep of the building and the students' sustenance. An awesome financial undertaking was thrust upon the broad shoulders of this young man, and it was a standard activity for him to use the fur collar and the gold watch that he had received as his wife's dowry as collateral for loans which he personally borrowed for the yeshivah's upkeep.

As rabbi of the town, he saw to all matters that pertained to its citizens. In a brief time he significantly elevated the educational level of the *cheder,* finally making it a viable option for academically-minded parents. Registration burgeoned, to the great consternation of the principal of the government school which was now left with a minimal Jewish enrollment consisting of weak students.

A vindictive man, the principal did not accept this situation passively. He warned Rav Kahaneman that if the children from affluent homes did not return to his school, he would inform the government about the opening of a non-accredited (hence illegal) school, which would surely result in the closing of both the *cheder* and the yeshivah as well.

Reb Yosef Shlomo was not intimidated and replied, "I have no doubt that you would inform on me, which would mean my banishment to Siberia. You should just be aware of the fact that in Siberia I will also open a yeshivah!" The principal concluded that there was no purpose in challenging this fearless young upstart, and abandoned his campaign.

In a harbinger of his future rabbinic life, Reb Yosef Shlomo demonstrated his leadership in every aspect of Vidz's communal life. One of his projects was to renovate the dilapidated old mikveh that was constructed of rotting wooden planks. The new mikveh would be *b'tachlis ha-hidur,* constructed of tiles that would be structurally sound and aesthetically pleasing. As he promised, the result was an exquisite, well-apportioned mikveh that cost a great deal in time, effort and expense.

Its debut was erev Yom Kippur, 1915. In less than 24 hours, the Rav and the rest of Vidzian Jewry were forced to flee because of the spread of World War I. Days later, the mikveh was totally destroyed.

With the advance of German troops, the Rav urged everyone in the community to flee. Many townsfolk felt that it was premature to pick up and leave, as numerous villages still separated the Germans from Vidz. The residents of those villages had not yet abandoned their homes.

But Reb Yosef Shlomo maintained that many factors can alter troop movements. And sure enough, the Germans changed course and marched into Vidz the following day. Sadly, this town would change hands numerous times during the war.

When relative calm returned to the vicinity, Reb Yosef Shlomo returned to the area to tend to the few Jews who remained in Vidz. He was appalled to discover that the Vidz Yeshivah had been taken over by the Germans and placed off limits. Typically, Rabbi Kahaneman's feelings always translated into action. He decided that he would speak directly with the German Field Marshal about the situation. A hen sprouting teeth would have been no less preposterous.

Although the rabbi had made up his mind with whom *he* would discuss the matter, the Kaiser's senior staff flatly refused an audience. Access to the Field Marshal was denied. To Reb Yosef Shlomo, however, this was merely a technicality.

He put on his Shabbos finery and managed to get past the guards. Earliest indications were that the Field Marshal was not in the mood for a visit from a chaplain. Not in the least. The officer began fulminating in the blackest, foulest and most unprintable invective.

Reb Yosef Shlomo replied in a soft and civil

tone. Then he drew himself erect, and in a strong voice accused: "You have taken our yeshivah, which is our home! How dare you?"

The Field Marshal was taken aback and apologized profusely. "I'm so... eh, sorry," he stammered. "I didn't know...!"

Right then and there, the Field Marshal ordered the yeshivah to be returned. But once Reb Yosef Shlomo saw that he had the man's attention, he appealed on behalf of the Jewish refugees in the area. The officer was impressed with the Rav's forthright manner and intelligence, and authorized the reunification of families that had been separated. Rabbi Kahaneman had but one remaining request: He realized that by meeting with the Field Marshal he had sealed his fate with the Russian forces. Always known for their swift punishments, the Bolsheviks would have had the Rav shot immediately for having established contact with the enemy. To protect him from such a fate, the Field Marshall awarded him a special pass that allowed him to travel freely throughout the German-occupied zone.

Reb Yosef Shlomo considered the reuniting of families to be a matter of *pikuach nefesh,* and he coordinated volunteers to collect food and other provisions so that those who traveled by train on

Shabbos would not go hungry. Additionally, the Rav paid a significant sum — on Shabbos — to unload the bricks that were already on the train, to make room for the Jewish passengers.

As the war zone moved further away from Vidz, the Rav and several families attempted to return to their former dwellings, only to discover that they had been burned to the ground. All that remained of his house were a heap of ashes and, oddly, an unscathed pillow and jacket. Viewing the carnage, the Rav was overwhelmed by the teaching of the Sages: "All that one does for his friend, ultimately he does for himself."

It was this pillow that he had lent to a boy in the Vidz yeshivah who had fallen ill, and it was in the lining of this jacket that he had managed to secrete the valuables of several villagers.

Twenty-two

REB YOSEF SHLOMO marshaled all of his spiritual talents as well as business acumen and entrepreneurial skills to serve his People. At the beginning of World War I, the Czarist government wrongfully arrested thousands of Jews on charges of spying for Germany. They were interned in the military camp of Poligian and endured unspeakable tortures. When the Central Powers gained the upper hand and seized the area, they did not liberate the innocent, starving hostages incarcerated because of their supposed loyalty to Germany. In fact, conditions worsened significantly under the new regime, providing a bitter foretaste of what was to become standard operating procedure under Nazi rule. The German captain of Poligian had no compunction announcing his intention that all the prisoners should perish from starvation. And in good German tradition, a threat to annihilate was a word of honor.

The few Jews who had remained in the area after the ravages of the war were hard-pressed to allocate any of their meager rations to Poligian's prisoners. To assuage their consciences regarding the seemingly hopeless plight of their brethren, they turned the matter over to Reb Yosef Shlomo.

As always, the Rav sought to approach the problem in a manner that would provide not merely cosmetic relief, but would offer a lasting solution. But what exactly could he do? An absence of options never deterred Reb Yosef Shlomo. He decided to employ a method that had withstood the test of time — but was so bold — that virtually no one had shown the ambition to try it on the conquering power.

Rabbi Kahaneman contacted his two associates, Gershon Rudnitzky and Hershel Kramer, and instructed them to retrieve his large sum of golden coins. How could the modest rabbi have amassed a veritable fortune? That is a tale of entrepreneurial brinkmanship, a result of the personal relationship that had developed between the Rav and the aforementioned German Field Marshal, who was also the regional commander.

The improbable connection between these two disparate men was forged in the stealth of the night, across a board of black and white squares. During discreet nocturnal chess games Reb Yosef Shlomo carefully probed the commander's mind to discover how the military situation might impact on the Jews in the area.

During one of their matches, the Field Marshall posed a query regarding how the region's verdant forests could best exploited and the timber exported back to Germany. "The right business mind knows how to capitalize and profit from every situation," the rabbi assured him. And I happen to know *just* the right connection."

The Field Marshal's eyes opened wide in anticipation of the profits that he could reap. He knew that he was sitting on a fortune, but was clueless how to set the wheels in motion. That is where the Rabbi's associates, Gershon Rudnitzky and Hershel Kramer, came on board. To the Field Marshal's mercenary delight, these two seasoned businessmen became the contractors of a hugely profitable wood exporting industry.

The military officer was so grateful to Reb

Yosef Shlomo for having brokered the successful enterprise, that he inserted a clause into the partnership agreement allocating him a steady commission. It was this royalty that was used to pay for the *pidyon shvuyim*.

The rabbi's request alerted some local individuals as to his intentions, and they tried to restore him to his senses. It was unheard of to bribe German officials, who were known for their pompous pronouncements placing them above any such temptations.

Reb Yosef Shlomo was undaunted. He had no problem attempting the unusual, and made the Germans an offer that he could barely afford… but one that he believed they could not afford to refuse.

And he was right. At a rate of ten golden rubles a head, thousands of Jewish prisoners were redeemed from the horror of the Poligian prison camp. The prisoners that the Rav did not manage to redeem with money, he emancipated through other means. One method that he employed was to ensure that the wagons used to transport meager rations into the camp never returned empty: somewhere underneath the rags and other junk heaped inside the cart was a Jew or two on his way to freedom. When this plan was uncovered, Reb Yosef Shlomo devised other daring schemes to redeem the remainder.

These clandestine operations required the assistance of numerous individuals, primarily volunteers to shelter the former prisoners upon their escape. Reb Yosef Shlomo appealed to the surrounding communities, but could not — at first — acquire their assistance in this undeniably dangerous activity. He then resorted to what he knew best, and *darshened* to the populace, no holds barred, with the passionate intensity that was his trademark. This time he earned everyone's support. Indeed, they felt so contrite that many begged his forgiveness for not hurrying to help in the first place.

Twenty-three

DURING one of Reb Yosef Shlomo's trips to Vilna to arrange assistance for the displaced, battles erupted that closed off the Vidz region. Stranded on a road now leading nowhere, the Rav fortuitously met Gershon Rudnitzky and Hershel Kramer, who lived in the nearby village of Koltianan. The two invited Reb Yosef Shlomo to become the Rav of their town, and he agreed on the spot.

Of course, Reb Yosef Shlomo's acceptance of a rabbinical position was contingent upon the Chofetz Chaim's criteria that there be a yeshivah in the town. So, despite the uncertainty of the time, in tandem with his rabbinic duties, Reb Yosef Shlomo set out with his usual determination and vision to establish a yeshivah in Koltianan.

For three fruitful years — until the roads to Vidz were reopened — Reb Yosef Shlomo remained the beloved rav of Koltianan, presiding over a flourishing yeshivah that was enthusiastically supported by the affluent locals.

But as long as Jews were still hungry or suffering, the Rav could not bask in his accomplishments. As Rudnitzky and Kramer continued to contract for the Germans, the government provided them with meals for their workers and fodder for their horses, among other (relatively) generous provisions. It occurred to Reb Yosef Shlomo that the surplus of this government issue could be rechanneled to hungry refugees in the area, and he wasted no time implementing his idea.

Reb Yosef Shlomo instructed Rudnitzky and Kramer to establish soup kitchens throughout the region. And it was not uncommon for Reb Yosef Shlomo himself to entertain between 50 and 100 ravenous souls at his Shabbos table.

When the German authorities learned that their food rations were being misappropriated,

Reb Yosef Shlomo was summoned by the German Commander of the Eastern Front, General Von Ludendorf.* With a chest full of decorations, and just as many deputies singing his praises, Von Ludendorf minced no words trying to intimidate this Jew who was privileged to be standing in his presence.

After detailing his "countless and impossible to enumerate" assets (yet he detailed them nonetheless) Von Ludendorf thundered, "I am the commander-in-chief of this entire area... the 'father' who determines who will eat, how much they will eat, and when they shall eat! What right, therefore, do you have to betray the Kaiser's army and take food earmarked for workers and distribute it to *Jews*?"

"Distinguished General," the rabbi responded, "true, you are the *father*, but you must remember that we Jews are all *brothers* from a common mother. Our 'father' has just been switched from Russia to Germany. You are well aware that brothers will remain brothers even if some of them receive a new father or stepfather. Regardless of this switch, it is only natural for a brother to share

---

* General Von Ludendorf was an associate of Hitler ימ"ש from the beginning and was even involved in the Munich putsch — although he escaped and Hitler was caught.

the little food that he has with his sibling."

Even General Von Ludendorf had to concede there was logic to this argument, and to admit that there was a blot in their patrilineal descent.

While in Koltianan, Reb Yosef Shlomo authored a commentary on the entire *Shas,* filling six cartons. Tragically, these boxes never left Europe. Later in life when he was asked why he didn't write novellae on the Torah he replied, "I have already written what I have to say; *min HaShamayim* it has never seen light."

To Rav Shach, who asked him the same question he replied, "It is my lot to write '*zeh sefer toldos adam*'... meaning, I must ensure that there will be *talmidim* to learn what is already written."

During the day the Rav would learn in the Koltianan yeshivah. There was no illumination at night, for during wartime it was next to impossible to acquire candles or oil. All he had were "*kinelach*" — slivers of splinters or fragments of toothpicks that were placed in the wall and lit. They provided just enough light to illuminate the *daf,* and create a mystical atmosphere of "*Torah Ohr.*"

For the rest of his life, Reb Yosef Shlomo would nostalgically long for the days when he learned

Shas by the light of the "*kinelach*." Years later, in a *mussar* discourse, he described how the medieval commentator the Rosh, had lived during one of the bleakest periods for Jews, daily facing murderous attacks from the Crusaders, yet never wrote a word about how he suffered. Jews in that period, he explained, managed to shut out the horrors and live in their own world suffused by the beauty of Torah. Those present realized how applicable those words were to Reb Yosef Shlomo himself.

In 1918, Reb Yosef Shlomo traveled to Vilna to consult with Reb Chaim Ozer. Early in their visit, the *gadol hador* cut him off in mid-sentence* and without any explanation instructed him to return at once to Koltianan. Reb Yosef Shlomo did as he was told, and miraculously was able to hire a hard-to-come-by wagon immediately.

As soon as Reb Yosef Shlomo arrived home, the borders to Vilna were sealed shut. Had he remained speaking with Reb Chaim Ozer any longer he would have been unable to return.

When Reb Yosef Shlomo left the wagon, he

---

*Four years would elapse before his next encounter with Reb Chaim Ozer, at the Knessiah Gedolah in Vienna. The great sage from Vilna picked up the conversation exactly where it had left off.

was greeted by a telegram inviting him to serve as the Rav of Ponevizh. He packed a few items and that very day the Kahaneman family parted farewell to Vidz.

Reb Yosef Shlomo did not depart Ponevizh until he had to, 21 years later. In the interim he would receive a *shtar rabbanus* — an invitation — from Dvinsk to fill the place of Reb Meir Simchah, an invitation to Frankfurt to succeed Reb Samson Rafael Hirsch, an invitation to Berlin to take over for Reb Ezriel Hildsheimer, and a *shtar rabannus* from the city with the greatest Jewish population in Palestine, Tel Aviv.

Twenty-four

REB YOSEF SHLOMO's inauguration in Ponevizh took place late at night. It was the 14th of Nissan, and Reb Yosef Shlomo, henceforth known as the Ponevizher Rav, had still not prepared the all-important document for *mechiras chametz.* Alone, without a version that he could copy, the Ponevizher Rav began to reconstruct the long and exceedingly complex text from memory when there was a pounding at his door.

His guests were a pair of armed Bolsheviks who ordered him outside. Clearly this was no social call to greet the new rabbi in town, and on his way down the stairs the Rav recited *viduy.*

Rabbi Kahaneman was led outside to the courtyard, and the younger soldier aimed his rifle. Moments later, a split second before the trigger was pressed, the older officer considered that maybe they had the wrong man. He suggested that his partner check the next entrance while he stood guard. Two shots rang out, and both soldiers left.

The Rav, who had come so close to breathing his last, hurriedly returned to his communal responsibilities, finishing the document at 4 A.M. as if nothing had happened.

It was commonplace in those days for there to be two rabbis in a city. One was the real spiritual leader, an erudite scholar possessed of fine character and sterling qualities; the other was *mitaam hamemshalah* — a government appointee who was inevitably an ignorant apostate whose appointment had no religious function. His sole purpose was to be an informant for the government.

Even though the two-rabbi system was standard, the Rav felt that it would undermine what he wished to accomplish as well as jeopardize the religious life of the town. Therefore, in a most radical move, he decided that *he* would serve both functions.

As far as the qualifications to be the "real" rabbi, he had everything that it took, but as far *mitaam ha-memshalah* qualification he lacked one essential prerequisite: the government appointee had to be conversant in the local language, and most yeshivah students could neither speak, read nor write Lithuanian. The Ponevizher Rav, always with a goal in sight, realized that there was a solution to this problem. Before leaving on a vacation he picked up a textbook on the language. The Ponevizher Rav experienced a rigorously studious vacation resulting in his acquiring an acceptably conversant level of the language that served him very well, then and in the future, and obviated the need for a second rabbi in Ponivezh.

People were amazed and rather envious at the Ponevizher Rav's ability to learn Lithuanian so quickly. Reb Yosef Shlomo could only comment, "I have been learning Torah for decades, and I still don't know it!"

Ponivezh, like most Lithuanian cities, had both religious and not-yet-religious inhabitants. And as in most cities, relations between the two groups were not always a harmonious symphony. The day Reb Yosef Shlomo took over the rabbinate in Ponevizh, he galvanized the office to provide assistance for the victims of World War I. This was a challenging assignmernt as there were various and opposed factions in Ponevizh, but with diplomacy, resolute leadership and a sharp focus on a common goal, he managed to persuade perennial disputants to unite for the common goal of rebuilding. There had been so much destruction during the war that someone with a clarity of vision and a grasp of priorities was needed to triage the restoration. Rabbi Kahaneman was just what the doctor ordered. He had a broad understanding of what needed to be done — spiritually and materially — but his first priority was always *hatzalas nefashos:* the saving of lives.

Among the homeless refugees in Ponivezh were widows, orphans, the ill and the infirm, the lonely elderly, the poor and the hungry. The Ponevizher Rav mobilized aid for all of the needy, and the results of his efforts sustained the lives of countless individuals. The Rav knew no rest until everyone was appropriately housed; he personally underwrote or raised the funds for whatever expenses were incurred.

No matter what the needy person's background, religious beliefs or allegiances, the Ponevizher Rav was there to provide assistance. As his concern was for *all* of the residents of Ponivezh, he quickly won the heart of every one of the town's inhabitants.

He also spearheaded the establishment of a top-flight hospital in Ponivezh, hiring the finest medical staff available both domestically and from abroad. The policy which he instituted was that doctors were entitled to charge whatever they deemed appropriate to those who could afford medical care, but the poor were to be treated free of charge. On opening day, the Ponevizher Rav offered the following prayer: "May it be the will of the Almighty that Your People Israel shall not need this facility. May it be used exclusively to assist the neighboring people, and our mothers in childbirth."

It was virtually unheard of for a rabbi, especially the rabbi of a town, to be a member of the *va'ad ha'ir* (city council). Yet the Ponevizher Rav was an active delegate representing Agudas Yisrael, and according to YIVO documentation, personally attended the meetings. In fact, he often took charge of the assemblies.

The Rav used his *va'ad* office and its influence to institute innovations previously never even dreamt of, such as the hiring of *melamdim* exclusively to teach boys from families too poor to afford tuition.

The Rav's house became the focal point of the town and the warmth that had glowed in his grandparents' and parents' home radiated just as intensely in his hearth. Every day dozens of men and women flocked to Rav Kahaneman to ask a *shailah*, seek advice, or lean on a shoulder.

Whoever entered the home was addressed as "*mein kind*" – my child, and was awarded tenderness and respect.

An eyewitness who lodged at the Rav's house recorded "A Night in the Life of the Ponevizher Rav." His diary chronicled the Rav answering *shailos* for four straight hours without interruption. The Ponevizher Rav then remembered that he had to visit a man in critical condition in the municipal hospital — a visit that could not be postponed as the Rav was a kohen.* When this visit was over, it was almost time to daven *shacharis.*

On his way to shul Reb Yosef Shlomo stopped off at the hovel of a poor widow and inquired about her son, who had not attended *cheder* the day before. He was the spiritual leader of a major town, yet he was aware of one boy who did not show up in the elementary school, and he wished to know why. Before departing he left some money for the household.

From there he headed to a different shack where a sick orphan lived. He inquired how everyone was feeling, and left some money there

* A kohen is forbidden to be in the same domain as a corpse.

too, to help purchase medications. Finally he was off to shul and to another full and exhausting day of communal and spiritual responsibilities.

Rebbetzin Kahaneman fully shared her husband's commitment to the community. An emotionally disturbed woman in Ponevizh lived alone without a semblance of hygiene. The Rebbetzin realized how desperately this embittered soul needed recognition and every Friday she graciously baked her a sweet challah (*bulkah*) for her. The most convenient method would have to been to arrange delivery of the *bulkah* and avoid personal contact, as this woman had a terrible odor.

But from the Rebbetzin's perspective, this would have been only half the mitzvah. Accordingly, she invited the unfortunate woman to her house every week to pick up the *bulkah* and to socialize. The first time she arrived, the Kahaneman children, before fleeing, thought that their mother had lost her sense of smell. For her part she carried on naturally as if nothing was out of the ordinary, as if the woman emitted the breath of angels! It wasn't until this woman had departed and was out of sight that the Rebbetzin threw open all the windows, and promptly vomited.

The Rabbi and the Rebbetzin were true partners in every facet of their lives, and they joined and complemented each other to help their flock.

When a certain poor person could not afford to pay his rent, his landlord summarily evicted him and his family in the middle of the night. They would have spent the night under the stars had it not been for the Kahanemans. They were all warmly received in the Rav's house (at that very late hour) and provided with hospitality.

A YOUNG orphan was sent to his poor relatives who lived in Ponevizh. After a while, the adult guardian, no longer able to afford his charge, reenacted a scene from medieval folklore. Late one night he brought the boy to the Ponevizher Rav's door, knocked and ran.

Rabbi and Rebbetzin Kahaneman raised the child as if he were one of their own. Every Friday the young lad would proudly walk the streets with his "father," hand in hand on their way to the mikveh. And this sight, the venerable rav clutching the hand of the orphan boy, was one of the most stirring and endearing for Ponevizh Jewry to behold.

Every *erev Shabbos* the Rav would personally visit all of the poor shopkeepers and saleswomen and inquire if they had enough for Shabbos. There were many other impromptu acts of kindness he performed that reflected the same care and concern for his brethren. He never spoke about fellow Jews without the tender appellation "*briederlach.*"

Indeed, the Rav considered that providing for all of the poor of Ponevizh was an integral part of his job, and he insisted that the charity be executed in a respectful, dignified and discreet manner. The recipients were always shielded from the providers, which meant employing a host of techniques and gimmicks to protect anonymity. His favorite method was to credit a bank account with funds that could not be traced. The recipient might imagine that the money had been transferred from a relative overseas or some other source, never suspecting that it was of local origin.

The Rav was so emphatic about guarding each person's privacy that an interesting, almost comical, irony often arose. When someone would stumble into dire straits, the Ponevizher Rav invariably learned about it and would organize an appeal to help. Because of the discretion involved, coupled with the extraordinarily charitable nature of Ponevizh Jewry — despite their poverty — the beneficiary of a collection would often contribute to a cause without ever knowing that he was donating to *himself!*

Twenty-five

KIMCHA D'PISCHA (Passover provisions) was a major, and highly organized, fundraiser for the needy. Reb Yosef Shlomo created a chart listing all of the Jewish residents of Ponevizh, and what he expected them to donate. He then apprised each family of the figure and to assure total participation had a list of everyone's name printed and posted prior to Pesach. This forced the hand of those who were not inclined to contribute, for alongside each person's name was a clear indication if their quota had been met.

One year the posted list showed two residents with glaringly empty boxes next to their names.

One of these "distinguished" citizens was a farmer who was simply not in the region during the time of the collection. When he arrived for *Yom Tov* he paid his quota right away and begged that he be spared the shame of an empty space next to his name. Reb Yosef Shlomo permitted the list to be reprinted again over *chol hamoed* with the correction, provided that the farmer covered the cost of the printing.

The other party who had not contributed was a nonconformist who had traveled to America before the holiday and returned a boastful and conceited individual with disparaging opinions (that he never hesitated to vocalize) about the Rav and all *talmidei chachamim*. This braggart made it abundantly clear that Reb Yosef Shlomo could not tell him what to do.

The man did not live out the year, and the *chevrah kadisha* would not bury him until his quota was paid. Word of this tragedy spread rapidly, and from then on no one took the Rav's list lightly.

One year, a wealthy merchant did not feel compelled to fulfill the quota for *kimcha d'Pischa* that Reb Yosef Shlomo had set for him. He offered in his own defense that he was a generous individual, and it was therefore inappropriate for the Rabbi to dictate what he should contribute to *kimcha d'Pischa*.

The Rav begged to differ, and informed the man that if he did not adhere to the head tax, the *hechsher* (kosher certification) on his food production plant would be removed. The *gvir* was yet to be intimidated and queried, "What right does Rabbi Kahaneman have to demand money from me, when he is delinquent in repaying my loan for the yeshivah?"

Reb Yosef Shlomo countered that one had nothing to do with the other. Regarding the loan [incidentally, he had just that day received enough money to repay it], it was borrowed by Reb Yosef Shlomo in his capacity as the "Yeshivah Dean"; the appeal for *kimcha d'Pischa* was undertaken by Reb Yosef Shlomo as the "Rav" of Ponevizh.

The *gvir* continued to insist that he should be absolved from a *kimcha d'Pischa* quota because *he* was the one who had financed the construction of Ponevizh's *yeshivah ketanah*!

Rabbi Kahaneman could not dispute this fact, but in his determination that the community's "haves" must underwrite its "have-nots," saw it as irrelevant. "For your generous donation you will surely receive a large portion in the World to Come, and I will personally guarantee this!" the Rav assured him. "I would crave to be your neighbor in the World to Come! But now we are dealing with *this* world, and down here I am the *mara d'asra* and you must listen to what I say!"

The *gvir* did not relent, so the Rav concluded that there was no more purpose to their verbal sparring, and resorted to the written word. He sent the recalcitrant man a copy of the *kimcha d'Pischa* poster with the obvious deletion as well as with the announcement that the *hechsher* on his plant had been withdrawn. In no time, the *gvir* paid his dues.

A liquor manufacturer approached the Ponevizher Rav for Kosher for Passover certification. He claimed that his liquor was made from potatoes and was therefore *chametz*-free, and was supervised by a particular rabbi who lived 80 kilometers away. Something didn't sound altogether kosher about this operation, and the Rav would have nothing to do with it.

The Rav's face-saving explanation was that as a matter of policy he did not, and would not, give a partial *hechsher*. Unless he actually supervised the manufacturing he could not permit his certification solely on the bottling. Reb Yosef Shlomo thought this was the end of the matter.

Weeks later he discovered that this locally-manufactured liquor was being sold in Ponevizh under the certification of a rabbi who lived far away. This only heightened Reb Yosef Shlomo's suspicions, and he printed an announcement in the local newspaper that he accepted no responsibility for the kashrus of this product. The shopkeepers promptly returned the liquor to the distributor.

The manufacturer did not take kindly to this reversal of his fortunes and started a rumor that Reb Yosef Shlomo's motivation was not kashrus but politics: the *rav hamachshir* was a *Mizrachist*, he claimed, and an ardent *Agudist* like Rabbi Kahaneman could not tolerate or respect those who espoused a different ideology. Many thirsty consumers chose to believe this interpretation and guzzled the spirits.

Government inspectors raided the plant after Passover and discovered that the "potato-based" drink was actually made from wheat (*chametz*). Because of the centrality of whiskey in Russian society, such tampering was considered a major felony, on par with murder or espionage. At least. The manufacturer was indicted on fraud and incarcerated, facing the full and ominous penalty of the law.

As the Ponevizher Rav was known to have strong government connections, relatives of the accused begged him to intercede. Reb Yosef Shlomo did as he was requested, never holding his personal affront against the man. The incident became famous throughout Lithuania, and was a story people loved to tell when describing the Ponevizher Rav's acumen and character.

There was only one shopkeeper in Ponevizh who publicly desecrated the Shabbos, a barber, who refused to close his business on the holy day. There are, perhaps, several ways of dealing with such a provocation, and as usual, the Ponevizher Rav adopted his own unique approach.

Every Erev Shabbos, with the shop filled with customers, the Ponevizher Rav would stand in the doorway and wish everyone "*A gut Shabbos*" in a loud voice. The barber was becoming very irritated by these weekly visits; still, the shop remained open Friday nights.

It was time to take further steps. One Friday night the Rav entered the shop and took a seat without saying a word. The Jewish patrons (though obviously not major *tzaddikim*) were too embarrassed to have their hair cut with the Rav — in all his rabbinic and Shabbos regalia — sitting right there. Thus the barbershop emptied out very quickly and no new customers (though they could not resist peering in from the outside) dared enter. Defeated, the proprietor asked the Rav to leave so that he could close the store, but the

Ponevizher Rav was in no hurry to depart. He remained seated until more and more clientele got a glimpse of the special guest. Finally, with what appeared to be genuine contrition, the barber solemnly promised that he would never publicly desecrate the Shabbos again.

A Ponevizh chocolate manufacturer also attempted to keep his wholesale operation open on Shabbos. The Rav went the route of gently explaining that public desecration of Shabbos was unacceptable in Ponevizh, but the merchant retorted that he took his instructions from market profitability, *not* rabbinic dictates. Little did he know whom he was up against. That Shabbos, Reb Yosef Shlomo announced in shul that it was forbidden to purchase any products manufactured by the *mechallel Shabbos* company. Needless to say, the Rav's word was law, and by Monday all the local outlets returned their merchandise, claiming that it was unsalable and was taking up shelf-space.

Accustomed to hard-nosed competition, this was one situation the manufacturer had never encountered before, so in the spirit of free enterprise, he launched a counter-measure. A delegation from the company's headquarters in Kovno arrived in Ponevizh to persuade the Rav to rescind his ban. They claimed that what he had done was a felony, declaring: "We shall not sit still until the full brunt of the law is brought to bear against you. And even if the court here in Ponevizh acquits you, we will appeal to a higher court in the capital, Kovno. Such legal proceedings will be debilitating for you, with expenses that will amount to a fortune. Do you think you can raise the capital for such an onerous battle?"

Reb Yosef Shlomo calmly replied, "Personally I do not have the money, but your competitor has plenty of money to cover my legal expenses..."

That very week the wholesale outlet ceased to open on Shabbos.

The Maccabi sport league organized a soccer tournament to be held in Ponevizh, with the opening game scheduled for Shabbos. When the Rav learned what was planned, he wished to score a goal for the sanctity of Shabbos, but the wealthy iron magnate who sponsored the league blocked his attempts. There was no way, he declared, that the Rabbi would interfere with something as important as a sports match.

Shabbos morning before the kick-off, Reb Yosef Shlomo and a large number of students from the yeshivah arrived at the soccer stadium to continue their learning. The Rav picked no place other than mid-field to deliver his *shiur*. The team captains, managers and the referees attempted to clear the field, but the students were engaged in matters far too significant to be relegated to the sidelines. Score one for the yeshivah team: this was the first and the last time that Ponevizh Maccabi ever attempted to play a match on Shabbos.

Twenty-six

IN THE AUTUMN of 1922, after Lithuania became an autonomous state, numerous edicts were enacted that threatened Shabbos observance. The municipality of Ponevizh was swept up in the nationalistic spirit and enacted ordinances of its own. One of these statutes forbade the opening of schools, including Jewish schools, on Sundays and all Christian holidays.

All attempts to annul this decree were stonewalled until the Ponevizher Rav stepped in. He approached the mayor of the town, a devout Catholic and reasoned: "If the throngs of Jewish children do not attend classes on Sundays, they will only get in your way. They will be out on the streets blocking the roadways and congesting the sidewalks. No doubt they will irritate the horses, climb onto the wagons and perpetrate other mischievous antics that children out of school are prone to do. Needless to say, we will do all that we can to avoid a confrontation, but you certainly have it within your power to eliminate the entire problem." The mayor immediately acquiesced.

In May of 1923, Reb Yosef Shlomo, capitalizing on his Lithuanian linguistic skills, was elected to Lithuania's new parliament, known as the *Sajm*. Though being a rav and a rosh yeshivah were already full-time occupations, he nonetheless viewed this as a rare opportunity to become an even greater *shaliach zibbur*. His assessment was not mistaken.

When the *Sajm* enacted a law forbidding *shechitah* (ritual slaughter) as cruelty to animals, the rabbis of Lithuania were at loss as to what to do. The Ponevizher Rav, however, acquainted with the government's power-brokers, knew that bribery (packaged just the right way) could do the trick. Single-handedly the Ponevizher Rav, walking the knife-edge of danger in an intricate plot whose sheer drama could chill blood in the veins, met secretly with Lithuania's Minister of

Health. All in one night he had to prevent his own constituents from launching protests against the governmental edict without explaining himself, acquire a colossal figure of money and deposit it into the right hands, and concoct a prototype of a newfangled, painless slaughtering mechanism.

The law was abolished, causing Reb Chaim Ozer — surely echoing the voices of thousands — to rejoice, "Lucky are we that we have the Ponevizher Rav!"

Reb Yosef Shlomo traveled to Kovno frequently for his parliamentary duties and was present for most votes. Most of his time in the *Sajm* he devoted to writing his Torah novellae, but he would always perk up his ears if the parliamentary debate bore relevance to the Jews. If a non-religious Jewish parliamentarian ever made disparaging comments about observance, the Ponevizher Rav would take to the podium and defend Torah values in a dignified and clever way.

Because of the wit that the Rav demonstrated in the *Sajm,* the President of Lithuania developed a fond admiration for him and saw to it that every public affair attended by Rabbi Kahaneman was equipped with kosher accommodations.

As a member of parliament* the Rabbi was

entitled to travel first-class on Lithuanian rail free of charge. He nonetheless preferred to travel third-class and explained his unusual behavior as a function of his priorities: "In the heated first-class compartments I am liable to fall asleep. *Chazal* teach that sleep is $^1/_{60}$ of death. There is no way that I would voluntarily submit to a portion of death. I don't have to worry about this eventuality in the frigid, uncomfortable third-class compartments, and I can use the time wisely to learn Torah!"

In the second elections for the *Sajm,* the religious factions were unable to unite as one party. The Mizrachi joined the nonreligious Zionist camp, leaving Agudah on its own. Tempers flared prior to the election, and the motto of the Zionist platform became "Cursed be the hand that votes for the Orthodox." Some of Agudah's rabbis wished to counter-attack by declaring a *cherem* (an excommunication) upon whomever voted for

---

* Fifty years later, Agudath Israel invited the Ponevizher Rav to be their member of Knesset, but he declined, saying that he didn't have the money to afford the office. There was no shortage of reasons to decline such an offer, but what — everyone wanted to know — did money have to do with it? The Ponevizher Rav explained that, halachah mandates that upon hearing apostasy one must tear ones garments (*kriah*). "Being in the Knesset would require me to rip my clothing on a weekly basis, and one may not repair the damage. How would I ever have the budget to buy a new wardrobe every week?"

the non-Orthodox. HaGaon Rav Avraham Dov Shapiro of Kovno announced that he would have no part in such a scheme. Still the plan was not scuttled until the Ponevizher Rav advised that the way to combat a curse is not with a *cherem.* "We should instead declare," he proposed, "***Baruch asher yakeem es divrei Ha-Torah hazos* — blessed** be he who votes for the Orthodox!"

Each *erev Yom Kippur,* the Rav would hurry out of his house to visit the elderly infirm who were not allowed to fast, and remind them of their prohibition. Persuading a Jew to eat on Yom Kippur was no easy task, but the Ponevizher Rav knew how to assert the weight of halachah until matters were perfectly clear. Some asserted that he was a *maikel,* unduly lenient regarding Yom Kippur. Reb Yosef Shlomo countered that he was, in fact, a *machmir:* stringent regarding *pikuach nefesh.* He would assuage the minds of those whom he compelled to eat, by relating Reb Chaim Brisker's pithy pronouncement: one who must make a *bris* on Shabbos has no regrets over the *chillul Shabbos.*

The Ponevizher Rav made special arrangements to provide kosher food for Jewish soldiers. In this regard he adopted the guidelines of Reb Yitzchok Elchonon, which mandated that the food was to be provided to every Jewish conscript, no questions asked. Even if it was manifestly clear that the soldier was merely seeking a free meal, it was not to be denied so that at least some kosher food would fill his belly.

In addition, Reb Yosef Shlomo worked tirelessly to secure furloughs for all Jewish conscripts on Seder night. He spared no effort in this regard, so that each young man would get an inkling what Judaism *and* freedom were all about. And here too, inquiries were never made regarding any soldier's level of observance.

PART of the Ponevizher Rav's uncanny genius was knowing how to add an uplifting Jewish message to any situation. One day he encountered the caretakers of the shul carting off the *shaimos* (*sefarim* that were worn and torn) to be buried. The Rav immediately let it be known that he was going to deliver an important address in the shul. As the good news spread, shops began closing down and people flocked to the shul. The Rav's remarkable oratorical ability coupled with his sharp wit made him the number-one attraction in town. No matter the intellectual ability of the listener, all emerged from the Rav's talks inspired, enlightened and, more often than not, amused.

As soon as the shul was full, the Ponevizher Rav made his entrance to the accompaniment of the *shaimos shleppers*. All rose, according honor to the famous scholar as well as his entourage. In keeping with his agenda, Rabbi Kahaneman had the *shaimos shleppers* seated on the *Mizrach*. These men, understandably, did not suffer from over-recognition.

As far as social status was concerned, *shaimos shlepping* had to be at the very bottom of the ladder, the only job requirement being stamina. Hence the honor those men received on that day was once-in-a-lifetime, and their wives in the audience were no less jubilant than their spouses. The Rav delivered a spellbinding *drashah* that made the audience beam with delight. But after his excursus was completed he still had a special message to share:

"Every parent exults over their youngsters' worn clothing, for there is no better sign of a healthy child. Clothing attests to how active and playful a child is. Woe to the parents who buy their children attractive clothing and it stays in mint condition! Bedridden boys and girls never wear out their clothing...

"*Baruch Hashem*, Ponevizh Jewry — young and old — have taken brand-new *sefarim* and rendered them *shaimos* because of constant use. The creation of so much *shaimos* that must be hauled away by our noble caretakers — to whom we are forever grateful — is a wonderful sign and a healthy commentary on our town. Allow me just to add my *birkas kohen* that we should be privileged to create much more *shaimos*!"

ONCE, during the mourning period of *bein ha-mitzarim* (the three weeks between the 17th of Tammuz and Tisha B'av), a couple came to the Ponevizher Rav to detail why they must be immediately divorced. The days for negotiation and counseling had long elapsed, they assured him, and there was only one option left. Reb Yosef Shlomo listened quietly to what they said, each party finishing the details for the other. When the bitter litany was finished, the Rav at first sat silently and still.

Then, in a totally theatrical maneuver, he leapt up as if shocked by a live wire, and exclaimed, "Do you realize what time it is?"

The couple looked at each other and shrugged. "It is *bein ha-mitzarim*!" the Rav thundered. "*Davkah* **now** you wish to divorce? You are liable to make a *kitrug* against our entire people! There couldn't be a worse or a more dangerous time than now."

The husband's eyelids began to flutter; his

wife's complexion turned as sallow as parchment. But the Rav wasn't finished. "Jeremiah the prophet upbraids the Jewish nation about the bill of divorcement we have brought upon ourselves! Are you trying to prove that your hatred surpasses everything? Don't you realize that by getting divorced now you could *prolong the Exile*?!"

The couple pleaded with the agitated Rav to stop. They had no idea how much trouble they had caused and how far-reaching were the consequences! They were so filled with contrition over the gravity of their plans that they begged the Rav's forgiveness, each other's forgiveness, the Lord's forgiveness... and eventually went on to lead a happily married life.

Twenty-seven

AFTER THE ARRIVAL of the Kahaneman administration in Ponevizh, its educational institutions flourished in both quantity and quality. The Ponevizher Rav oversaw each and every one of them, and nothing was delegated away from his control. Whenever a new boy would come to the yeshivah, or to any of the Ponevizh institutions, he would always approach the youngster and ask a short and simple question whose warmth defies translation, "*Yingeleh, ma'ayin atem v'shel me attem*? (Little boy, where are you from and who is your family?") He always phrased his questions in the plural, as a sign of respect — even to a pre-bar mitzvah boy. The Rav's next question was always about accommodations, lodging and food. He insisted upon knowing what might be lacking. This sincere and loving introduction would capture each boy's lifelong allegiance and devotion.

Reb Yosef Shlomo established nothing less than an educational empire in Ponevizh, with over a thousand youngsters enrolled in the various institutions. The citizenry used to quip that it didn't pay to pave the roads in Ponevizh because sooner or later the Rav would use up every centimeter by breaking ground for a new school or expanding an existing one.

In addition to the yeshivah and elementary school in Ponevizh, Reb Yosef Shlomo established a local high school for girls. This was a major undertaking, especially as there already was a well-appointed secular high school for Jewish girls. By comparison, the girls' school established by the Ponevizher Rav paled to the competition as it was located in a dilapidated, poorly-lit building. He once addressed the inferior conditions by commenting, "Do you know why the secular high school is so well lit? Because there rages a fire within that consumes Jewish souls!"

Notwithstanding, the Rav was aware that it would take more than hyperbole to make the religious school a viable alternative. He therefore hired the finest teachers from abroad, and convened weekly PTA meetings that he personally addressed. In a short time, his methods proved effective, and the religious school's reputation and its enrollment increased dramatically, while that of the competition shrank noticeably.

But he wasn't done. In 1922 the Rav spoke about the critical need to establish a *network* of religious schools for girls, as well as vocational schools for boys who did not intend, or who were unable, to continue in yeshivah. And as always, talk from the Ponevizher Rav invariably led to action.

WHEN the yeshivah in Ponevizh outgrew its quarters, the Ponevizher Rav contemplated purchasing the "Polish Gymnasium," a spacious facility that stood vacant in the center of town. The Ponevizher Rav entered into negotiations with the building's owner, a local judge. He ended up closing the deal for a very fair price, contingent upon each payment being made precisely as agreed.

The seller subsequently learned that he had charged too little for the building, and tried to wriggle out of the deal. The Ponevizher Rav was protected by the signed contract, but the "payment-on-schedule" clause loomed threateningly. Coming in even slightly short or late on a payment would not only invalidate the contract, but would also forfeit all that had been paid to date.

Reb Yosef Shlomo threw all his energies into raising the necessary capital, but on one occasion he could not meet his goal. The day before a payment was due, Reb Yosef Shlomo sadly realized that he had nowhere left to turn. The imminent loss haunted the Rabbi, affording him no rest. Although it was already late at night, he could not fall asleep. "I did all that I could," he told the Almighty, and tried to resign himself to the situation.

Nevertheless, he was still not at peace and went to visit his brother-in-law, Reb Asher Kalman, who also kept very late hours. Reb Asher Kalman was deeply distressed by Reb Yosef Shlomo's predicament. But once the Ponevizher Rav got the matter off his chest, his mind was cleared and he immediately delved into a Talmudic excursus and even related *chiddushim* as if nothing were bothering him.

Then, in the middle of the night, there was a sudden pounding on the door. There stood two local butchers, announcing that they had just finalized a *shidduch* between their children and in the midst of the engagement celebration, they had decided that one-third of the dowry should be deposited with the Rav and used with his discretion until the wedding.

The figure represented precisely what was needed for the purchase of the gymnasium. The Ponevizher Rav returned home and Reb Asher Kalman rejoiced at the miracle from Heaven, joining the *mechuttanim* at the ongoing festivities.

It was almost morning when Reb Yosef Shlomo heard a knock at his door. There, with his head hung low, stood one of the *mechuttanim*, bearing the news that the engagement had been cancelled. He had come at that hour to make sure that the Rav did *not* return the money to *either* side until a *din Torah* could be conducted to settle the account. In the interim, the Rav could use the money to meet the mortgage payments.

When Reb Asher Kalman met his brother-in-law later that day, he commented that the "on/off" engagement party was surely the most bizarre *simchah* that he had ever attended. The whole thing seemed contrived; perhaps a Divine arrangement to enable the yeshivah building to be purchased. It took years for the butchers to settle their differences, years in which the

Ponevizher Rav was able to buy the building.

Ponevizh's *yeshivah ketanah* building was also acquired with a hefty helping of Divine assistance... and astute salesmanship. One Shabbos, the Ponevizher Rav accidentally-on-purpose arranged to meet Dovid Langer,* a well-known entrepreneur and the owner of the largest flourmill in the area. During their "chance encounter," he asked Langer if he knew who owned a particular building. Upon Langer's affirmative reply, the Rav then inquired if that building had *always* belonged to that owner. "No," Langer replied, only to be further quizzed if the present proprietor would always remain the owner. "Unlikely," Langer replied, mystified by the line of questioning. "These kind of buildings belong to one person today and to another the next..."

The Rabbi then asked Langer if he knew the story behind "Glickele's Kloiz" (a beis midrash named after its benefactress). "Sorry, I don't understand the question," the businessman responded.

"I wish to know," the Rav said slowly, "whose was it, and whose will it be?"

"Oh, this is a whole different story," Langer

---

* The name has been changed.

swiftly rejoinded. "It's a holy building that will *always* remain Glickele's."

Reb Yosef Shlomo fell into a pointed silence, knowing that his message was understood. After Shabbos, Langer called the Rav to inform him that he was willing to sponsor the purchase of the *yeshivah ketanah* building, to be named after him [for the ongoing spiritual holiness that would accrue to him name].

To keep the educational empire afloat, the Ponevizher Rav was regularly forced to borrow staggering sums of money. People felt duty-bound to warn him of the risks that he assumed, cautioning that the consequences could be disastrous for himself and his family. With understanding eyes and a kind smile he calmly assured them: "If I had large sums of money, it would be wrong for me to expand the yeshivah, or dream up new ideas whose implementation would exceed the amount of money that I have. But as I do not have a single penny, and I must rely exclusively upon the hand of God, why not think in broader terms?"

It once happened that all the debtors and banks converged at once, demanding that their loans be repaid immediately. Innovative strategist that he was, this time the Rav was caught thoroughly off guard. He hadn't a clue how he could repay, and had zero resources at the time. Reb Yosef Shlomo stalled his creditors, saying he would need a few days to get the money together.

But the gentile collection agent appointed by the bank refused to extend the due date. And with an apparent sense of glee, he warned that any delinquency in reimbursement would result in the fullest penalty of the law.

No sooner had this bearer of grave tidings departed, when an unknown fellow appeared at the Kahaneman door. The man had the look and the manner of a troublesome and time-consuming nudnik. "The Rabbi is very, *very* busy regarding a most urgent matter," family members insisted, "and he absolutely cannot be disturbed!"

The strident stranger refused to budge, repeating over and over that he must be allowed to speak with the Rav concerning a personal matter. Rabbi Kahaneman overheard the commotion, and despite the fact that every second was precious in the race to generate funds and avoid arrest he agreed to see the visitor.

The man explained that he had just received a large sum of money from the American government as compensation for his son having fallen in the line of duty during the Great War. It was not wise, he believed, to hold onto so much money, especially since his employer might discover his true assets and decide to reduce his salary. He therefore wanted the Rav to discretely hold onto the money, with full permission to use it for *klall* purposes in the interim.

Saved from yet another crisis! But the story doesn't end there. The man finally came to collect his money on *chol ha-moed* when the stores and businesses — possible sources for a quick loan – were all closed. Reb Yosef Shlomo sat his guest down and inquired about his welfare as if he had the sizeable sum in his pocket, ready to pay back. Without betraying a hint of concern, the Rabbi offered, "As you have just come from a journey, let me first serve you a meal before we set off to the bank to retrieve what is yours."

As the Rav waited upon his unexpected guest, his mind raced, seeking a plan to instantly generate a pile of money. For once, not a single idea sprang to mind. During *bentching,* just as the Rav reached, "May we be lacking nothing," the mailman arrived, with a large check for the yeshivah...

Twenty-eight

MANY YESHIVOS were uprooted when the Bolsheviks spread into eastern Poland. Some of the rabbis and their students managed to relocate — at least temporarily — in Ponevizh. Among these transients were famous *gedolim* such as Reb Yeruchem Levovitz, the *mashgiach* of the Mir, and Reb Naftali Trop, the rosh yeshivah of Radin. Reb Yeruchem became the Ponevizh yeshivah's *mashgiach,* causing enrollment to swell overnight. It was just a transitory stop for Reb Yeruchem and he insisted that Reb Yosef Shlomo's brother-in-law, Reb Asher Kalman Baron, be appointed the yeshivah's official *mashgiach* in addition to the *shiur* that he delivered. Rabbi Baron was so modest that he refused to say his *shmoozin* or *shiurim* inside the *beis midrash.* Reb Naftali Trop also delivered *shiurim* in Ponevizh and contemplated remaining there, but Reb Yosef Shlomo feared that this might distress the Chofetz Chaim, and advised him to return to Radin.

The Ponevizher Rav was a man of many loves. His decades in the rabbinate in Lithuania demonstrated his passionate love for his fellow Jew; his words and actions conveyed his deep love for the Land of Israel. But clearly his greatest love was that for Torah itself. His devotion to Torah, his intoxication with its sweetness, was so powerful that there were often times that he would grab his head as if possessed and exclaim *Briederlach, lohmer b'emmes lernen Torah! Oy, vee zees is dee Torah*! Dear brothers, let us truly learn Torah! Oh, how sweet is the Torah!"

Later in life he would recall with pangs of nostalgia the deep commitment Ponevizh's Jewry had for Torah learning. Simple people who toiled all week for a meager living, their only free night was *leil Shabbos* and they used this opportunity to its fullest. All the seats in the shul were filled every Friday night by Ponevizh's residents diligently learning late into the night.

The *shiurim* commenced at midnight (!) and the elderly residents of the town were anxious to attend. But what could they do? In the winter the streets were sheets of ice and walking in the dark was extremely hazardous. Their solution to the problem was reminiscent of the Hillelian example of the ultimate Torah dedication: to avoid slipping and falling the old and the infirm would crawl to shul on their hands and their knees!

Because of the Ponevizher Rav's unswerving attachment to Torah learning, he was willing to endure enormous anguish and humiliation to bankroll the educational institutions. Nothing could stop him from the perpetuation of Torah learning.

"What I want, what I really want," he used to say, "is nothing more than Torah! And thus the Lord has promised (*Tehillim* 145) '[You] satisfy the want of every living thing.'"

The Rav also reflected that all of his efforts to establish a genuinely profitable enterprise, or a business whose revenue would finance the yeshivah's budget, had failed. "From here I have concluded that Torah belongs to *all* of *klal Yisrael*, and no financial venture can have a monopoly on Torah support," he declared.

At one point, when he could no longer pay for his students' meals (prior to the construction of the dormitory and dining room), he devised the following solution: he printed "Yeshivah Currency" and dispensed the "bills" to the students every *rosh chodesh*. Local shopkeepers had agreed that these vouchers could be exchanged for food in local stores. When the proprietors amassed a tidy sum of these papers, they would go to the Ponevizher Rav to have them redeemed. This system was one of countless clever techniques the Rav devised, and bought him extra time to pay his bills, plus an additional benefit: the shopkeepers, acutely aware of how poor the yeshivah was, often did not have the heart to demand payment.

Reb Yosef Shlomo never personally benefited from the yeshivah's assets. Once, while on a fundraising mission in Königsberg, he wrote to his wife on yeshivah stationery and apologized that he could only relate "yeshivah business" so as not to be *moiel b'kodesh* — to benefit from consecrated charitable funds. He was in Memel when a friend informed him that he would be traveling to *Eretz Yisrael* and would be delighted to deliver something to the Rav's mother, who lived in Tel Aviv. Reb Yosef Shlomo was eager to take advantage of the offer, but first asked if he could borrow a pen in order to write a letter. The pen in his pocket, he explained, belonged to the yeshivah, and thus could not be used for any personal business.*

As Lithuanian Jewry was engulfed in poverty, the time had come for the Ponevizher Rav to look to other lands for financial support for the educational institutions he had fought so hard to build. The Rav maintained that a rosh yeshivah who is not involved in his yeshivah's fund-raising is delinquent in his job. Nevertheless, whenever Reb Yosef Shlomo traveled abroad to raise funds for Ponevizh, he never directly addressed the issue of money. Instead, with eloquence and wit, he described his love for Torah and the Jewish people. Only upon rare occasions would he drop an oblique reference to the yeshivah's dire straits.

Once he recounted the parable of a poet in the countryside who awoke one morning to discover that his goat was missing. The poet assumed that the blustery wind of the previous night had blown open the gate, allowing the animal to escape. He could think of no other way to retrieve his loss than by placing an advertisement in the newspaper, so off he went to the tabloid's office.

---

* Years later, the Rav, and the yeshivah's first *mashgiach*, Rabbi Abba Grossbard, paid for all meals that they ate in the yeshivah's dining room. Indeed, the yeshivah's records show the Ponevizher Rav's full payments for every repast. Similarly, the invitations for his son's wedding were sent from the yeshivah, but he was particular that the worker who took care of this chore did it only after hours, and was remunerated from Reb Yosef Shlomo's personal funds.

However, the poet within got the better of him, and he ended up penning a sextet of homophonic brilliance and such exquisite cadence that he forgot what had brought him to the newspaper and never even mentioned the lost goat!

Needless to say, the audience ate up the Ponevizher Rav's clever analogy regarding how *he* had neglected to mention the plight of his own yeshivah.

It was standard procedure for the Rav to use the podium to talk about the splendor of Torah study and how this gift was for the *entire* Jewish People without singling out Ponevizh's fame in this regard. His exclusive appeal was to get others to join in the study of Torah and encourage those who were already learning to increase the time that they devoted to this holy pursuit.

At first, his mission brought him to nearby countries, but eventually no continent was off limits. German Jewry, especially its leadership, always received Reb Yosef Shlomo warmly. Rebbetzin Naftali Carlebach, for example, sold her jewelry and delivered the proceeds to the Ponevizher Rav.

Rav Kahaneman spent a full three weeks in Cologne, lecturing to the Jewish residents. In accordance with his standard policy, he never mentioned in a public lecture his yeshivah or the reason he had come to town. Most of Cologneian Jewry had assumed he was a representative of Agudas Yisrael who was dispatched to teach and to be *mechazeik* — strengthen the people in their faith.

In Frankfurt, Rabbi Shlomo Zalman Breuer — meaning no harm — introduced Reb Yosef Shlomo to his congregants as a Lithuanian rosh yeshivah who had come to collect donations for his school. Reb Yosef Shlomo became ashen and protested vehemently. He considered his mission the dissemination of Torah knowledge and one aspect of this goal was bankrolling Torah institutions. To refer to him as a fund-raiser would be like calling a surgeon an individual who fills out insurance forms. It is a tiny — yet essential — aspect of a noble calling. *Chazal* teach, the Rav declared, that one who donates to charity may not contribute more than 20 percent of his income. To enlightened Jewry, you need not even request — you need caution lest they give too much!

"I am here exclusively," he said firmly, "to promote the cause of Torah learning."

During the same visit, Rabbi Breuer, contrary

to his standard policy,* invited the Ponevizher Rav to deliver a *shiur* in his yeshivah. In his inimitable way, Reb Yosef Shlomo made the most of the situation. He asked the boys what they were learning *aside* from their main study, adding, "For your main subject, you hear *shiurim* from *Ha-Gaon*, HaRav Breuer, and there is surely nothing that I could add to the dazzling *chiddushim* that he presents to you!"

The students replied that their secondary study was *Eruvin*. The Rav immediately proceeded to deliver an erudite discourse on that difficult *mesechta*. The caliber of the *shiur* — delivered without any preparation — amazed Rabbi Breuer who could only comment, "Such an incredible genius, and he spends his time collecting money!"**

---

*He usually did not permit guests to address the *talmidim* for fear that an unfamiliar learning methodology might confuse them.

**Reb Shimon Schwab was present at that very *shiur*, his first exposure to the Lithuanian methodology of Torah learning. The young man was so impressed that he wished to accompany Reb Yosef Shlomo directly back to Ponevizh. He followed Rabbi Kahaneman back to his lodging and requested an audience.

After an interview that lasted an hour, Reb Yosef Shlomo concluded that the Telshe Yeshivah would be better suited to develop the bright youngster's talents, and the Rav's advice was adopted. (After beginning in Telshe, Rabbi Schwab later studied in Mir.)

On a different trip to Frankfurt, the Ponevizher Rav met with Rabbeinu Yaakov Rosenheim, whom he had earlier befriended at Agudas Yisrael's Pressberg Conference. Rabbeinu Rosenheim could not bear to watch the Ponevizher Rav shuffle from home to home collecting funds, so he instructed him, "Go to my office. There you will find a beautiful Vilna *Shas* and you can learn in comfort, while I go to solicit in your stead."

That is exactly what transpired. After a few days, Rabbeinu Yaakov Rosenheim returned to his office and presented Reb Yosef Shlomo with a most impressive sum of money that supported the yeshivah for an entire year!

A later visit resulted in Rabbeinu Yaakov Rosenheim arranging a meeting between Reb Yosef Shlomo and a wealthy man who was vacationing in a distant village. The Ponevizher Rav took a night train to the scheduled meeting, arriving in the early morning. Exhausted from the sleepless night, the Rav checked into a hotel for a brief rest.

That morning, for the first time ever, Rabbi Kahaneman overslept, waking just a few minutes before the scheduled appointment… and he had not yet *davened*! The Rav was in a quandary. Logic dictated that he keep his appointment with the *gvir* as *mitzvah d'rabbim adifa* — the public good always takes priority. Still, his inner voice insisted, first things first, and he launched into his devotions.

The meeting was scheduled for 8:30 A.M., and the Rav arrived at the venue a half-hour late. The *gvir* was nowhere to be seen, and the Ponevizher Rav had the horrible feeling that he had made an irrevocable mistake, and that the yeshivah would pay the price.

Just then a man rushed in, huffing and puffing with non-stop apologies unspooling from his lips. "Will the Rav *ever* forgive me?" panted the *gvir*, who was of German extraction and obsessively punctual. "I cannot explain my behavior, for this has never happened before! I overslept by a *full hour*!"

The Ponevizher Rav tried to look sympathetic, but the rich man could not stop flagellating himself. He felt so guilty for having "kept the Rabbi waiting" that he significantly upped his contribution to a total that would cover the yeshivah's expenses for several months!

When these funds were depleted, the Ponevizher Rav departed to the British Isles on yet another fundraising expedition. This trip turned out to be a dismal failure, and new sources of revenue were desperately needed. The Ponevizher Rav contemplated traveling to South Africa, but he could not resolve whether or not he should embark on such an extended journey. Eventually, he brought his quandary before Reb Elya Lopian, who performed the *goral ha-Gra*. The *goral* landed on a detail relating to the construction of the Tabernacle (*Shemos* 25:9), "*v'ken ta'asu* (And thus shall you do.)" Rashi's commentary on this verse is, "For all generations." This explanation was interpreted to mean that the Rav should depart immediately on a trip that would sustain the yeshivah for a *long* time.

The Ponevizher Rav quickly captured the hearts of South African Jewry. He took to the pulpit every day, exhorting the masses to increase their commitment to Torah study and mitzvah observance. On one particular Shabbos, he spoke three different times at three different shuls, but no one seemed to be able to get enough of him. In fact, followers began trailing him from one talk to another. When he noticed the same familiar faces in the morning that he had seen the night before, he declared, tongue in cheek: "I am of course delighted to see the same people who have already heard me, but this places me in an awkward dilemma. If I present a superior talk to what I delivered last night, those who have already heard me will think I wasn't fair to *them*.

Yet, if I deliver an inferior talk to what I said last night, those who have already heard me might become haughty over the preferential treatment that I have afforded *them*. I have therefore no other recourse but to repeat the *exact same speech* I gave last night, to avoid any hint of favoritism on my part!"

The Ponevizher Rav encountered significant success in South Africa, and contemplated how to get the best yield from the harvest. His conclusion was a far-sighted plan to provide long-term income for the yeshivah by purchasing some near-prime, local real estate. Johannesburg Jewry, however, felt that it was unwise for the Rav to invest in property when he was already bowed under such crushing debts. In no uncertain terms, members of the community made their position known to the Rav, and even sent a telegram to Reb Leib Vilkomeer, his father-in-law, in order to lobby support for their opinion. The venerable rabbi, however, had this to say in his succinct return telegram: "My son-in-law knows precisely what to do."

And so he did. In the end, against the advice of his friends in Johannesburg, the Rav bought a residential building in a respectable working-class neighborhood. Almost immediately after the purchase the price of the real estate trebled when the South African Supreme Court relocated to the area. Virtually all of the buildings within a quarter-mile radius were converted into offices that commanded substantial rents.

Even with this boom, however, the yeshivah did not realize any immediate proceeds, because the building was encumbered by a huge mortgage. It was not until the Rav's visit in 1934 that he was able to make the final payment.

Ultimately, the Ponevizher Rav sold the office building in Johannesburg for a handsome profit. In the mid 1940s, these monies financed the construction of the yeshivah in Bnei Brak, which became a haven to segments of decimated European Jewry who ascended to the Land of Israel with the hope of reclaiming a fraction of what had been lost.

V'ken ta'asu, explains Rashi, "For all generations."

Twenty-nine

AS HIS CAREER as an international fund-raiser blossomed, the Ponevizher Rav realized that even the most successful excursions to Switzerland and Germany could not provide enough revenue for his burgeoning complex of institutions. He had no other recourse, he concluded, but to travel from Lithuania to distant America.

But before embarking on such a momentous journey, the Ponevizher Rav sought the counsel of the Chofetz Chaim. He made the grueling trek to Radin and was closeted with his rebbe in a private meeting that lasted 18 hours. Reb Yosef

Shlomo never revealed any details of their marathon discussion, but he would forever claim he never forgot a single word that was said in that room. Moreover, he stated that based upon that talk he was able to solve the majority of problems that would arise during the next 36 years of his life.

During the Rav's subsequent visit to America he crisscrossed the country, alternately achieving successes and encountering challenges.* Chicago's Jewish Federation prohibited Reb Yosef Shlomo from delivering a talk, in accordance with its policy of not permitting fund collectors to make public addresses. This irritated the Ponevizher Rav, who never mentioned his yeshivah when he spoke in public. But policy was policy, and his

---

*The Bostoner Rebbe recalls that from the end of World War II on, Boston was on the itinerary of most prominent — and some not-so-prominent — rabbis collecting money for their institutions. The Rebbe was invariably asked to provide the visiting rabbis with a list of prospective donors and to join them in visits to the homes of potential contributors.

But the Ponevizher Rav was different from all the others who routinely came to town for the very same purpose. His visits to the Rebbe's residence were to convey his rabbinic respects and extend proper courtesy. Despite the Bostoner Rebbe's relative youth, the Ponevizher Rav would discuss Torah matters with him, and then be on his way, never asking for any assistance, and deliberately steering clear of the main supporters of the Bostoner Rebbe's court.

only opportunity to speak in the Windy City was given him by a fledgling Young Israel congregation.** The Ponevizher Rav was visibly hurt by the affront that was conferred upon him, when

For several years this "uneven" relationship — as the Bostoner Rebbe refers to it — persisted, until he finally asked the Ponevizher Rav if he could be of some help. Absolutely not, the visiting rosh yeshivah replied. "Collecting money is like going to a *shvitz-bad* (Turkish bath). Meaning, first you have to undress which is naturally very embarrassing. You then lie down on the massage table so that the masseur can give you a rubdown.

"What are you thinking as you lie on the table? Here I am, a distinguished individual, lying naked, as a fully-clothed attendant — no great genius — works me over. The whole situation is thoroughly humbling, but your consolation comes from the knowledge that in a few minutes you will be on your way and never have to see the masseur again.

"That's what makes collecting money bearable," the Ponevizher Rav concluded. "But *you*, my esteemed host, *you* must remain in the *shvitz-bad* even after I leave town!"

**The Ponevizher Rav always ate his Rosh Hashanah night meal by himself. The origin of this custom dates back to his first visit to America in 1929, when he traveled to Chicago to meet a wealthy man who was not affected by the depression that had devastated the country. The meeting took place *erev Rosh Hashanah* and the *gvir* was enchanted by Reb Yosef Shlomo and invited him to eat at his house that night. The Ponevizher Rav wasn't sure how to decline the invitation of a man who had just contributed generously to the yeshivah, but whose standard of kashrus was not likely to be on par with his own. He therefore replied that he always ate his meal on Rosh Hashanah by himself. Once the words had left his lips he made sure not to violate them for the rest of his life.

his sole topic was the strengthening of Torah learning and mitzvah observance.

Another *non*-highlight of that trip took place in Miami Beach, where over 1,000 individuals congregated in a shul to hear the Ponevizher Rav speak. The address was followed by an appeal that raised only $18(!). The Rav's associates were heartbroken, but Reb Yosef Shlomo did not appear fazed by the paltry proceeds. As everyone wrung their hands and mourned the disaster, the Ponevizher Rav simply wanted to know exactly "what kind" of synagogue had hosted the event. When he was informed that it was a house of worship where men and women sat together during prayer, he was not surprised. In fact he was relieved that money for the holy Ponevizh Yeshivah was not raised in an institution with ideals antithetical to its own.

During the Rav's trip to the United States an audience with the Lithuanian consul was arranged for him by a Jewish federal judge in Philadelphia. As a result of their meeting, the Ponevizh Yeshivah was awarded the status of a theological seminary and its students were absolved from the Lithuanian military draft. It was a major achievement, but the Rav had not finished. Ponevizh was not the only yeshivah in the country! By the time Rabbi Kahaneman was ushered out of the consulate, both Telshe and Slobodka were also awarded the same exempt status.

A driver would take the Ponevizher Rav from town to town during the night so his days could be maximized for collecting. On one occasion, the driver fell asleep. Though the Ponevizher had never learned how to drive, he grabbed the wheel and steered the car to safety. Rav Kahane-man would point to this episode as proof that in times of danger, there are revealed in man abilities that he did not even know existed. Others pointed to this event as proof that the Rav was always in the "driver's seat", never abandoning his responsibility to display leadership.

A portent of the Rav's future was also drawn from an eye examination he had undergone as a young man. The assessment of the ophthalmologist was that he would never need glasses, for while one of his eyes was far-sighted, the other was near-sighted. This meant that one of his eyes was always resting while the other was doing what it could do best. This was preferable, the doctor assured him, to wearing glasses and have both eyes exert themselves. This condition was considered an apt description of the Rav's visionary acumen. One eye was keenly focused on the present and the other, like the *chacham*, was *ro'eh es ha-nolad* — set toward the future.

Thirty

WITH THE OUTBREAK of World War II, Lithuania was thrust into turmoil.The teetering government had no consistent policy and appropriated whatever it deemed to be in the national interest. Among the many casualties of the wanton panic was the Ponevizh Yeshivah building, which was impounded and placed under lock and key. It was time for the Ponevizher Rav to institute a call-up of his own.

On *erev Rosh Hashanah* 5700 (1940), Rabbi Kahaneman approached the Chief of Staff of the Lithuanian army and explained that, in the current crisis, *everyone* had to be mobilized, even the spiritual army. "We are eager to do our share for the national cause," the Rav explained, "but we need to be let back to our barracks!"

The reasoning appealed to the General, and he even apologized for sealing the building.

Reb Yosef Shlomo possessed the proper documents to escape from Europe and travel to Palestine, but he did not wish to abandon his community. Furthermore, every day he was of inestimable assistance to the flocks of refugees that streamed into Lithuania. One disoriented refugee approached the Rav and asked him the whereabouts of the "*hachnasas orchim* (hospitality)" home. "What's wrong with staying with me?" Reb Yosef Shlomo demanded.

Such largess notwithstanding, it was obvious that a more sweeping solution would have to be found for the large number of refugees that was multiplying hourly. As the Ponevizher Rav was gathering funds and provisions to accommodate the influx, it was brought to his attention that with the proper amount of money some Jews in Poland could be saved. Without a second's hesitation he signed a check to the person who had supplied him with this information, leaving the amount blank.

"There must be some mistake," the man said, pointing to the empty line.* But the Ponevizher Rav had not erred. "You will know how much is needed, so *you* must fill in the amount; I can only tell you how much I currently have in my account."

The last public assembly of the Ponevizh Yeshivah, prior to the Nazi invasion, was Simchas Torah. No one knew what the future held, but it was apparent to all that they might not live out the year, or see each other ever again. Accordingly, they gave this Yom Tov celebration their all, and the Ponevizher Rav commented that the participants all received ample *tzeidah laderech* for the upcoming difficult days.

How the Ponevizher Rav managed to escape

---

*Years later, this man with the check became an official in "Aliyat Hanoar," an Israeli governmental office in charge of the absorption of young immigrants, which helped subsidize the *Batei Avos* for orphans that the Ponevizher Rav had established in Bnei Brak. It was highly unusual for Aliyat Hanoar to provide money to a religious institution and this very fellow was instructed to snoop around the *Batei Avos* and see if there wasn't a reason or two to disqualify the institution from funding. But he refused to cooperate with the plan, announcing unequivocally that there was no need to make an inspection, for the Ponevizher Rav was above reproach.

Europe is a mystery that even he never fully understood. Certainly it was not a deliberate plan of his to be far away from Ponevizh, his family and his yeshivah in the winter of 1940, and thus be spared the horror of the Nazi infiltration. His absence was caused by his involvement in a misguided attempt by the Lithuanian government to solve the Jewish refugee problem prior to the inevitable German takeover.

Equipped with a diplomatic passport, Rabbi Kahaneman was selected to be Lithuania's "ambassador" to persuade the United States to authorize the immigration of all stateless Jewish individuals. The idea was that American Jews should bring their substantial influence to bear upon Washington. The naivete of the plan was a tragic reflection of the common misconception about America's humanity and largess towards outsiders (read: Jews), and the supposed clout of its Jewish citizens.

Keenly aware of how precarious the situation was, the Ponevizher Rav announced prior to his departure that anyone to whom he owed money should inform him forthwith. A week before he left, the villagers of Ponevizh, whose love of Torah could never be dampened, celebrated a *siyum ha-Shas,* accepting upon themselves to learn through the cycle again.

It was time for their beloved rabbi to say goodbye, to part from his family and the learning empire that he had created, believing that someday soon all would be reunited. The entire town escorted the Rav to the train station, and just as he was about to board, the youngsters began to chant, "*Rebbe, Rebbe, nemt unz mit*! Master and teacher, take us along!"

Soon the chant caught fire and everyone — the men and the women, the tinsmiths and the cobblers, the seamstresses and the bakers — all joined in the same refrain. According to the Rav, this haunting chant would stay with him forever. Most of these precious Jewish lives would soon be engulfed in the Nazi inferno.

In what was undoubtedly one of the oddities of the war, the Ponevizher Rav — resplendent in his rabbinic regalia — stopped in Berlin, Vienna, and in fascist Italy as he made his way to Palestine: a route that was supposed to lead him, ultimately, to Washington, D.C. It was a demanding journey whose seeds had been sown, on a certain level, a decade earlier.

Hitler had already declared his intentions, and for those wise enough to read it, the writing was on the wall. Rabbi Moshe Landinsky, a rosh yeshivah in the Radin yeshivah, approached the

Chofetz Chaim and asked if the Germans would actually succeed in carrying out their diabolical plot to annihilate the Jewish People. "It is not possible," the sage carefully replied, "to destroy the entire Jewish People..."

Rabbi Landinsky understood from the response that the Nazis would not achieve their full goal, but they would not be thoroughly unsuccessful either. This ominous prediction begged the next question: What contingency plan should be made?

The Chofetz Chaim quoted the policy of Yaakov (*Bereishis* 32:9): "If Esau comes to the one camp and smites it, then the remaining camp shall survive."

Now remained the most critical question of all: Where is that camp that shall survive to be located? Once again the Chofetz Chaim resorted to the scriptures for his reply. "On Mount Zion," he declared, "there will be refuge, and it will be holy" (*Ovadiah* 1:17).

The content of this conversation was conveyed to the Ponevizher Rav, and was duly contemplated. Even though it was never the Rav's intention to abandon his family and town, it was obviously destined that he be spared. He would devote his salvation exclusively to the fulfillment of the prophecy, and indeed Ovadiah's declaration would be mounted on the buildings of the Ponevizh Yeshivah* — and etched upon Rabbi Kahaneman's heart.

---

*The *gematria* of *Ponevizh* (with *kollel*) is the word "Zion".

Thirty-one

IN 1940, the near sexagenarian Ponevizher Rav arrived in *Eretz Yisrael*, commencing the most remarkable chapter of his life. The Rav looked out at the few scattered homes nestled in the Zichron Meir neighborhood of Bnei Brak, and at the hill overlooking it all, and thought to himself that this would be a perfect location for a yeshivah. The Ponevizher Rav's escort explained that the land was private property, and was currently being bid on by a Professor Zitron. The doctor had his eye on the plot as the site for a large sanatorium.

Rather than rely on hearsay, the Ponevizher Rav investigated the matter and discovered that the owner was offering the plot for the relatively low price of 500 Lira Sterling on condition that the purchaser would break ground within twelve months. Such a condition was in no way a deterrent to the Ponevizher Rav, and without any further deliberation, he bought the land.

People were reluctant, however, to wish him mazel tov on the purchase. It was the middle of World War II, Nazi forces were raging across Europe, and appalling reports had begun filtering in about atrocities and the mass murder of Jews. It did not seem to be the right time to think about, let alone *build*, new yeshivos. Furthermore, although no one wished to actually articulate the thought, the Nazi juggernaut seemed to be invincible, and Palestine was clearly in Hitler's crosshairs.

The feeling that prevailed in Eretz Yisrael at the time was that of sinking despair. All were absorbed with the catastrophic losses in Europe, and the Ponevizher Rav was no less consumed than anyone else. However, he was even more consumed with the necessity to rebuild.

His plan was to erect a building that could accommodate at least 500 students. Indeed, as he ascended the hill of the not-yet-built yeshivah he was heard to declare, "I can already hear the sound of Torah that will emanate from this place!"

Nothing could have sounded more preposterous, for the youth in the country at the time were singularly focused upon finding employment. And whereas there may have been a few exceptions, they probably didn't number more than a dozen. Five hundred students sounded no less absurd than 50,000. But the Ponevizher Rav was characteristically unfazed by the critique. "Days will soon come," he predicted, "when there will be millions and millions of Jews who will live in Israel. Then there will not be enough room for the students in Yeshivos Chevron and Ponevizh!"

The Ponevizher Rav's outrageously unrealistic pronouncements raised some eyebrows, but none of this daunted the man. In a sea of skepticism and despair, the Ponevizher Rav proceeded undeterred with his plans. No one could place a damper on his enthusiasm.

When the Rav detailed his ideas to the Chief Rabbi, Ha-Rav Isaac Herzog, the scholar listened patiently, thinking, perhaps — like so many others — that after all this man had lost: wife, children, yeshivah, novellas on the entire Talmud, *nebach*, the misfortune had affected his ability to reason. Yet the Ponevizher Rav contended with perfect clarity that with the Almighty's help he would indeed build an enormous yeshivah and an educational infrastructure that surpassed the network that he had established in Ponevizh.

"You're dreaming," the Chief Rabbi said at last.

The Ponevizher Rav replied, "Yes, I *am* dreaming, but my eyes are *open*. This dream shall be fulfilled through days and nights of *not* sleeping!"

Not long after this encounter, Reb Shneur Kotler, son of the Lakewood Rosh Yeshivah, Reb Aharon, visited Bnei Brak. The Ponevizher Rav took him to the desolate hill upon which the yeshivah would be erected to give him, well, a "scenic" tour. At the very top of the barren knoll, Rav Yosef Shlomo cupped his hand in a gesture fraught with significance, and then whispered, as if he were revealing the secret of the century, "Here, from right *here*, the Torah will emanate."

Rabbi Kahaneman had no confusion about his life's mission. As the noted Ponevizh rosh yeshivah in Bnei Brak, Reb Shmuel Rozovsky was wont to elaborate, Rav Kahaneman willfully removed the mantle of leadership of *klal Yisrael* from his broad shoulders — although he always continued to direct Torah-oriented life — and focused exclusively upon what he was convinced was his true calling in life: the reestablishment of the centrality of Torah learning in Jewish life.

Prodding him incessantly was the agonizing memory of the millions of martyrs who perished, including his own wife and children, the only exception being one son, Avraham. All his life, he kept a photograph of his children in his wallet, and engraved on his heart. These were not the only kindred he deeply mourned: only a handful of over 1,000 students from the Ponevizh educational network survived the war, and nearly all of his rabbinical colleagues from Lithuania were sacrificed together with their flocks. Despite these devastating losses, when an American once asked him to explain God's intent in the Holocaust, he replied, "I lost everything in the *churban*, and I have no *kashas* — questions!"

Rebuilding Torah institutions was the most meaningful expression of his grief, and he had no doubt that he had been spared in order to fulfill the Divine guarantee, *"ki lo tishachach mipee zar'o."** He encouraged others who had suffered

*In 1948 Rav Kahaneman established the *kollel* of the Ponevizh Yeshivah. He explained to the young scholars on numerous occasions that their obligation was to save the generation from spiritual disaster. And, echoing the mandate that the Chofetz Chaim had issued him so many years before, he charged his *avreichim* to establish a yeshivah wherever they accepted a rabbinic position.

to find for themselves a proper mode of consolation. He constantly uplifted the spirits of the downtrodden and saved them from despair in his inimitable way, revealing illumination in the heart of darkness. His message was that God was undoubtedly with them, and that they must immerse themselves in Torah study so that the nation might heal itself. Together, then, they could all join in speedily fulfilling the prophecy of Ovadiah that not only *"B'har Zion t'hiyeh pleitah"* [On Mount Zion there will be refuge]... but also *"v'haya kodesh"* [and it will be holy]! This verse appears in large letters across the front of the main yeshivah building.

Thirty-two

THE YESHIVAH's cornerstone was laid on the 28th of Iyar, 1942, the 55th birthday of the Ponevizher Rav. The Rav fasted and prayed the entire day with great devotion. The ceremony was graced by the presence of a few invited guests including the Chazon Ish and Rabbi Yaakov Landau, the Rav of Bnei Brak.

It was not your typical ground-breaking ceremony. There were no broadly-grinning governmental officials donning hard hats, gripping shovels and posing for the cameras. In fact, there were no cameras, balloons, streamers or champagne to speak of.

It was a lightly catered affair; a few sheets of newspaper were hastily arranged atop some planks of wood from the nascent construction site, upon which were placed some modest drinks and a few baked goods. But the food went untouched, for it was not for refreshments that they had gathered.

The Ponevizher Rav led the assemblage in a few *pirkei Tehillim* and then scooped up cement with a spade. His hands began to tremble as he gripped it near his chest and tears coursed down his cheeks, dampening the mortar and preparing it for its august mission. The Rav then tossed the contents into a shallow hole in the ground to serve as the *even pinah* — the cornerstone.

And with this, the ceremony was over and the *talmidei chachamim* began to descend the hill. The Chazon Ish commented that when you launch an endeavor with cake and schnapps, you never know if it will succeed. However, when you sow with tears, you are assured that *b'rinah yiktzoru* — you will reap in joy.

Tumultuous events and political developments would eventually put the creation of a yeshivah on the back burner. Of more immediate urgency was the creation of a warm and spiritually nurturing facility for orphans. Notwithstanding his noble goal of rebuilding the

Ponevizh Yeshiva in the Holy Land, the Rav could not ignore a spiritual holocaust he saw unfolding there.

Orphans who had been raised by their parents to be God-fearing individuals were being sent to environments where neither law nor tradition were observed. The appalling situation was a source of enormous anguish for the Rav, and he railed against the wrong that was being perpetrated.

Speaking at a gathering in memory of the Holocaust martyrs, the Ponevizher Rav declared: "I shall not eulogize; all I can say is that the *kedoshim* are in the presence of Rabbi Akiva and God Himself, and no one can stand in their presence or their holiness. We owe these sacred souls a debt, and that is to become the fathers and mothers of those few orphans who have miraculously survived. The wish of those that perished is that their children should not forget their Judaism and the Oneness of God. It is therefore imperative that we establish for them *Batei Avos,* homes that will nurture and educate these precious children."

The audience, composed of blue-collar, low-income wage earners, was so affected by the Ponevizher Rav's words that a collection was held spontaneously. That "kitty" comprised the initial funds for the first of the *Batei Avos** erected on the yeshivah property.

Further incentive to expedite the project was the arrival of the *yaldei Teheran*. This group of 1,000 young orphans managed to escape the Holocaust via a tortuous Iranian route. They arrived in Israel to resume the lives that the Nazis had all but destroyed, but the Jewish Agency had other plans in mind. Their political agenda was for these children to begin anew in irreligious — make that anti-religious — kibbutzim. Only the handful of youngsters that the Ponevizher Rav managed to divert to the *Batei Avos* were not robbed of their heritage. The Ponevizher Rav considered this a spiritual "inquisition" and was aghast that less than four percent of the youngsters — all from deeply religious households — were assigned to the *Batei Avos*.

But there was no time simply to protest, given the prodigious task at hand. It was time to act. Rabbi Kahaneman received word on Friday that the first group of orphans would arrive on Sunday morning. The Ponevizher Rav quickly assembled a staff and swung into high gear. There was less than one working day to create accommodations.

---

*Less than a jubilee after the first of the *Batei Avos* opened its doors, the system had educated and matriculated over 10,000 students!

Piece by piece, a makeshift dormitory swiftly developed. Because of the collapse of the citrus market that year, the Rav's son was able to buy a shack at a very low price from an orchard owner in Petach Tikvah. This structure was transported to Bnei Brak to house the children. Juxtaposed was a kitchen hastily erected from cinderblocks. Steel bed frames were secured the same day, but try as they might, the Rav and his assistants could not locate any bedding; during those difficult times in Palestine, most items were at a premium, and some were just impossible to acquire. The Ponevizher Rav was beside himself, for how could he bring orphans to a new home without linens and other basic amenities?*

Time was running out. Somehow, he would have to acquire what the stores could not provide, and he did so in his inimitable style. That Shabbos he *darshened* in the largest shul in Bnei Brak, rallying everyone's passions in a frenzy of

---

*At a later date, a group of children arrived from Tripoli in the middle of the night, and once again the Ponevizher Rav did not have sufficient bedding. Together with his secretary, Binyamin Zev Deutsch, the Rav went to the home of Eliyahu Eisenstat, the proprietor of a bedding store in Bnei Brak. The Ponevizher Rav knocked loudly on his door and proclaimed, "Reb Eli, Reb Eli... arise, arise to the calling of Your Maker! *Yiddishe kinderlach* are coming to learn Torah, but we do not have linen or pillows for them. Reb Eli, open the store!" Needless to say, Eisenstat fulfilled his calling...

emotion. Immediately after Shabbos, the pillow and linen shortage became a thing of the past. As a matter of fact, it even turned into a surplus. One person was so eager to donate all of his pillows that he rushed to the *Batei Avos* right after Shabbos — even before *havdallah* — and he was *not* the first one there!

Considering the horror and upheaval these youngsters had already endured — coupled with the typical challenges of adjusting to a new environment — simply providing them with a well-appointed dormitory would not suffice. Emotional stability does not flourish by chance. The care and the love showered upon these traumatized children had to be carefully considered, and a delicate balance struck between "head" and "heart." This aspect too, the Ponevizher Rav oversaw with fatherly concern, and meticulous planning.

The cuisine at the *Batei Avos*, as all other facets of the institution, was superior to the standard in other Israeli schools, with a far more varied and bountiful menu. One member of the community felt that the operation was not cost-effective, and he had a number of suggestions to reduce expenses. His first recommendation was that the students themselves fetch the institution's food, in order to avoid delivery fees. This fellow never detailed his other proposals, for the

Ponevizher Rav cut him off. The Rav firmly explained that he was *not* running a commercial, for-profit venture, that the institution was filled with hundreds of "only children," — *his* children who were his *bnei zekunim* (children born in old age) as well as *udim muzalim m'aish* (brands snatched from the burning fire).*

The *Batei Avos* became such a central component of the Ponevizher Rav's life that it was not uncommon for him to drop everything in the middle of the day to go and *schmooze* with the youngsters. The discussions that he conducted were peppered — often highly seasoned — with Torah thoughts. At night, frequently in the very dead of night, he would quietly stroll through the dormitory to replace a wayward blanket, or plant a kiss upon a tousled head.

The Ponevizher Rav lavished unbridled love upon the children of the *Batei Avos*. As it was, he could never contain his joy when he saw any little boy learning Torah. If this child was one en-

---

*On the first night of Rosh Hashanah, hundreds of men and boys would file past the Ponevizher Rav to receive his priestly blessing. The Rav would place both hands above the heads of each and every one and chant the benediction that his ancestor, Aharon *Ha-Kohen*, had recited. Each person had the distinct impression on that night, at that moment, that he were the Rav's *only* son.

rolled in the *Batei Avos*, the Rav's delight knew no bounds; it was broadcast in his facial expression — and throughout the neighborhood. He would supply an update to anyone who would listen about the progress and achievements of the *Batei Avos* pupils. His truly greatest *nachas*, it seemed, was when the student was one of the embattled *yaldei Teheran* that the school had absorbed.

Yosef Meir Glicksberg was the youngest among the first group of seven *yaldei Teheran* to arrive at the *Batei Avos*. "The Ponevizher Rav hugged me in his arms for the longest time," Glicksberg remembers. "He would be with us all day long and stroll with us in the orchards. We were like one family."

Indeed, in the early days of the *Batei Avos*, the Rav ate his Shabbos meals with the children and sang along when they would chant Yiddish songs from the ghetto. He would also join them in the sukkah for a *simchas beis ha-shoeva* and delight in the selling of the *kibbudim* for commitments to learn pages of Gemara by heart. It was the very highlight of his *chag simchaseinu*, and he would repeat over and over, "*Noch* (more) *Torah! Noch* (more) *Torah...*"

Once the Ponevizher Rav personally ordered a large quantity of mattresses for the *Batei Avos* from a furniture store on Rechov Herzl in Tel Aviv. But even after the price had been negotiated and a promise of delivery assured, the Ponevizher Rav was not still finished. He insisted that he actually see, feel and "test drive" one of the mattresses. Right there, in the center of Tel Aviv's furniture district, the distinguished Rabbi Kahaneman climbed aboard to assure himself that the mattress would offer adequate support and comfort for his dear children.

Originally, the *Batei Avos* catered exclusively to children who had survived the Holocaust. Over time, its doors were opened to any child from a difficult or poverty-stricken background. The Rav's devotion to these students was no less zealous.

In the course of Rabbi Kahaneman's numerous excursions overseas to raise funds for his educational institutions, he once encountered a fabulously wealthy lady in Detroit, Michigan. The woman was amenable to the idea of providing a warm home for war-ravaged orphans, but supporting *religious* institutions was not part of her agenda and she had no compunction about saying so explicitly. In no uncertain terms, she stipulated to the Rav that she did not want her money supporting a school where the boys wore yarmulkes, "fringes" or ear-locks. And just to make certain that her English was understood with dread clarity, she put her hands behind her ears and wiggled them back and forth, with a resounding *"NO!"* that no one could misinterpret.

Even for one schooled in the intricacies of talmudic logic, or any other, *l'havdil,* reasoning, this woman did not leave much room for manipulation or maneuvering. Apparently, the Rav would be forced to politely and regretfully refuse the donation, or hope to find a loophole allowing him to accept the money while fulfilling the stipulations.

The Ponevizher Rav, with characteristic brilliance and foresight, opted for the second choice: he graciously accepted the woman's donation, and used it as the seed money for... a *Batei Avos* for *girls*!

The Rav wasted no time turning the girls' school into a warm and tender home to raise the future mothers of our People. Whenever a young woman from the *Batei Avos* became engaged, an elegant and beautifully catered party was thrown for her, with the Ponevizher Rav in attendance.

A guest at one of these exhilarating *simchos* recalls that the gala gathering was graced by rabbis, educators and public figures who all offered their wishes that the couple build a lasting and faithful home in Israel, basing their comments upon the weekly Torah portion and other rabbinic passages. The Ponevizher Rav was the final speaker, and to everyone's surprise adopted a different approach. He spoke to the hearts of the couple, particularly the orphaned bride, and wished them in plain and simple language a life of peace and tranquility, free of upheaval and removed from harm. His words were those of a loving father to his only daughter.

On another occasion, a Sephardic young woman raised in the *Batei Avos* became engaged to a student from the Porat Yosef yeshivah in Jerusalem, and once again the Ponevizher Rav participated in the festivities as if he were the father of the bride. Not long after the engagement, however, some problems arose and the couple decided to call off the nuptials. The Rav begged to differ, and he was very outspoken in his position. Eventually his will prevailed, and the couple was married in a grand ceremony that took place at the *Batei Avos* and at which the Ponevizher Rav himself officiated.

This couple was not blessed with children for a long period of time, but when good tidings finally did arrive, the precious baby contracted a rare, life-threatening disease. He was hospitalized in Jerusalem's Shaarei Zedek Medical Center where his situation remained grave and unstable. On numerous occasions the Rav traveled specifically to Jerusalem to visit the family and meet with the doctors of Shaarei Zedek. His concern was no different from that of any doting grandparent.

The Ponevizher Rav, along with many other relatives and friends of the family, pursued spiritual avenues as well, and a recovery — deemed miraculous by the doctors — occurred. The baby returned home and was later followed by numerous brothers and sisters. All are part of a distinguished and learned Jerusalem family.

Rabbi Kahaneman often said that he had established Ponevizh's *yeshivah ketanah* primarily for the children of the *Batei Avos*. It was standard procedure for the Ponevizher Rav to enter the *yeshivah ketanah* and walk directly into a classroom where a *shiur* was being delivered. He would sit on one of the benches just like any of the other students — though all were at least 50 years his junior — and listen intently for an hour or two.

Like a true father, the Ponevizher Rav would never abandon any child of the *Batei Avos*. One day, as he was riding in a taxi down Bnei Brak's Rechov Rabbi Akiva, he spotted a former student named Avraham in the company of friends with whom he would never have associated had he remained in the *Batei Avos*. The Rav instructed the driver to pull over. He then rushed out of the cab and urged Avraham to join him, but the troubled youth refused. The Rav's eyes began to swim and he cried, "*Avram'ala, chazor b'cha! Avram'ala, chazor b'cha*! Avram'ala come back, come back *to yourself*!" But the boy turned away and departed with the smirking thugs. The Ponevizher Rav never saw him again.

This boy descended deeper and deeper, yet every time that he was about to "hit bottom," the plaintive cry of the loving Ponevizher Rav — "*Avram'ala, chazor b'cha*!" — held him back. Decades later, it was the resonance of that very call, he declares, that changed the course of his life, rehabilitating him to a life of mitzvah observance.

Thirty-three

IN 1943, WITH the *Batei Avos* fully operational, the Rav declared that it was high time to resume the construction of the yeshivah. In his mind, there was an added time pressure as well: The aging rabbi had begun feeling weak and exhausted, but he rejected the recommendations of his close associates to consult with a doctor. "The world is afire!" Rabbi Yosef Shlomo would intone. "*Every second is precious*, there is no time now!"

As his health steadily deteriorated, he concluded that if he wished to see the yeshivah operational in his lifetime then he had better implement the opening earlier than he had originally planned. The initial enrollment was but six students. As the building was still on the drawing board, Bnei Brak's Heiligman Shul became the temporary venue for the Ponevizh-Israel yeshivah. The lunchroom, where the students dined together with the *yaldei Teheran,* was a shack that stood on the slope of the yeshivah's hill.

The lodging of the yeshivah students was also an ad-hoc affair, the arrangements initiated by the Chazon Ish. He recommended that the students sleep in an apartment rented from a particular *avreich* who was struggling financially. The sage's reasoning was that it would be appropriate for the yeshivah to open with this *chesed,* in keeping with the teachings of *Chazal*: "*Torah, techilasa chesed* — the Torah commenced with kindness."

It was the Ponevizher Rav's explicit intention that the new yeshivah be an extension and direct continuation of the yeshivah in Lithuania which had been engulfed in the flames. It was therefore no coincidence that the daily *shiur* he delivered after davening in *Magen Avraham* commenced with *siman* 56. The last *siman* that he had taught in Ponevizh, Lithuania, was *siman* 55.

Once, someone expressed the thought that the

Ponevizh yeshivah in Bnei Brak was actually a *matzeivah* for the yeshivah in Lithuania. Clearly this individual did not understand the Rav's goals. The Ponevizher Rav did not take offense, but instead quipped, "Did you ever see a tombstone grow and expand larger than the grave itself?"

At the end of the first winter *z'man* the Rav approached the only one of the yeshivah's six students who did not wear a hat, and whispered, "In a short while the yeshivah will expand, and with it so will the expenses. When this happens I won't be able to help you buy a hat. But now that the expenses are not too great I still have the means. Therefore take this money and buy yourself a hat."

IN 1946, as the shell of the yeshivah was taking shape, a small, makeshift *beis midrash*, office and *shiur* room were pressed into service. (Today, those rooms are only the base of the main staircase!) The Rav and 32 students moved in and set about *their* work. Amidst the din of the workers, and the banging of construction, the *kol Torah* rang out.

Area residents began to complain that the noise from the *beis midrash* was disturbing their afternoon siesta. The Rav was confident that this problem would soon be resolved. "Soon," he declared, "not tens, but *hundreds* of students will be learning here, and not just during the regular *sedarim*, but 24 hours a day. By that time, the *kol Torah* that emanates from here will be so treasured by the neighbors that if it stops during the rest hour, the sudden quiet will disturb their sleep!"

In those early days, the Rav's vision of the yeshivah-to-be was so vivid that it was rare for him to speak of it in the future tense. When the architect brought him a sketch rendering an overview of the entire campus, he was awe-struck by its beauty and grandeur. The drawing was immediately hung in the yeshivah's office, and the Rav summoned his closest students. "This," the Rav proudly announced, "*this* is how the yeshivah *looks*!"

As the yeshivah grew, the Ponevizher Rav worked to ensure that the adjacent residential area would be occupied exclusively by *bnei Torah*. He referred to this as a "security zone" (*der gartel*), and, together with a local businessman, conceived a building project known as "Kiryat Hayeshivah" (today known as Rechov Rabad), with affordable housing for the appropriate tenants. The Ponevizher Rav maintained that it was critical that a conducive environment surround the yeshivah, and that there was no other option but to create it.

He envisioned that in the future he would open an elegant luxury hotel on the hilltop adjacent to the yeshivah. He planned to accommodate those accustomed to such amenities so that they would be able to vacation within arm's length of Torah learning. When it was pointed out that such a costly venture had a negligible chance of being profitable, he was not discouraged. "I would be willing," he asserted, "to invest two million dollars in such a scheme, if as a result one Jew would learn half-an-hour longer than he would have otherwise..."

The Ponevizher Rav took heart from the degree of diligence and scholarship prevalent in Israel. In his opinion, the level of learning was even higher than it had been in Europe before the war. He derived from this fact a modicum of consolation for the tragic losses in the Holocaust, commenting on one occasion, "I have *derech eretz* for this generation; its imbued with a *neshamah yesaira*."

Because the Ponevizher Rav's family was virtually annihilated during the Holocaust, he was not forced to wrestle with the temptation to fill the yeshivah's teaching slots with relatives. "My personal tragedy contains at least one asset for the yeshivah," he maintained, "enabling me to go after the most talented teachers available." Certainly no one could debate the stellar qualifications of Ponevizh's prestigious staff: Rabbis Eliyahu Dessler, Chatzkal Levinstein, Benzion Bamberger, Dovid and Baruch Dov Povarsky, Shmuel Rozovsky and Eliezer Menachem Shach.

The Ponevizher Rav used the same discriminating eye when hiring employees as administrators of the yeshivah, in compliance with the Chazon Ish's directive that a yeshivah treasurer is an integral part of a yeshivah's *spiritual* administration. Reb Yosef Shlomo could not offer his employees handsome salaries, but he did provide each one with the distinct sense that the Rav could not manage without their invaluable assistance.

The Ponevizher Rav's relationship with his staff was warm and personal. One of them related how he had traveled to South Africa with Rabbi Kahaneman in order to lessen the elderly rabbi's load. But the aide was thoroughly unsuccessful... Wherever they went, the Rav waited upon his escort, who was many years his junior, tending to all of the younger man's needs.

Thirty-four

THE YESHIVAH began to burgeon, but the Ponevizher Rav's personal assets remained nothing more than the scant items that he had brought with him from Europe. He did not even own the utensils to cook a simple meal — not that this disturbed him in the least. His room was no different from any other in the dormitory — austere, institutional, with just the bare necessities. He did not even have a clothes closet, and his Shabbos frock hung unceremoniously from a nail driven into the wall. Because he lived just like one of the boys, it was not uncommon for a student to forget to bring supper to his room. When this occurred, the Rav similarly decided to "forget" to eat his evening meal.

Many students have attested that the Rav barely slept, certainly not more than three hours a night, and even that short stretch was never uninterrupted. He usually returned to Bnei Brak on the last bus from Tel Aviv, where he had spent his days engaged in monetary matters for the yeshivah. He would then enter the *beis midrash* for about an hour, deriving enormous pleasure from the *masmidim,* and then retire to the yeshivah office where he would continue dealing with the yeshivah's affairs.

When the Israeli War of Independence broke out, the Ponevizher Rav was forced to hold the reins of the yeshivah single-handedly, as Reb Shmuel Rozovsky was isolated in the blockade of Jerusalem. Aside from his weekly *shiur klalli,* the Rav also had to deliver a daily *blatt shiur** in Rabbi Rozovsky's stead. He also filled the role of *mashgiach,* and delivered the weekly *shmuez.*

The yeshivah was forced to abandon its building; located on a hilltop, it was a likely target for aerial attacks. Ponevizh thus relocated to the packing plant of a nearby orange grove. During the day, the *talmidim* learned out in the open air with *shtenders,* assembling inside the plant for the

---

*One of the innovations that the Rav brought to his yeshivah was the institution of a daily *iyun shiur;* a weekly *shiur klalli* was the standard in the yeshivos of the time.

shiur. Despite wailing air raid sirens and crashing bombs in the too-close-for-comfort vicinity, the students' diligence was astonishing.

The civil guard instituted a black-out, prohibiting the use of lights at night; all learning was thus restricted to the daylight hours. But the Ponevizher Rav could not make peace with this restriction, so he developed his own version of "Daylight Savings Time" by setting his wristwatch back by two hours. As a result, the yeshivah davened *Shacharis* at the crack of dawn, at five o'clock, instead of at seven, and *Maariv* at 7 P.M., which was really 9:00.

Just in case anyone thought that the Rav was taking extraordinary liberties with his time management, he put their minds at ease by assuring them that the government would soon adopt the same policy. In fact, no more than a few days elapsed before the Israeli government instituted "Ponevizh Time."

After the War of Independence, restrictions against immigration were abolished. As *aliyah* swelled, so too did the yeshivah's ranks — and its expenses.

The Ponevizher Rav ran himself ragged traversing the country in his efforts to increase the yeshivah's coffers. He commented ruefully that he sometimes didn't know if he was coming or going, sighing, "I no longer know if I am Yissachar or Zevulun!"

With the financial strain mushrooming daily, a major temptation arose when an extraordinarily wealthy man offered to "buy" the *beis midrash* of Ponevizh for half-a-million dollars, on condition that it be named in his honor. The prospective purchaser's stipulation was by no means unreasonable for this sort of bequest. Furthermore, if one were to tally the sheer amount of exertion, embarrassment, time abroad, hours away from the students, *bitul Torah,* and the host of other difficulties the Ponevizher Rav would undergo in order to raise that amount of money, the offer was nothing less than the bargain of the century!

But before he would consider closing the deal, the Ponevizher Rav needed to know the source of this millionaire's assets. He was informed that the tycoon owned a chain of beachfront hotels in America. The Rav's next question was more detailed, and the reply confirmed his fears: An integral part of the hotel's appeal was the ways it pandered to man's vices.

The Ponevizher Rav did not need to hear any more. The deal was off. "I shall not sell the yeshivah for this type of money," he stated in a tone that left no room for negotiation.

Thirty-five

THE PONEVIZHER RAV embarked on his fundraising missions with Herculean vigor and unmatched dedication. He gave nary a thought to physical comfort or convenience. On one trip to England, he was accompanied by a member of the yeshivah staff who was thirty years his junior. This novice, however, was no match for Reb Yosef Shlomo, and after just a few days the younger man saw that he had neither the stamina nor the physical agility of the elderly rosh yeshivah, and planned his return to Israel, suffering from acute exhaustion.

There were occasions during the course of his

numerous trips abroad that the Ponevizher Rav was accorded the "red-carpet treatment" appropriate for a Torah scholar of his stature. But there were just as many times when he was subjected to callous indifference, and worse. As a rule, he never discussed the humiliations he suffered during his travels, alluding to them only occasionally via oblique references in correspondence or conversations with his closest confidantes and relatives.

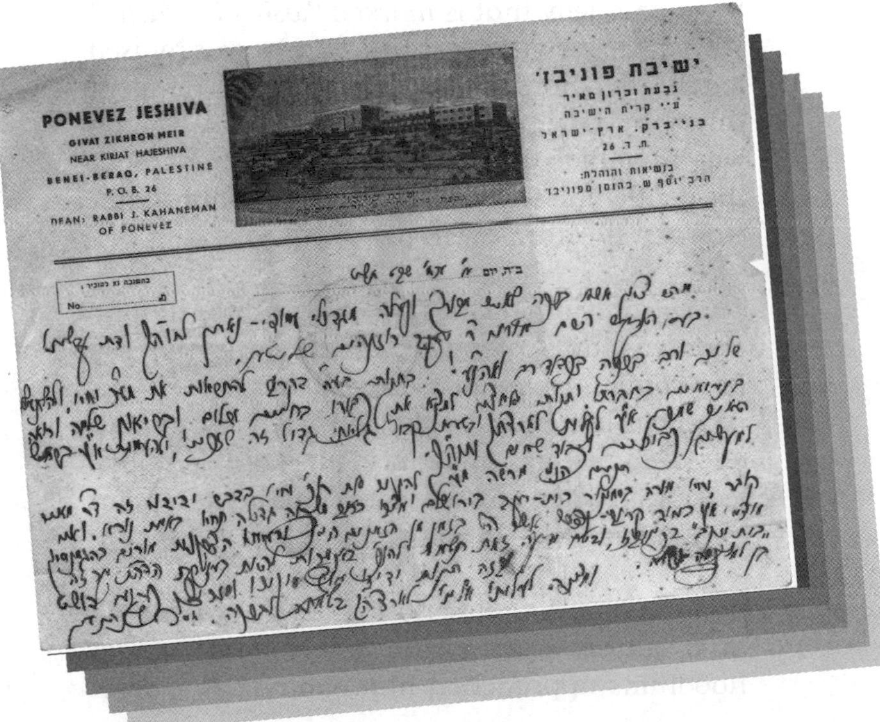

PONEVEZ JESHIVA
GIVAT ZIKHRON MEIR
NEAR KIRJAT HAJESHIVA
BENEI-BERAQ, PALESTINE
P. O. B. 26

DEAN: RABBI J. KAHANEMAN
OF PONEVEZ

ישיבת פוניבז'
גבעת זכרון מאיר
ע"י קרית הישיבה
בני-ברק. ארץ-ישראל
ת. ד. 26

בנשיאות והנהלת:
הרב יוסף ש. כהנמן מפוניבז'

בתשובה נא לזכור:
No. ....

ב"ה, יום

One might imagine that people would stand in line for the *zechus* of hosting a rabbi of such eminence, but sadly, this was not the case. In one poignant letter, Rabbi Kahaneman wrote: "Shabbos is imminently coming, and I have purchased a disposable plate for my meals." In another correspondence he wrote that he had located a local *shochet* whose kashrus he felt he could trust, and therefore he would eat in this man's house. His menu, however, was still rather lean: "I have brought matzos from Israel and I shall garnish them with jelly that is marked *'kasher l'Pesach.'*" Yet a different letter describes how he was refused lodging in a hotel for "various reasons." He spent the night under the stars until daybreak, when it was brought to the attention of the manager that the gentleman who had been denied admittance was a "VIP" from overseas.

The only other clues to the hardships that he endured may be gleaned from the stories that the Rav sometimes related as a *mussar haskel* — a practical lesson to be derived from his experiences. Sometimes these incidents "accidentally" leaked out when he used them to elucidate a point in a *shmuez*.

One anecdote described how he was riding on a subway in New York City when a gang of hoodlums approached him. Object? Not *divrei*

Torah. The Rabbi had no doubt that he was about to be mugged, and there was no one else in the car that he could summon for help. Armed with only his wit, he appeared to be at a distinct disadvantage, given the arsenal of the brawny opposition. But appearances can be deceiving...

The Rav pulled out a slip of paper upon which was written an address in the area. He nonchalantly approached the young men, who were closing in for the kill. In faltering English, he asked if they recognized the location and could inform him when to get off the train. The "brainy bunch," certain that they had never encountered an easier mark, instructed the rabbi to get off at the next stop along with them. They reasoned that a victim was always easier to attack on a dark, deserted street than on a well-lit train where they might be interrupted at any time.

As the subway pulled into the station, the youths leered in anticipation of a Mickey Mouse mugging. When the doors opened, the venerable rabbi, with a sweeping gesture of his hand, gave the gang the honor of disembarking first... and then delayed his own exit for but a moment, until the train door slammed shut. The Ponevizher Rav claimed that Yaakov *Avinu* gave him the idea, referring to *Bereishis* 33:12, when Eisav offered, "Let us travel on together..." to which Yaakov replied, "Let my lord go ahead of his servant..."

WHEN THE PONEVIZHER RAV heard that Hebrew University had amassed debts exceeding 40,000 Lira, he let out a long and mournful *krechtz* and wailed, "What's wrong with us? For their *narishkeit* they have invested millions of Lira, but for the learning of Torah we have spent but a paltry sum!"

As fundraising was such an integral part of his life, he naturally tried to get the most mileage out of it. "*Kinderlach,*" he once began a *shmuez* aimed at increasing the diligence of the students, "do you know what gives me the strength and the determination to be a globetrotter, overcome my bashful nature and knock on the doors of doubtful donors? Your learning. When I see your immersion in Torah study it gives me the impetus to do the impossible."

Once the Ponevizher Rav returned from overseas quite late, arriving at the yeshivah at 2:30 in the morning. The senior *talmidim* waited for him in his house and the Rebbetizen* had set the table with a meal. The students sat with the Rav for about an hour while he ate and talked, until he turned to them and said, "*Nu, bachurim...*"

They were sure that the end of the sentence would be, "Good night," but they couldn't have been more mistaken. What he said was, "Let's go to the yeshivah where I will deliver a *shiur.*"

---

*In 1953, the Rav wed Hinda Porath, a descendant of a distinguished Lithuanian family. The Sages teach that *zivug sheini* is according to *ma'asav* — one's second marriage partner is awarded by virtue of one's deeds. Rabbi Kahaneman suggested that perhaps this means, "according to one's profession." "There is nothing that I wouldn't do for the yeshivah, but I cannot be its *baal habusta,*" he explained. "Now both the yeshivah and I will be blessed with what we have been missing..."

They used to quip that in the Ponevizh yeshivah there was no need to deliver *shmuezim* about the love of Torah, for the Rav was the very embodiment of that attribute. His passion was not only related to his enjoyment of learning, but a result of his deep love of God. On Simchas Torah the Rav would dance as fervently as his strapping young students, whispering to them *"klor verren Shas,"* meaning: accept upon yourself *now* to learn diligently, so that you will be an expert in the entire *Shas*.

The Ponevizher Rav was certainly in the position to issue such exhortations. His personal mastery of the Talmud was precise and total. He once took a seat and grabbed the closest gemara in the vicinity. An onlooker observed that the Rav opened the volume at random, and asked him why he was learning that particular page. "This is where I am holding," Reb Yosef Shlomo replied, meaning that he was at home anywhere and everywhere in *Shas*.

On Simchas Torah, the verses of *Atta Hareisa* were auctioned to the highest "bidder" — that is, learner — usually those who committed themselves to learn the entire *Shas* during the course of the year. The Ponevizher Rav personally oversaw the auctioning and enjoyed every moment. He claimed it was the best "business" he did all year long.

Thirty-six

SOON AFTER the Ponevizher Rav arrived in America during Chanukah of 1950, he began suffering from a kidney ailment. He was hospitalized in Manhattan's Mt. Sinai Hospital; his condition was categorized as critical, his chances for survival poor. The doctors believed that the Rabbi's only hope was to remove the damaged kidney in what would be a complicated and risky operation.

Prior to surgery one of the doctors frankly informed the Rav of the peril involved in the procedure. As his "last wish," as it were, Reb Yosef Shlomo summoned four survivors from Lithuania to his bedside, and asked them to recount any accomplishments they had been able to achieve because of him. Those assembled were happy to comply, but found it a puzzling request at that crucial hour. The Ponevizher Rav explained that he stood on the verge of his Judgment Day, which would undoubtedly entail a *din Torah* with the true Judge. "I am endeavoring," he told them, "to prepare my case."

Tefillos in behalf of the Ponevizher Rav were organized all over the world. During the actual operation students in the yeshivah learned all night long, interrupting themselves every half-hour to recite *pirkei Tehillem.* The operation was successful but serious complications developed during post-operative care. He did not fully re-covered until five months later.

A gala *seudas hoda'ah* was hosted by the yeshivah, graced by an exuberant Chazon Ish. "I was already summoned to the World to Come," the Ponevizher Rav said at the occasion, "but as the expression goes, 'when you need a thief you remove the noose from his neck...' Apparently I am still needed for the building of the yeshivah.

"While in the hospital I prayed, 'Master of the Universe, there are plenty of *lamdanim* and *talmidei chachamim* in the world, but where will

You find another '*meshugeh l'oso davar*' to build the Ponevizh Yeshivah?'

"I have no doubt that it was in the yeshivah's merit that I was spared."

No one was more relieved over the Ponevizher Rav's recovery than the Chazon Ish. The two Torah giants enjoyed a warm relationship that was forged upon mutual respect.

Someone once criticized the Ponevizher Rav to the Chazon Ish, questioning the necessity of building so many buildings. The Chazon Ish shot back, "Don't you see that he is being instructed from Heaven, *build!* No mortal has a right to intervene..."

Regarding these two scholars, people used to joke that Bnei Brak was doubly blessed with the Chazon Ish and the "Ish Hachazon."* The love and admiration of the Ponevizher Rav for the Chazon Ish knew no bounds, and his commitment to uphold the Chazon Ish's opinion was total. Students who learned with the Ponevizher Rav as he prepared his *shiur klalli* noticed that if, as he paced his room thinking of a *svara*, his eyes

---

*"Ish Hachazon", a twist on the name Chazon Ish, meaning visionary, refers, of course, to Reb Yosef Shlomo.

stumbled across a volume of the Chazon Ish, he would stop, hug the *sefer* and kiss it.

Two highly intelligent *talmidim* in Ponevizh were neglecting their studies. The Ponevizher Rav was concerned and discussed the issue with the Chazon Ish. The Gaon proposed that the two become his *chevrusas* for a fixed period of time every day. This arrangement was maintained almost to the last day of the Chazon Ish's life and as a result, both of these students developed into *gedolei Torah*.

Reb Moshe Portman was one of the very few *talmidim* of the original Ponevizh yeshivah in Lithuania who survived the Holocaust, and was therefore understandably close with the Rav. After his marriage, he and his wife spent their Seder with the Ponevizher Rav. When their first boy was born, they were eager for Reb Yosef Shlomo to be the *sandek*.

A jubilant Rabbi Kahaneman arrived at the bris in the company of the Chazon Ish. The Rav awarded the Gaon the honor that was to have been his, reasoning: "Had this been the bris of *my* son's son, I would have preferred the Chazon Ish be the *sandek* over myself. Today's *simchah* is the same to me as if it were my own grandson's, and therefore I acted accordingly...."

The Ponevizher Rav never missed a *talmid's simchah*. Even in his later years, when he was weak and ill, the Rav always had time for his students. And he did not make mere cameo appearances at such gatherings; he participated as a full partner in the festivities. If the joyous occasion was the marriage of an orphan, he was supremely happy!

One boy who managed to survive the horrors of World War II arrived on Israel's shores an orphan without a living relative. He attended a yeshivah in Tel Aviv but was embarrassed to celebrate his *aufruf* there, thinking that it would appear odd that he had no family and few acquaintances.

He therefore opted to spend his *aufruf* in anonymity and traveled to the Pension Reich hotel in Jerusalem. That very Shabbos, both Rabbi Kahaneman and the famous rav of Petach Tikva, Rabbi Reuven Katz, were also guests of the hotel. When they noticed a *ben Torah* alone during the *z'man*, they feared something was amiss and inquired as to his health. The young man fidgeted and became flustered, but finally explained that he was about to be wed and had come to the hotel to get away from the premarital jitters and chores.

The acutely perceptive Rav Kahaneman gently asked the anxious fellow if that Shabbos was his *aufruf.* The young man, after clearing his throat and turning a few shades redder, conceded that it was.

When the *chassan* opened his door the following morning, he found the two elderly *gedolim* waiting to escort him, *shoshbinim*-style, to davening. The groom objected vigorously, as he was headed for the distant outskirts of Bayit Vegan, but the rabbis would not absolve themselves from this mitzvah. The two locked arms with the groom and escorted him all the way, in a scene that could only conjure up a glorious procession led by the *malachei hashares.*

Thirty-seven

THE 27TH OF SIVAN, 1953, was the yeshivah's official *chanukas ha-bayis*. This date was deliberately chosen by the Ponevizher Rav, as on that very day, twelve years earlier, the Nazis had entered and conquered Lithuania, bringing about the destruction of Lithuanian Jewry. The Ponevizher Rav had planned to mark the occasion as a fast, with all-day learning capped by *shiurim* by the Chazon Ish and the Brisker Rav, ending in an uplifting *seudas mitzvah*. The plan did not work out as envisioned, yet the Rav's tearful address was still heartrending to all those present.

Soon after, however, the Ponevizh yeshivah

fell upon hard times. In 1954 — after the devastating loss of the Chazon Ish — the yeshivah's financial situation deteriorated rapidly. The Ponevizher Rav had to undertake an emergency fundraising trip to the United States; and not long after his departure he received more tragic news regarding the passing of the yeshivah's *mashgiach*, Reb Eliyahu Dessler. The trip, however, was successful thanks to the extraordinary generosity of Rabbis Eliezer Silver, Velvel Yaffa and Shaul Satiansky, each of whom contributed $50,000. The Ponevizher Rav referred to them as the *malachim ha-tovim* who saved the yeshivah.

Upon his return, Reb Yosef Shlomo was sobered by the fact that although the past debts were canceled, the future still loomed ominously. He sat down and calculated the yeshivah's expenses and was appalled by the enormity of the sum. But after a little more arithmetic he concluded that this enormous figure tallied only $330 a day. This information put his mental wheels in overdrive.

In the past, yeshivah students had eaten their main meal in the homes of *baalei battim*, in a tradition known as "*teg*" (the daily meal). By supplying nourishment, a *baal haboss* could earn a share in the student's learning. But because of inequities in the system, often at the expense and the pride of the student, Reb Chaim Volozhiner abolished the "*teg*" system.

The Ponevizher Rav realized it would be advantageous to all if he were able to revive the concept of "*teg*" — without its drawbacks. It occurred to him that individuals could provide *teg* on the yeshivah's turf, where no student's dignity would be compromised. Those benefactors who were willing to underwrite one day of the yeshivah's expenses, he called the *Nitzavim*.

The Rav quickly implemented the system, and quipped that the only difference between the old version of *teg* and his innovation was that "in the past the students would eat in the homes of the rich; now, the rich eat *their 'teg'* in our home!"

The idea of dividing a yeshivah's expenses into 365 days and then apportioning them out was not that novel a concept, but it took a *gaon* the caliber of the Ponevizher Rav to put the system into practice. It was also the destiny of the Ponevizher Rav to be the one to introduce an idea that has since been adopted by numerous yeshivos the world over.*

---

*In fact, Reb Elchonon Wasserman in Baranovitch, and Reb Meir Shapiro in Lublin, had proposed the "on-campus-*teg*" notion earlier, but they could not find an attentive ear for their plan. Indeed, when one wealthy individual finally agreed to initiate the program, *Dos Yiddishe Tagblatt* in Warsaw gave the phenomenon a headline, "*Dos Ven a Gvir Farshteit...*" ("When a Rich Man Understands...").

Thirty-eight

ALTHOUGH Reb Yosef Shlomo's official title was the rosh yeshivah of Ponevizh, he accepted upon himself the responsibility to enlighten all of *klal Yisrael.* His premiere vehicle for achieving this goal was the *Yarchei Kallah* learning program, which he organized every summer for those in the work force.

As usual, the Rav's ideas were on a grand scale,* his plan envisioning the involvement of

*The Ponevizher Rav was in America at the time that he was planning the debut of the *Yarchei Kallah*. In the course of his travels, he stumbled upon an opportunity to purchase used, U.S. Army surplus platoon-sized tents for next to nothing. The Rav was certain that such an overflow

all of Israel's residents in the *Yarchei Kallah,* which was to be launched in numerous shuls throughout the country. Rabbi Kahaneman's precedent was Rabbi Akiva, who had the original yeshivah in Bnei Brak. "It was illogical to assume, the Rav argued, "that Rabbi Akiva's 24,000 students were all congregated in *one* yeshivah."

The Ponevizher Rav also firmly believed that Torah was the possession of *all* of *klal Yisrael,* but its owners had to truly deserve this treasure as well as be cognizant of its value. While *bnei Torah* were privileged to learn Torah the entire year, with a two-and-a-half week intersession, the *Yarchei Kallah* would provide those not enrolled full-time in yeshivah a two-and-a-half week *z'man* to counterbalance the *bein hazmanim* they endured the rest of the year. "Thus," he told the *Yarchei Kallah* participants, "despite your lengthy *bein hazmanim,* you will remember that you are first and foremost *talmidim* who belong in our yeshivah."

With characteristic modesty, the Ponevizher Rav claimed that the idea of *Yarchei Kallah* was not his, but a practice that had functioned biennially in the time of the *tannaim* and *amoraim;*

---

crowd of *Yarchei Kallah* participants would descend upon Bnei Brak, that the tents would be drafted for further use, this time by the Army of Hashem.

and therefore, he was merely reinstating the custom with a few revisions. This age-old tradition (which hardly anyone had ever heard of) he found alluded to in the writings of Rav Sherirah Gaon.

The Rav threw all of Ponevizh's resources into the absorption of the summer learners and their families. This meant dormitories and *maggidei shiurim*, classrooms and *baalei mussar*. The Rav made a point that all of the accommodations should be top-shelf, so that nothing would detract from the experience. Participants were divided into various categories and sub-categories according to their learning levels and areas of interest.

The early risers were invited to the Ponevizher Rav's home, which was adjacent to the yeshivah, for a hot drink before davening. And from that hour until late into the night, the Rav was continuously at the disposal of the learners. Under no circumstance would he ever cancel, or absent himself from a *shiur* he was to deliver to the *Yarchei Kallah*. Even if a *talmid* was scheduled to be wed in Jerusalem — an event he would otherwise always have made sure to attend — he would send his regrets, explaining that he was unable to abandon the *Yarchei Kallah* — even were it his own son's wedding.

Over time, the idea of *Yarchei Kallah* was adopted

in numerous locations both in Israel and abroad, and the Rav was suitably elated.

JUST AS THE *Yarchei Kallah* was predicated upon the belief that Torah belongs to the entire nation, the Rav likewise never viewed Ponevizh (in Israel or in Lithuania) as "his" yeshivah, or other yeshivos as the yeshivos of "others." In the early years, when roshei yeshivah came to Ponevizh, Lithuania, to solicit funds, Reb Yosef Shlomo gladly escorted them to the local men of means.

He didn't alter this policy when he came to Israel. Once a wealthy tourist visiting from America offered a large donation to the Ponevizh yeshivah as a tribute to his parents. In the course of his discussion with the Rav, the gentleman remembered that his father had learned in Slobodka in his youth, at which point Rabbi Kahaneman suggested that it would be more fitting for him to make his contribution to the Slobodka yeshivah (also located in Bnei Brak).

On another occasion, a rosh yeshivah from Jerusalem who was on a fund-raising mission in America, entered a shul on his itinerary and found it packed. At first the rabbi couldn't believe how fortunate he was, in that all of the town's potential donors were congregated under one roof. That was until he realized why they were there. The large and enthusiastic crowd had gathered to hear a celebrated guest speaker from overseas: Rabbi Yosef Shlomo Kahaneman. As the Ponevizher Rav began to deliver his legendary, electrifying appeal for greater learning and Torah observance, his colleague became crestfallen and began calculating his losses.

The rosh yeshivah wearily girded himself for the Rav's segue into the wisdom of contributing to Ponevizh. He was thunderstruck when the Ponevizher Rav, having noticed the visitor's entrance into the shul, appealed for the audience to contribute handsomely to the Jerusalem yeshivah that he represented!

The Ponevizher Rav was in New York when Reb Aharon Kotler passed away. He eulogized the *gaon* at his funeral and then convened an emergency meeting in the home of one of Ponevizh's greatest supporters, Charles Bendheim — not on behalf of his own yeshivah — but on behalf of Lakewood! Reb Aharon's yeshivah was burdened by a debt of $100,000, and the Ponevizher Rav labored assiduously to erase it. This required so much time and energy that it appeared to some that the Rav had forgotten that he had traveled to America to raise money for Ponevizh. But the fact of the matter was that the Rav's central goal — his only goal — was the building of Torah wherever he went, and he did not limit that goal to Ponevizh.

Sometimes the worth of his actions was not immediately apparent. He used to make an annual pilgrimage to a distant community in England in order to provide them with the merit of contributing to Torah learning. If that sounds a tad supercilious, it is nonetheless the veracious truth. The donations that the Ponevizher Rav collected there never compensated for his time or expenses. Still, the Rav made his yearly visit, encouraging the locals to increase their Torah learning. Little did he realize how effective he was.

Thanks, in part, to his impassioned pleas, some community members decided to dig deep into their pockets and open a *kollel*. The next year, when the Rav arrived, they explained that they had nothing to donate to Ponevizh as all available money was invested locally. Rabbi Kahaneman was overjoyed by the news, and tickled that he had had a share in it — despite Ponevizh's (negligible) loss.

Rav Kahaneman was instrumental in getting the court of the Vizhnitz chassidus to move to Bnei Brak. The Vizhnitzer Rebbe's agents were doubtful that they would be able to afford the property, until the Ponevizher Rav took over the negotiations. Serving as an ombudsman to purchase the land, the Rav knew no rest until the deal was consummated.

The Rav's longtime associate in Britain, Yaakov Levinson, arranged a key appointment between Rabbi Kahaneman and a renowned *gvir* in London. Putting this meeting together was by no means a facile endeavor, and Levinson worked tirelessly to coordinate it. Just prior to the long-awaited encounter, the Rav learned that Levinson had a regular learning session scheduled for the same time that the meeting was to take place. He therefore insisted that Levinson not accompany him, even if it meant canceling the appointment.

This was a real insight for Yaakov Levinson. Up until then he had thought that the Ponevizher Rav would do anything for the sake of the yeshivah. He then learned that the Rav would do anything — even sacrifice the yeshivah's interests — for the sake of learning Torah. Even for one single individual.

Thirty-nine

LONG BEFORE the winds of change and the dark clouds of terror had cast their shadow over Europe, the Ponevizher Rav yearned to transport his extraordinary educational empire from Lithuania to Eretz Yisrael. He always said that a Jew, no matter where he is, must always remember where he belongs, and that is *Eretz Yisrael.*

After the Holocaust, the establishment of a State of Israel was foremost in everyone's minds. In the religious camp, a heated debate escalated regarding the merit of this venture. The Ponevizher Rav declared that we should not delude ourselves that the State would function according to Torah precepts — at first. Eventually, however, a Torah authority would govern the land.

After the State was established, one naysayer predicted that it would definitely fall. The Ponevizher Rav's face contorted with pain, and he thundered, "After the spilling of so much blood?!"

His outlook on the nascent State and what would transpire there, like everything else in his purview, was visionary. The Ponevizher Rav was fully convinced that the length and breadth of Eretz Yisrael would be filled with *chozrim b'tshuvah* busily engaged in Torah study. This anticipation found expression continuously.

One day as he was walking down a main street in Bnei Brak, he observed construction workers at the building site of the radically secular/socialistic *Histadrut HaOvdim*. The Rav, who had acquired significant knowledge of architectural and engineering matters while overseeing the construction of the Ponevizh campuses in both Israel and Lithuania, was not happy with what he saw. He rushed over to the workers to verify that they were using reinforced steel and concrete in the foundation.

The jaws of the *Histadrut HaOvdim* employees gaped in amazement over the Ponevizher Rav's interest in their building. "I have no doubt that one day this building will become a yeshivah," the Rav explained serenely. "I am therefore concerned that it should be properly built."

It was on *Issru chag ha-Shavous,* 1941, at Agudath Israel's third (Israeli) convention that the Ponevizher Rav made his famous declaration, "Write tefillin and mezuzos for the children of Ein Charod, and we will yet need to build *chadorim* and yeshivos for the children of Nahalal!" (These two kibbutzim in Emek Yizrael were leading centers of secularism at the time.) And to this he added a clever twist of topography, by announcing, "It will not be long before the sound of Torah in the *emek* will be heard *b'rama...*"

On a different occasion he declared that tefillin and tzitzis should be placed in the knapsack of every soldier in the IDF. "If they don't use them today," the Rav expounded, "they will surely use them in the future."

The Ponevizher Rav's second wife had not-yet-religious relatives in Kibbutz Ashdot Yaakov in the Galil. At his wife's request, the couple traveled to the kibbutz. The Rav's visit had a dramatic impact upon the residents, especially the youngsters who had actually never before seen a religious man! The Ponevizher Rav's infectious love and warmth captured the hearts of the kibbutznikim. Gently, he proposed that they place mezuzos on their doors.

The Rabbi wisely did not over-request, and his entreaty was accepted. Just a few days later he was back with the goods, equipped with hammer and nails. The Rav derived such enormous joy from the performance of this mitzvah that he practically danced from one house to the next. Now each home, he declared, affirms that there is a God within.

Not long after the Rav's triumphant visit, a group of 11- and 12-year-olds from the kibbutz were invited to the *Batei Avos* for Shabbos. Included in their itinerary was a trip to the Ponevizh

Yeshivah and a visit to the Rav for *seudah shlishis*. It was quite a sight to see these children from anti-religious homes crowding around the Rav, as he patiently explained to them the meaning and significance of the blessings before and after food.

On the eve of the *shmittah* year (the sabbatical year during which the Torah mandates that the land must lay fallow), the Ponevizher Rav traveled to the *shmittah*-observing agricultural kibbutz, Chofetz Chaim. His visit caused quite a sensation, and he used the opportunity to speak passionately about how critical it was for Torah law to dominate life in the Holy Land. Before the onset of the *shmittah* he suggested that every farmer go over and wish a tree, "Gut Shabbos, *boimelah*." He himself kissed the ground and wished it "Gut Shabbos."

As always, the Ponevizher Rav practiced what he preached, and his *shmittah* observance delayed the construction of the yeshivah's dining room by one year. Some orange and grapefruit trees grew on the site, left over from the orchard that had once flourished there. The Rav ruled that because of *ba'al tashchis* (the prohibition against waste, which includes the destruction of a fruit tree) the trees may not be uprooted but must be replanted — which involved digging up trees along with their roots, a labor that is forbidden during *shmittah*.

Forty

TOWARD THE END of his life, Reb Yosef Shlomo Kahaneman became deeply concerned about building a financial infrastructure that would facilitate the influx of funds when he would no longer be there to solicit them. Hence, during a period when the financial obligations of the yeshivah were overwhelming, and every day the debtors pounded at the door, he took all available resources and invested them in a plot of land for a cemetery to be called "*Netzivei Ponevizh.*" He believed this would provide a valuable source of income for the future.

Rabbi Moshe Akiva Druk, editor of the newspaper *Hamodia,* asked the Rav, "What is a *kohen* doing with a cemetery?" Rab Yosef Shlomo had this to say: "Ponevizh has only one *meshulach* who travels all over the world in its behalf. I am looking for a method that can continue my work even after I am gone... If people wish to be buried here, I hope that they will contribute handsomely to the yeshivah for their resting place."

It was standard procedure for the Ponevizher Rav to commence the construction of a new building at the same time that another project was in the stages of completion. And while a shortage of funds was always a problem, he was never at a loss for ideas. It was his fervent goal to establish exactly the same number of yeshivos in Israel as had been destroyed by the Nazis in Lithuania, in order to perpetuate the memory of the *kedoshim*.

This project got underway during *chol ha-moed Pesach,* 5722 (1962), when the Ponevizher Rav visited Ashdod. At the time the area was barren, and the august plans for the town's future as a burgeoning port city were merely sketches on the City Planning Commission's drawing boards. The Rav was overtaken by the beauty of the area, and actually bent down and kissed the sand.

It occurred to him that no Jews had set foot in the area from the time of *churban bayis sheini*. It was only appropriate, he reckoned, that with so much urban development astir, Torah should also gain a foothold in the area. His plans called for a large yeshivah with an attached community, which he would name Grodna after the yeshivah of Reb Shimon Shkop.

The Ponevizher Rav wanted to hold a grand ground-breaking ceremony for Grodna in the presence of *gedolim* and thousands of *bnei Torah* from all over the country. The fifth of Kislev, 1964, was selected for the big day, as on that date twenty years earlier the yeshivah had opened in Bnei Brak. But the night before the event, all of the plans were placed in jeopardy when a terrible storm erupted.

The arrival of the Rav and Rabbi Chatzkal Levinstein at the Ashdod ground-breaking.

It would take more than a ceaseless downpour, however, to force the Ponevizher Rav to postpone this gathering. Many who were aware of the Rav's legendary resolve grudgingly headed for Ashdod in howling winds and blinding rain. But just as the caravan of 25 buses arrived, a gorgeously sunny day unfurled. The Ponevizher Rav stepped up to the makeshift podium and reminded the audience of his credentials: he was the sole survivor of the communal rabbis of Lithuania, and felt personally bound to reestablish the yeshivos that had been destroyed.

Forty-one

AMONG THE RAV's greatest attributes was his extraordinary empathy with the suffering of his fellow man. During one of his domestic fund-raising appeals, he knocked on the door of a simple Jew in Givat Olga. The timing did not seem overly providential at first, as the homeowner was on the verge of tears and whined that he could not contribute.

"I'm just a simple wagon driver," the man explained, "and my horse has suddenly died."

The Rav immediately set aside his reason for coming to Givat Olga, and inquired how much a new horse would cost. He lifted the broken man's spirits, assuring him that God's salvation can come instantaneously. And it did.

For as soon as the Ponevizher Rav returned to Bnei Brak he located a livestock merchant and negotiated, as only he knew how, the purchase of a healthy horse, enabling the poor wagon driver to go back to work.

One day, a highly agitated mentally ill man came to visit the Rav. Rabbi Kahaneman demonstrated boundless patience hearing out the poor soul. When some students became aware of the marathon filibuster, they hinted that visiting hours were over. The Rav, who respected all of God's children, put an end to their intercession, enabling the intruder to continue rambling. The Rebbetzin then tried to come to her husband's rescue by announcing that it was dinnertime.

Rav Kahaneman, however, didn't feel that he needed rescuing, and in a burst of gracious cordiality, he offered, "Would you please be so kind as to honor us with your company for a meal?" To the spectators' dismay, the answer was affirmative, and the repast was followed by an additional hour-long installment of intensely strange musings.

During the Eichmann trial, which included testimony from numerous witnesses who had endured unspeakable suffering, Rav Kahaneman was in a somber state. Throughout the protracted trial he was never able to sleep more than two hours a night. When two Iraqi Jews were hanged for allegedly spying for Israel, the Rav fasted all day and went to bed in anguish, sobbing unrelentingly.

Reb Yosef Shlomo once met the elderly Reb Aharon Yaakov Klepfish, who had been the *Av Beis Din* in Shniadova, Lithuania. The esteemed rabbi could not control himself and broke down crying, relating that he had heard that the Nazis had incinerated the Talmud Torah that he had built. The Ponevizher Rav shed many sympathetic tears before offering yet a greater consolation: "If only I would have received such good tidings!" he wept. "If only I would have heard that all of the buildings that I erected for Torah were burned to the ground! I live with the ongoing fear that my buildings still exist, and that the impure have placed a *tzeilem* upon the holy domain."

The Ponevizher Rav truly felt the anguish of Russian Jewry, and he never failed to mention their plight in his addresses. When Chazzan Lange from Moscow was miraculously liberated, he led the davening in a shul in Bnei Brak. The Ponevizher Rav attended the service and afterward had this to say: "Moscow's chazzan is here, but where are his *mispallelim*?"

Forty-two

THE PONEVIZHER RAV ultimately had to travel to America for an operation to save his life. Even though the surgery was successful, the Rav remained a sick man whose prognosis was bleak. As he recovered in a convalescent home in upper Manhattan, a visiting friend asked about the quality of the Rav's care and whether anything was lacking.

The answer to the second question is the true gauge of a human being. To ask what one is missing, is a roundabout way of asking what is truly important. For one recuperating from surgery, the answer would almost inevitably be in the realm of health: missing a sense of balance, an appetite, the ability to fall asleep, and the like. Others might respond with a wish for a favorite dish, or for some form of entertainment. Yet others defer to traditional values and will always say that they miss their mothers, their friends, or the comfort of their home surroundings.

Without hesitation Rabbi Kahaneman replied: "I am missing seeing a *ben Torah* learning."

This want was promptly filled. It was arranged for a yeshivah student to come to the home and learn near the Rav. Nothing the doctor might have ordered could have been as effective. The turnabout in the Ponevizher Rav's condition was manifest and remarkable. Seeing the boy learn and hearing the *niggun* of the gemara brought a broad smile to his wizened face, and joy to his body, which was racked with pain. The Rabbi's spirits were restored. To Rabbi Kahaneman, involvement in Torah learning was not a *want*, it was a *need*. When the leaves rustled outside his window, he perked up and commented, "Now I can hear the *kol Torah* of the *talmidim* from the yeshivah in Bnei Brak."

Two days after Shavous the Ponevizher Rav returned to Israel weak and infirm. One day his son saw him crying and asked why he was sad. Surely in Bnei Brak, on the yeshivah compound, he was in the epicenter of scholarly pursuit! Nothing ever made the Rav happier.

"I received so much *chesed* in America," the Rav sighed, revealing the cause of his ailment, "I know not if I am deserving…" This was a source of great hardship for the Rav as all of his life he had dedicated himself to helping his brethren, and now he was reliant upon the help of others.

Early Wednesday morning, the 20th of Elul 5729 (1969), the Rav ceased to rely on the assistance of others, and was summoned to the Celestial Yeshivah where he was able to bask in all that he had accomplished during his phenomenal lifetime. From everywhere, mourners came to express their grief for the man who had enriched their lives in his building for Torah.

הרב כהנמאן, פאניעוועזשער רב
נפטר געווארן אין בני ברק

הרב יוסף כהנמאן

אגודת ישראל באמריקה
מבכה מרה את פטירתו של אחד מגדולי מרביצי התורה בדורנו,
ראש ישיבת פוניבז המפוארה
הגאון
מרן ר' יוסף שלמה כהנמאן
זצ"ל
הנשיאות וההנהלה

Epilogue

AMONG THE Ponevizher Rav's unfathomable losses which included his wife, all his children but one, his yeshivah and every other facet of the Ponevizh educational empire that he built, were also his novellae on the entire *Shas*. Of six cartons filled with his writings only one thin notebook remained. Once, upon consulting this worn notebook he commented to a friend, "This is all that will remain of me in the end."

His humility prevented him from seeing the true value of his work. Hardly anyone is aware of that notebook, but the accomplishments of the Ponevizher Rav are the stuff of legend.

To wit, in 1969 a tremendous debate raged throughout America and the world's scientific community. Was there, or was there not, life on the moon? The catalyst of this debate, of course, was the scheduled manned landing by the Apollo 11 Lunar Excursion Module.

Before this "one giant leap for mankind" actually transpired, opinions flew as to the possibility of life in space. It was, perhaps, a hypothetical question until — from the most unexpected quarter — someone *not* from the scientific community expressed a definitive opinion. This outspoken expert was none other than the Satmar Rebbe *zt"l*, who asserted with total certitude that there was *no* life on the moon.

And where, many wished to know, did this scholar, not famous for astrological insight, glean this information? "Obviously," the Rebbe responded, "if there were life on the moon, the Ponevizher Rav would have gone there collecting!"

As long as the cause benefited the Jewish People, how much more so if it concerned Torah specifically, the Ponevizher Rav would overcome any hurdle to enable it.

One man, a product of a very fine yeshivah, had a lot to say about Torah academies, rabbis and anything connected with observant Judaism — all negative. The man's rabidly vitriolic assaults were far more acerbic and potent than the average religion-basher, for this fellow was a genuine *apikorus*. He was by no means an ignoramus and he used his years of learning to his perverse advantage.

To make things worse, he was exceedingly wealthy and his sphere of influence was significant by any standard. If one would have to pick the least likely candidate to contribute to a yeshivah on a scale of one to a hundred this individual was undoubtedly in the top one percentile. And because his opinions were so well known, people were certain that the Ponevizher Rav was truly pushing it far too far when he announced that he intended to visit this man for a solicitation.

"Waste of time," was the kindest comment that was offered. Still the Ponevizher Rav was yet to be daunted by a challenge. With the bravery and conviction that had marked his entire life he knocked on the door of the *apikorus* and was begrudgingly let in.

A few minutes later Rabbi Kahaneman emerged with a multi-digit check for his efforts. Even the loyal optimists had trouble subscribing any rate of success in this "mission impossible" and they were burning with curiosity to know how the Rav had pulled it off. "Simple," he smiled, "I explained that an *apikorus* could never develop without a yeshivah..."

After the passing of Reb Aaron Kotler, the Ponevizher Rav applied Herculean efforts to assist the Lakewood yeshivah and save it from financial collapse. His extreme exertion resulted in a severe case of pneumonia, and a period of hospitalization in the Intensive Care Unit.

The attending physicians ordered the Ponevizher Rav to cease and desist from any further activities. It was nothing less than suicidal, they pleaded, for a man of his age and in his medical condition to run all over the world without sleep and regularly scheduled meals.

But what the Bolsheviks and the Nazis could not manage, a few placid doctors were not about to achieve. The Ponevizher Rav had a mission to accomplish and *no one* could stand in his way. The Rav explained that he needed the doctors for only one thing: to sign his release. He had a job to do and he wished to resume his work at once. The head of that department declared, "This is the most stubborn patient in the entire hospital!"

He could not have awarded Rabbi Kahaneman a greater compliment. "The most stubborn patient in the entire hospital!" Reb Yosef Shlomo repeated several times, so proud was he of the doctor's evaluation.

Rabbi Kahaneman had every right to be stubborn. He was the only communal rabbi to survive from all of Lithuania, and he bore the burden of these martyrs and all of the others upon his shoulders. And this may be one of the Rav's most enduring legacies.

If he felt responsibility for those who are no more, how should we feel toward those among us who are alive and well, yet bereft of Jewish education or upbringing? The Ponevizher Rav used to say, "Just as a Jew may never despair, we may also never despair of any Jew; and just as we want one-hundred- percent Jews, we also want one-hundred-percent of the Jews."

It does not take great imagination to ponder the kind of building that he would be doing today — brick and mortar, souls and minds.

מרן
הרב דפוניבז'
יוסף שלמה הכהן
זללה"ה
בהרב החסיד ר' יהודה ליב זללה"ה
כהנמן

Frau Sarah Schenirer

If not for Beis Yaakov,
there wouldn't be a Lakewood Yeshivah.
— Rabbi Aharon Kotler

Agudath Israel has provided
two diamonds for the Kesser Torah:
Daf Yomi and Bais Yaakov.
— Rabbi Yosef Shlomo Kahaneman

Forty-three

SPREADING the garishly tinted skirt before her, the young woman pondered a tear which slashed the length of the hem. She fingered the edge of the rip where the elaborately woven pattern was starting to fray. Could she insert a seam here that would be invisible? She scanned the sweep of the skirt — such a lovely pattern. Had its owner brought it in sooner, the damage might have been minimized. Deftly, Sarah's fingers began to pin, matching the pattern across the gap, joining it perfectly. Perhaps the new seam would be obscured by the gores of the full skirt.

As her hands worked, her thoughts wandered to the owner of this beautiful garment. A new customer, true, but to all appearances like so many who comprised the clientele of this expert Krakow seamstress: young, attractive, with time and money to adorn herself to best advantage. Every seam must align perfectly; every dart and gather must flatter. For Sarah's skills, these young ladies were willing to wait patiently, wiling away the time during the fitting sessions with Polish novels, gossip and small talk.

Sarah shook her head. If only they would pay half as much attention to their inner selves. She sighed again as she positioned the skirt under the needle, checking and rechecking the position so that the new seam would be straight. She leaned on the treadle. If only it would be as easy to repair the rip in the fabric of Jewish life — before it unraveled completely.

A bell interrupted Sarah's thoughts, and a young man in his late teens entered the shop, staring awkwardly at the floor. "Is Steinwurtzel's order ready?" mumbled the boy.

"Oh, yes, a dress and two blouses." Sarah quickly wrapped the package while the young man attempted to balance a few coins atop the sewing machine. "*A danke*" he whispered, and fled.

Sarah imagined the scene which led to this errand: Deena Steinwurtzel, busy preparing for her examinations, needs her newly hemmed frock for tonight's party — would it be so terrible if her brother stopped off for it on his way back from yeshivah?

Mrs. Steinwurtzel, caught in the middle, does not wish to infringe on her son's learning, yet she is even more afraid of alienating her daughter, whose path is leading further and further away from home. Her husband is oblivious to all this tension for when he isn't working, he is busy learning, or visiting the court of his Rebbe. Sarah wondered if anyone realized how such minor snags soon became major rents within a family. Jewish life was coming apart at the seams — who would be able to mend it?

Trimming the loose thread and examining her stitches with satisfaction, Sarah thought about her own situation. A family tragedy had left her divorced at a young age; her profession reminded her daily of her own solitude. Tracing patterns for petite dresses, she wondered now and then if she would ever design clothing for her own children. But, not one to brood aimlessly, she consoled herself with a new side business—producing wardrobes for the poor of Krakow. She placed a small sign in her window: "Inexpensive Dresses for Little Girls."

Never was there a more effective advertisement. Dozens of mothers and daughters crowded into the shop, the din echoing through nearby alleyways in the Jewish section of Krakow. Ignoring the chaos, Sarah took measurements and displayed fabric, while mothers chattered and children whined. Over the raucous bedlam, Sarah announced that if she were to join two remnants together to make a garment, the cost would be but pennies, far less than the price of newly-cut yardage. The mothers were thrilled.

"Please God, I shall make their wedding gowns as well," the dressmaker murmured as one group left, barely making room for a new batch of customers.

"Dresses, we want dresses for Chanukah!" the children demanded. Suddenly, Sarah's usual quiet and dignified demeanor froze, sphinx-like. In an instant, she was transported two hundred miles to a synagogue in Vienna, where the story of the Chanukah heroine had first been introduced to her.

Awakening from her stunned silence, Sarah Schenirer called out over the surrounding cacophony, "Have any of you heard of the great Yehudis, from the Chanukah story?"

There was no response from any of the small

patrons. Sarah tried again. "Whoever can tell me about Yehudis will get a special prize." She waved her hand high in the air. "Whoever can answer my question will get a beautiful ribbon like this, to tie her hair."

The girls, wide-eyed, gazed up enviously at the ribbon, but not one opened her mouth. An ocean of silence washed over the shop. Finally one mother whispered, "How could they possibly know who Yehudis was? They don't go to a Jewish school that teaches about our holidays. They can tell you about the Apostles, and they can tell you about Easter, but if you want to know about Yehudis, then you have to ask the boys."

"So then why," Sarah murmured, "don't we worry about our daughters' education the way the men worry about their sons'?" She then turned to the girls. "I want you all to come back to my shop for the first night of Chanukah. There will be plenty of *latkes* and other treats. And then," she added, her voice warm with passion, "then you will hear the story of Yehudis."

Forty-four

A BLANKET of snow covered Krakow's cobblestone alleys, topped by a lacy spread of powder that had just dusted down. The air was cold and sharp, and the moon, nearly a quarter full, cast an eerie pink glow across the whiteness. Frosty needles pricked the young girls' nostrils and lungs as they trudged towards Sarah Schenirer's shop. They hesitated outside the door; what sort of Chanukah party would the seamstress make?

A bright menorah beckoned from the window. The door opened, a burst of warmth from the wood stove enveloped them, and they bustled

Krakow winter in the time of Sara Schenirer.

inside. The room was crowded with early arrivals, and many mothers had squeezed into the outer hallway. Still, no one complained and no one fidgeted. Inside, all was as silent as the snow-covered streets. Mothers and daughters sat spellbound as Sarah Schenirer spoke. Yehudis and the Chashmonaim, Chana and her seven sons, all took life and played out their stories before the women and girls of Krakow.

That night a miracle occurred in Krakow. The news spread quickly: the so-called "simple seamstress" was a genius who could mesmerize anyone — even little girls — with her encyclopedic knowledge.

Thus was the Bais Yaakov movement born. Sarah Schenirer's dilapidated dress shop would soon be transformed into a classroom, the only vestige of its former function the blackboard, its sketches and measurements replaced by block Hebrew letters.

But that first night of Chanukah, as the last little girl filed out of her shop, Sarah was too excited to sleep. She sat up late, writing in her diary: "Until now I was a seamstress for our little children. May the Almighty only enable me to prepare spiritual clothing for the souls of our girls."

Forty-five

BORN IN 1883 to a devout family of Belzer Chassidim in Krakow, Poland, Sarah Schenirer claimed a rich family tradition of scholarship. Her father, Bezalel HaKohen, was a descendent of the *Schach,* and her mother, Shainah Faigah, stemmed from the *Bach*.

Together with her peers, Sarah Schenirer attended the local public school, achieving academic honors. She was taunted as the *Chassidonis* (righteous girl) because her piety and religious zeal were so pronounced. Addicted to reading, her very favorite volume was the *Chumash*, which she studied with the explanations of the *Chok l'Yisrael,* a gift from her brother, as well as the Yiddish classic *Tzenah U'renah.* In Torah literature, there were few other choices available, and the secular novels favored by other girls held little interest for her. While her friends gathered on Shabbos afternoons to play and gossip, Sarah Schenirer would be lost in the world of her *sefarim.*

Sarah's formal education was almost terminated after sixth grade, when her parents wished to find her a trade. This was a common practice among poor families seeking to make ends meet. Sarah pleaded to be allowed to finish elementary school, and in the end, her parents relented.

But eighth grade was the limit. Upon graduation, Sarah was given a choice: would she prefer dressmaking or sales? Sarah was allowed little time to mull over this decision, for her elder sister Mania was to be wed, leaving one less breadwinner in the family. Then, the family's small business collapsed, and Sarah was forced into full time employment.

Sarah refused to become a saleswoman. And so, she quickly learned the art of dressmaking. Sarah was under enormous pressure to hone her skills, spending hours upon hours practicing at her workbench. Still, she never neglected her thirst for reading and learning. Her quest for knowledge was as natural to her as her need for food or sleep; she was baffled by—and perhaps intolerant of — those who lacked her passion. Sarah did not mince words with Mania's friends who would come over to squander their time with frivolous activities.

At first Sarah would mend for the younger sisters of her friends, but her reputation as a superior seamstress brought her an ever-widening circle of customers. Still, she was no entrepreneur. Her clientele grew naturally, yet she never sought to expand her small shop into a more lucrative business. For Sarah Schenirer, work was simply a means to an end; achieving a modest income left her free to focus on what was truly important in life.

This quiet existence came to an abrupt halt with the outbreak of the First World War. Sarah and her family followed the streams of refugees fleeing war-torn Poland for safer territory. Their wanderings landed them in Vienna, where they joined thousands of homeless, spending the nights in one alley or another in the back streets of that beautiful city.

Eventually they discovered an availability of sorts, a dark and cramped apartment for rent in

District VI, a predominantly Christian section. The family was elated to at last enjoy a roof above its head. All, that is, except Sarah, who was keenly disappointed with the location: it was more than an hour's trudge through snow and ice to the nearest shul.

Having found shelter, Sarah was able to set up shop, the opportunity for which she was certainly grateful. But staving off hunger in Vienna required far more hours at her workbench than she had ever spent in peacetime Krakow, and, by the end of the week, Sarah was starving for spirituality too.

One day, the Schenirer's Christian landlord mentioned the existence of a nearby Orthodox shul. News of a rent decrease would not have been more welcome. Sarah followed the directions to the Stumperfergasse shul but her excitement was quickly dashed by a glimpse of the "Rabbiner." In a finely-brushed fedora and three-piece suit, he looked like he had just stepped from Mariahilferstrasse, Vienna's posh shopping boulevard. To Sarah, a rebbe or a rav dressed the part: *streimel* or *spodek*, caftan or a long coat at the very least. Her consternation was clearly evident, for the woman next to her smiled and whispered, "Pay no attention to his attire. Wait until you hear the *drashah.*"

It was the Shabbos of Chanukah and Rabbi Dr. Moshe Flesch spoke about the heroism of the Maccabees and the role of women in the revolt against Greece. "Was it not Yehudis who was willing to sacrifice her own life in the time of the Hellenists so that future daughters would be able to carry on our tradition? This battle," the rav thundered, "is not yet over. The war must be waged on all fronts and the women of today like Yehudis long ago — must join in the struggle!"

Sarah Schenirer was thunderstruck. She was certain that Rabbi Flesch was speaking to *her*! She was even more certain that he ought to be speaking to the young women of Krakow — but how would they ever hear his message? And then, in an epiphany, Sarah understood her task. She would be the conduit to carry this message — the message of Yehudis — from Vienna to Krakow. And why stop at Krakow? She would convey this message to all the daughters of Galicia, to those of Poland, indeed to *every* Jewish girl who had forgotten her heritage.

From that day on Sarah never missed a class or a sermon by Rabbi Flesch, who was an adherent of the Hirschian school of thought. She would assiduously write down every word. Her mission — to transmit the *mesorah* — required absolute accuracy. The weight of that mission pushed aside Sarah's natural reticence, and she showed her notes to the rav.

Rabbi Flesch was impressed with the exact detail of the notes — all recorded after Shabbos from memory. Recognizing Sarah's keen desire to learn, he recommended that she study the works of Rabbi Samson Raphael Hirsch and the books of Rabbi Marcus Lehmann.

Sarah eagerly accepted the Rav's advice. Obtaining such expensive *sefarim* posed a different problem, but Sarah arrived at a simple solution: she would henceforth eat only one meal a day, dedicating the savings to expanding her library. The investment was well worth it, for it fortified her determination. Had she not already formed her plans to educate Jewish girls, she confessed, reading Rav Hirsch's *Chorev* would have brought her to the very same conclusion.

Forty-six

WORLD WAR I was now over, but its aftermath would last years. The Schenirers returned to Krakow to discover that after the Treaty of Versailles, the detritus of war lay not only in the battlefield. Amid the rubble of innumerable buildings and entire cities lay countless humans, and even worse, humanity. At the conclusion of the Great War, chaos prevailed in every corner of war-beleaguered Europe, and the Jewish world was no less a victim.

Soldiers far from rehabilitated to civilian life gallivanted through the streets with nothing to do but brandish their weapons and flourish their bayonets. The Jews, of course, were their favorite targets. Pillage and plunder were standard procedure; the ensuing desperation produced an atmosphere ripe for values antagonistic to Torah ideals. Ready to plunge into this breach feet-first, the secular Jewish thinkers had a field day like never before.

The devout men were protected by their strong ties to their yeshivah and their rebbes; they could cling to a still-vibrant support system. But women — even from the most religious homes — were easy prey for the secular ideals that were rampant and on the rise, for they lacked any formal Jewish schooling. The Minorities Treaty signed at the end of World War I promised support for all cultural minorities in eastern Europe. But each year the subsidies to Jewish schools in Poland dwindled.

In her book, *And all Your Children Shall be Learned,* Shoshana Zolty points out that originally Polish public schools catered to the children in heavily Jewish neighborhoods. These schools were closed on Shabbos and holidays and open on Sundays. Using state funds, the schools also provided Jewish instruction, but they gradually were closed. Although it was unthinkable for Jewish boys to attend secular schools, the girls were enrolled in Polish *gymnasiums*, as their parents could not afford private schooling.

Sheltered Jewish girls were exposed to modern, secular culture and attracted to non-Jewish philosophies. Influenced by Marxism and other ideologies, many of the girls began to question the religious values and traditions of their parents; some were swept into the small but growing feminist movement in Poland. Zolty records how young girls appeared at their Shabbos tables attired in stylish, immodest fashions and responded brazenly to their elders. Matchmakers and arranged marriages were no longer accepted willingly, and yeshivah students — their own brothers — were regarded as pathetically unworldly.

Sarah understood that the time to act had arrived. The question was, how? She knew what she wanted to do, but felt that she must first obtain rabbinic approval for her project. There were those, including prominent rabbis, who shared the opinion of Sarah's brother: Torah education for girls was at best a waste of time, and at worst, a transgression of halachah! Her brother encouraged Sarah to find another outlet for her energies. When his advice failed to stifle her ambition, he invited her to his home in Tchabeen.

He had a plan to nip his sister's madness in

the bud. The Belzer Rebbe, Reb Yissachar Dov, was visiting in nearby Marienbad. Sarah's brother would take her to see the *tzaddik*, and pose the question: is it worthwhile to provide girls with a Torah education? A sincere chassid, the brother was loath to waste the Rebbe's time with such a trivial — and obvious — matter, but he was desperate to quash Sarah's delusions.

Brother and sister approached the Rebbe's court, submitting a *kvittel* stating Sarah's intention. The rebbe was known for his brevity and the Schenirers could not have hoped for any lengthier a reply than "No." In fact, the response was a bit longer: "*Brachah v'hatzlacha* — Blessing and good fortune." It is hard to imagine which was greater: the brother's shock, or Sarah's relief.

The Rebbe not only approved of Sarah's plan; his two-word consent was said with great enthusiasm. It was the opinion of the Belzer Rebbe, and, as the Schneirers later learned, of the Chofetz Chaim, that Sarah's idea was no *chiddush* — it contained nothing novel; it was authentic Torah ideology. The saintly scholar explained that historical practices of the past, which had ignored women's formal religious education, needed to adjust to the changing times. Joining the Chofetz Chaim in endorsing the new project were Reb Chaim Ozer Grodzinski, Reb Zalman Sorotkzin and

Reb Yosef Yitzchak Schneerson, the Lubavitcher Rebbe.

Sarah Schenirer later made the grueling trek to Gur to seek additional support from Reb Avraham Mordechai Alter, the *Imrei Emmes*, who was known for his concern with Jewish education. The Rebbe's sister apprised him of Sarah's

ב"ה, יום כ"ג לחדש שבט, תרצ"ג

אל כבוד האלופים הנכבדים הובבי ומוקירי תורה החרדים לדבר
זשר בעיר פריסטיק יצ"ו.

כאשר שמעתי שהתנדבו אנשים יראים וחרדים לדבר ד' ליסד
ים בי"ס בית יעקב ללמוד בו תורה ויר"ש מדות ודרך ארץ זו תורה
זת אחב"י. אמרתי לפעלם הטוב יישר ד' חילם ומעשה ידיהם יכונן
נין גדול ונחוץ הוא בימינו אלה. אשר זרם הכפירה ר"ל שורר בכל
ו והחפשים מכל המינים אורבים וצדים לנפשות אחב"י וכל מי
עה יראת ד' בלבבו המצוה ליתן את בתו ללמוד בבי"ס זה. וכל
שות והפקפוקים מאיסור ללמוד את בתו תורה אין שום בית מיחוש
בימינו אלה. ואין כאן המקום לבאר באריכות.

כי לא כדורות הראשונים דורותינו אשר בדורות הקודמים הי'
בית ישראל מסורת אבות ואמהות לילך בדרך התורה והדת ולקרא
צאינה וראינה בכל ש"ק. משא"כ בעוה"ר בדורותינו אלה. וע"כ
עוז רוחנו ונפשנו עלינו להשתדל להרבות בתי ספר כאלו ולהציל
מה שיש בידינו ואפשרותינו להציל.

הכותב למען כבוד התורה והדת

ישראל מאיר הכהן

Letter from the Chofetz Chaim regarding Bais Yaakov schools.

activities in Krakow. Again, the endorsement was complete and enthusiastic.

Having obtained the blessings of such prominent *gedolim*, Sarah was ready to begin her work. She gathered some neighbors, all very religious ladies, who surely would back her project. But as she began to outline the plan, explaining the details with great passion, the women began to titter. Such ideas, they protested, were mere fantasies. She should not waste their time with such foolishness.

Briefly discouraged, Sarah refused to let narrow-minded criticisms inhibit her dreams. With arduous effort, she assembled in Krakow's Jewish orphanage a large cross section of the community, including a number of prominent rebbetzins. This time, Sarah was able to complete her presentation, and several in the audience were impressed, not only with the plans, but with Sarah Schenirer herself. Among them was Rebbetzin Halberstam, the granddaughter of the Tzanzer *tzaddik*, the Divrei Chaim. On the spot, the rebbetzin pledged her allegiance and her support to Sarah's proposals. That was the last day Sarah touched her sewing machine.

Forty-seven

WITH THE BLESSINGS of *gedolim*, and the support of the leaders of her community, Sarah was ready to set up shop. But a teacher must have students, and a school must have an enrollment. Sarah's goal was not to create an exclusive academy, catering to an elite few.

Jewish education would be for all Jewish girls; as such, its existence could not be kept secret. If the school was to cure the plague of secularism raging throughout Europe, then all of Europe had to hear about it. The word had to spread!

At this early stage, the school was still a one-person enterprise. And that person was Sarah. Teaching, recruiting, advertising, fund-raising — the ex-seamstress had to do it all. Frau Schenirer's appearance in the many Jewish communities of Poland was an unimaginable novelty: A religious woman campaigning!

And Sarah seemed the most unlikely candidate to ignite a revolution. She was extremely modest and unassuming, so quiet and refined that it was difficult to picture her speaking with such passion and emotion. But when she opened her mouth, fiery intonations and irrefutable moral suasion hypnotized her audiences. The legend spread from house to house, from town to town: "Such an intelligent woman, from Vienna! She speaks so many languages perfectly, and with such ardor and wit. She brings tears to our eyes!"

Meetings were organized for her across the country, and shuls in every city opened their doors to her. Women who had never gathered before assembled to hear the convictions of a Krakow seamstress.

And what was her message? She told them what they already know, if only they would open their eyes to the reality of the situation surrounding them. The message was heartbreaking, but the truth.

In countless homes, the oldest daughters were running away. The Jewish home was too confining, too restrictive, and so they flocked to the big cities, living on their own, throwing off the authority of their parents, abandoning Judaism altogether. They were running away, and they were not returning. There were those in the audience who, tragically, had experienced Sarah's scenarios first-hand. Many more had witnessed such calamities among their neighbors and acquaintances. But now came Sarah's challenge. *These girls seem lost, but what will become of their younger sisters?*

She spoke with an urgency that would have been strident, had it not been tempered by an overwhelming compassion: "If we do not provide these girls with a Jewish education, then it is no wonder they feel foreign in their own homes."

This bleak reality was evident to everyone, but its causes were not so clear. Sarah Schenirer proceeded to analyze the roots of the problem, so that all would understand her proposed solutions. She explained that Judaism has been presented to girls in an entirely negative way: They were not permitted to keep the company they choose, nor wear what they wished, nor attend popular lectures and entertainments. No positive experiences of Jewish life had been provided to counterbalance the endless restrictions. There existed no Jewish schools, no clubs, no literature, magazines or classes. All was "do this" and "don't do that," with no understanding or appreciation of the lifestyle imposed upon them.

She appealed to the mothers: "The tragedy will not affect only the girls. The future of all of *klal Yisrael* is at stake. Look at our history. Whom must we thank for the self-sacrifice of Yitzchak A*vinu* if not the education that Sarah *Imainu* provided him? Thanks to whom was Yaakov raised as a God fearing individual? Was it not the merit of Rivkah *Imainu*? Surely the cardinal responsibility for the children's education is the mother."

On occasion, Sarah even castigated the fathers: "What purpose is there in all of the prayers and learning, if the next generation is disappearing? And who is to blame if not the parents, who spend so much effort providing material resources for the children while neglecting their spiritual needs?"

Reactions to Sarah's stark message were mixed: Mothers were ashamed, recognizing their daughters in Sarah's sorry descriptions. Fathers, who perhaps had been so obsessed with their work that they had become oblivious to their own families, began to look around them. The elders were put to shame by this little woman from Krakow, or was it Vienna, who admonished them for having neglected their families. But there were others who rationalized that all this ruckus was only about girls, and if they can't read Hebrew or prefer not to pray, still, it was only a bunch of women. *Nu nu...*

Sarah countered: "Is there anyone in the audience who hasn't seen the trains filling up each Elul with chassidim, flocking to spend Yom Tov with their rebbe? While fathers and sons climb spiritual peaks, their sisters descend into the morass of stagnation and boredom. Worse, they are dragged to shul by their mothers, who *daven* piously while their daughters, chafing in contempt, yearn to be anywhere else. There exist no Jewish schools, no clubs, no literature, magazines or classes."

Returning to the images of her erstwhile profession, Sarah Schenirer wove a somber tapestry of Jewish domestic life. "The fabric of the home has been shorn, and the few seams remaining are stretched to the snapping point. Centuries of tradition are unraveling in a decade and we are the ones to blame." The audience flinched under the seamstress's accusing finger, but they were quiet. They knew that she was correct.

After the accusation, came the consolation.

"Send your daughters to Krakow. In Krakow we will repair the breach. In Krakow we will rebuild. Let us begin a school where Torah values are taught, and Jewish ideals are cherished, where Jewish pride, the glory of the Jewish daughter, will be discovered. There is no need to despair; there is need to take action. Now!"

Forty-eight

SARAH SCHENIRER'S powers of persuasion netted her an enrollment that doubled and tripled from year to year. But opposition to the very concept of formalized Jewish education for girls remained strong, even to the point of hostility. When opponents threw stones at the fledgling school, she would pick up the rocks and, cradling them lovingly in her palm, tell her *talmidos*, "We will turn these into bricks to build Bais Yaakov." This was the genius of Sarah Schenirer: to turn attacks into opportunities, slung stones into stepping stones.

The source of the opposition was not mere

prejudice or ignorance. Indeed, it was rooted in the words of *chazal*: *Kol ham'lamed es bito Torah k'ilo m'lamda tiflus*—whoever teaches his daughter Torah, it is as if he has taught her thoroughly inappropriate material. It would have been nearly impossible to challenge the conventional understanding of that *chazal*, were it not for the Chofetz Chaim's assertion, "This generation is *indoctrinating* its daughters with *tiflus*. If only they would teach them Torah!"

Still, how could a seamstress go about the unique and revolutionary task of teaching Torah to young girls? She herself had never received formal Jewish schooling, nor had she learned any teaching methodology. As there was no curriculum, she designed one, based upon the lectures she had heard in Vienna and on her own studies of Rav Samson Raphael Hirsch. The content was plentiful, but the format, geared originally to adults, had to be recreated entirely.

The initial student body came from observant homes, but to accomplish her broader goals, Sarah Schenirer felt she had to begin from *aleph*. She would devote a battery of classes to each of the holidays, to Shabbos, to analyzing the *siddur* in detail. A single *brachah* was a subject in itself. Little girls who observed the holidays, who kept Shabbos, who habitually made *brachos*, went through a visible metamorphosis.

"Why are blessings so important?" Frau Schenirer asked. "Everything in the world belongs to Hashem. Therefore, anything we enjoy in this world is like a present from the Almighty, for which we must thank Him. Whoever enjoys food or drink — or any pleasure — without first making a blessing is like a thief. He has taken something without permission."

The next morning a mother rushed over to Sarah Schenirer in excitement. "My little Esther'ke caught her brother Arah'leh drinking without a brachah. '*Goniff!*' she cried. 'You took something without permission!'" The novice teacher shed tears of joy.

Other, more subtle, changes occurred as well. No longer did the girls respond in Polish when addressed in Yiddish, nor did they speak with arrogance and defiance. They looked forward to shul, and, unlike their elder sisters, who rolled their eyes and fidgeted as their fathers recounted the great deeds of their rebbes, past and present, these young girls craved stories about *tzaddikim*. Exposure to the pure faith and idealism of Sarah Schenirer had opened their hearts to spirituality.

The school enrollment increased daily, and mothers who escorted their daughters to class would linger to learn a little themselves. Occasionally, even fathers would do the same.

One day, a distinguished-looking Jew, dressed in chassidic garb, entered Sarah Schenirer's classroom and remained for close to an hour. Finally, he addressed Frau Schenirer. "What precisely are you trying to do?"

"My intention," she explained, "is not to teach these girls how to pray from a prayer book. They knew this without me. I wish to make these girls so excited about their religion and so proud of their Judaism, that they will become true *bnos Yisrael*!"

Having observed her in action, the man needed no more convincing. He introduced himself as the head of Agudas Yisrael in Krakow. Agudah, he said, was committed to helping her achieve her goal. First, he promised, they would transform her makeshift classroom into a full-fledged school.

With Agudah's support, Sarah Schenirer left her seamstress shop for a much larger room. This, too, was quickly outgrown. There were now 80 girls in the school — too many for Sarah Schenirer to manage alone, so an assistant, or at least an apprentice, had to be hired. Sarah naturally turned to the woman who had helped her in her seamstress days, now enlisting her to aid in mending souls. Student enrollment was up by about 130% and the staff had doubled!

Agudas Yisrael set up a founding committee to monitor the activities of the school. One of the committee members suggested that the institution be named "Bais Yaakov" as per the verse in which G-d instructs Moshe, "*Ko somar l'vais Yaakov* — Say this to the house of Jacob." Rashi comments, "*Eilu ha-nashim*, these are the women" (*Shemos* 19:3). Torah was to be given first to the women. The recommendation was unanimously accepted — Torah for girls would be recognized under the rubric "Bais Yaakov."

With Agudas Yisrael assuming financial responsibility, Sarah Schenirer was able to focus on

לעגיטימאציע

און צייגניס

בית יעקב.

אגודה ,שלומי אמוני ישראל".

שרה שענירער

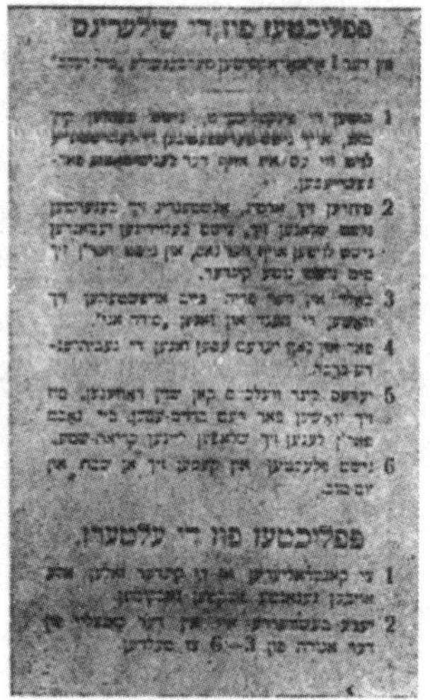

פפליכטען פון די שילערינס

פפליכטען פון די עלטערן

School regulations from the first Bais Yaakov school in Krakow, signed by Sarah Schenirer.

her far-reaching goals. For from the beginning, her vision was not limited to founding a school; she knew — perhaps instinctively — that she was launching a movement. Still, her primary occupation was providing quality education for her own *talmidos*. In this, she acted alone, for there was no one else competent to teach.

When the small Bais Yaakov swelled to 280 *talmidos*, Sarah made her next ambitious move: she selected her two best students to become teachers, providing them with an intensive training course. They were both thirteen years old!

These two young women were soon burdened with far greater responsibilities than merely delivering lessons, for Frau Schenirer would spend a great deal of time on the road. Bais Yaakov was not to be merely a Krakow innovation — it had to spread throughout Poland. Meanwhile, the home branch continued to blossom, under the aegis of two thirteen-year old girls.

Forty-nine

FROM TOWN TO TOWN, city to city, throughout Poland, Sarah Schenirer tirelessly pursued her cause. While she could convincingly counter oppositional arguments with precise quotations from midrash and *Chazal*, she never developed an assertive style. Nor did she engage in bombastic rhetoric regarding how vital her work was. Her approach was anything but slick, and thoroughly foreign to public relations. There is no question in hindsight, that had she adopted a more aggressive approach, it might well have solidified the opposition, hindering her success.

Instead, Sarah Schenirer 's devotion to her People, her love for the daughters of Israel, was tangible to all who heard her speak, friend and foe alike. Some compared her to one who, having discovered a starving, naked child, was driven to look after the abandoned creature. The urgency she felt, as if she were saving lives, was not lost upon her listeners. She herself made the metaphor explicit, referring to the restoration of Jewish pride as the only way to acquire true "*chaim.*" Admittedly, this did not translate smoothly, but her audience understood what she meant by a "*chaim*-true life."

After the initial Bais Yaakov was well established — even after the idea had caught on elsewhere — Sarah Schenirer still operated in a virtual vacuum. Parents throughout Poland sought to send their daughters to local versions of the school in Krakow. But there was one apparently insurmountable obstacle to the creation of new schools: there were no teachers. Even Sarah's own students, her initial class, were now barely 13 and 14 years old!

Yet considering the alternative — no schools at all — this was an obstacle that would have to be overcome. As a first step, Sarah Schenirer relied upon her old strategy, which had enabled her to embark on her recruiting missions. She placed a young girl, barely a teenager, in the classroom. This protégé far exceeded Sarah's anticipations! A natural teacher, the girl's finesse, enthusiasm and responsibility made her an immediate success. A thrilled Sarah entered into her diary, "My heart wept from joy; my dream is becoming a reality!"

A cadre of 14-year-olds, veterans of Bais Yaakov's brief existence, was drafted into service. These young women would later lovingly reminisce about the days that they put up their hair, donned high-heels and adapted serious demeanors to play the part of mature teachers.

Beyond the illusion of age and experience, Sarah Schenirer provided her girls with genuine tools to educate. After a full day of teaching, she would sit up all night, writing lesson plans and lectures on every subject in the curriculum. These precious notebooks remained the key reference work for all of her teachers, even decades later when they were respected teachers and leaders of their own schools.

Once a girl had been sufficiently groomed for her new position, Sarah would escort her to a distant town, and instantly a new school would be founded. At a public meeting, Frau Schenirer would first address the audience, and then introduce her well-rehearsed *talmidah*. After a brief presentation by the tenderfoot teacher, Sarah

Schenirer would retake the podium and pose the usually rhetorical question, "Who wouldn't wish for a teacher like this to instruct her daughters?" And so would sprout a new branch of Bais Yaakov.

This meant that Sarah had to take to the road again and again, and each trip bore fruit. A dynamic was underway, and there was hardly a Jewish community in Poland that Sarah Schenirer had not visited. Branches of Bais Yaakov were initiated in hundreds of towns.

While the response to Sarah Schenirer's challenge was usually positive, the groundwork having been laid months before during Sarah's earlier visits, occasional adversaries sought to block the opening of a Bais Yaakov school. One student records how Frau Schenirer handled such opposition:

> She went with me to S. to open a school. We arrived there in the middle of the night. The next day she called a meeting of mothers and girls, and she spoke to them. A few disturbed the meeting, opposing the idea of a Bais Yaakov. She did not rest until they accepted her invitation for a private meeting, which lasted the entire night. They became the best friends of Bais Yaakov and helped me substantially in establishing the school. I then realized that she had been reluctant to leave me alone with the opposition in town, until she had converted every last one to my side.*

Though young in age, these apprentice teachers were mature in experience, having benefited from the constant tutelage of Sarah Schenirer. They had absorbed her burning passion and were eager to spread the flame. Many of these young girls would become important personalities in the towns where they assumed positions.

How successful were these pioneers? The early Bais Yaakov magazines feature photographs of young women, each not much older than the group of *talmidos* surrounding her. These pictures speak volumes about a relationship and a bond far deeper than the standard student-teacher association. The photographs were not the province of the magazines alone. They could be found framed and hung in living rooms, on mantelpieces, over bedroom dressers, throughout Europe, and they were clutched in handbags and hidden in pockets, treasured amidst the last, most precious possessions of the *talmidos* — even to their tragic journey's end.

The model, of course, for this special *morah-talmidah* relationship, was Sarah Schenirer herself. She always referred to her students as "*banos.*" Denied children of her own, these girls were truly her daughters, fulfilling the words of the Sages

---

* Joseph Friedenson, *Dos Yiddishe Vort*

that one who teaches a child Torah is considered that child's spiritual parent.

Unlike her student-teachers, Sarah Schenirer was in fact considerably older than her protégées. Nonetheless, Frau Schenirer was never deemed an elderly or an old-fashioned woman. The result was a synergy between youth and experience that was as complementary as it was productive. The *banos* had no difficulty relating to and confiding in their mentor, and her will and directives were followed with total discipline, obedience and love. She was sorely missed during her frequent absences.

In fact, Sarah's return to Krakow from any of

her many journeys was celebrated with a hero's welcome. Word would circulate that Frau Schenirer had arrived in the city. Pens would drop, and the girls would pour out of their classrooms to greet their mentor. They would escort her into the building, where Frau Schenirer, fatigued undoubtedly from nights of traveling and speaking, would nonetheless hold court. Vividly she would describe the experiences of her travels, painting rich lessons with each anecdote, whether serious or humorous.

Like children craving the presence of a long absent parent, the girls drank in her stories, savoring the renewed kinship as much as the tales themselves. But Frau Schenirer did not allow time to be wasted. Her narrative complete, she rushed the girls back to class, the lessons continuing as if uninterrupted. Still, each girl's face reflected a feeling of relief and contentment: Sarah Schenirer was home.

Late each night, after preparing the next day's lesson plans, Sarah would stroll through the dormitory and tuck in each student, making sure that she was adequately covered. Small wonder that she earned the title, *"Eim b'Yisrael."*

Beyond her host of teenage assistants, Sarah Schenirer sought other solutions to the thorny problem of providing teachers. In Germany, she had heard, girls were provided with instruction in Jewish subjects, and some of them received formal education in teaching methodologies. Surely some talented girl could be persuaded to make the trek — as far culturally as geographically — from western to eastern Europe, for the sake of her less educated sisters.

Frau Schenirer's idealism was contagious, and she managed to convince Dr. Judith Rosenbaum to join her in her great project. For the Berlin-born and -bred academic, it was as foreign an adventure as joining the Peace Corps would be to a suburban American; the eventual wife of London's Dayan Grunfeld nevertheless rose to the challenge.

Hiring young Judith was a courageous step for Sarah Schenirer as well. It meant introducing a vivacious and attractive woman, who possessed charismatic qualities and an outward appearance that Frau Schenirer lacked. Yet Sarah Schenirer was oblivious to any personal interests, focusing exclusively on the benefits to the Bais Yaakov movement.

The Keren Torah division of Agudah established a "World Center for Bais Yaakov" in Vienna directed by Dr. Leo (Shmuel) Deutschlander.

Dr. Deutschlander was a gifted and dedicated *askan*, who managed to turn the fantasies of a dress-maker into a tangible program, thanks to his organizational genius and educational training. He developed and systemized all of Sarah Schenirer 's ideas into a concrete syllabus and methodical curriculum, complete with a battery of examinations and a roster of continuation courses.

Eventually, Dr. Deutschlander would oversee the financial foundation of the Bais Yaakov network and ultimately, the costs for the new building. This would mean arduous fundraising throughout Europe to raise funds. Bais Yaakov could not have survived without him, and never did he tire, never did he complain about the burden he had assumed.

In addition to helping to recruit Dr. Rosenbaum, the World Center for Bais Yaakov dispatched two more pedagogic experts to assist Sarah Schenirer: Betty Rothschild-Werner and Chava Landsberg. All three had been born in Western Europe and were graduates of Heidelberg and Bonn Universities.

In the presence of these gifted instructors, each with advanced university degrees, Sarah wondered if there were anything left for her to contribute to the students. The educators themselves provided the answer in unequivocal terms. "We cannot manage without you. There is no alternative!"

These pedagogic experts understood Sarah Schenirer well, and worked harmoniously with her. There was never a clash between eastern and western cultures, for Sarah had no interest in imitating the lifestyle that she had observed during World War I. She also knew that her students would not be able to adapt to it without further jeopardizing Jewish life in Eastern Europe. Thus, the Bais Yaakov girls of Poland were never exposed to the trappings of western life. The faith and strength that resulted from the rigorous study of Judaism — this was the message conveyed by the new teachers.

Fifty

BY 1924, the Krakow Bais Yaakov school was the flagship of a movement encompassing most of Europe. Sarah Schenirer traveled to Warsaw to participate in Agudas Yisrael's annual convention. The proposed agenda of Poland's most influential Jewish organization included full sponsorship of the Bais Yaakov network.

At the convention, rabbis, educators, distinguished guests from abroad — were unanimous in lauding Bais Yaakov. As the leaders of the Jewish people praised her accomplishments, Sarah Schenirer all but melted with embarrassment.

According to the figures quoted at the conference, the first Bais Yaakov in Krakow opened in 1917; four years later, Bais Yaakov schools opened in other cities; later 22 more Bais Yaakovs opened, followed by an additional 28 — totaling 54 schools with thousands of students by 1924.

For Sarah Schenirer , these statistics were anything but dry figures. She personally had founded each school, developed the curriculum and provided the teaching staff. She could see before her the children in each school, their classrooms and every detail of their school day.

Conjuring up images of these little girls — whose elder sisters had been lost to the Jewish people for the lack of a Jewish education — Sarah was oblivious to the proceedings. Suddenly, her reveries were interrupted. A voice from the podium announced: "We now intend to expand the original Bais Yaakov in Krakow, renaming it 'The Seminary for Teachers.'"

Sarah gasped. A teacher's seminary was *precisely* what was required to accommodate the numerous and nationwide appeals for teachers! But who was this speaker who had divined just what was needed? He was a man so much ahead of his time that he perceived the needs of the next generations, decades in advance. Earlier, he had visited the humble school in Krakow and, recognizing its vital purpose, had immediately dispatched a class of students from his hometown. Now, Rabbi Meir Shapiro, founder of the Chachmei Lublin yeshivah and originator of the *Daf Yomi* system, was to prod Bais Yaakov to its next stage of development.

Although Rav Shapiro's pronouncement meant that Sarah Schenirer would have to double her already grueling workload, she accepted his visionary plan and all that it entailed. With an ever heightened sense of mission she returned to Krakow to resume her instruction and augment her work. Her diary entry reads, "A seedling is still pliable and can be swayed. My plan can only be fully implemented with the young." The infrastructure was now being sown for these seedlings to sprout into a veritable forest.

Fifty-one

CULTIVATING A grassroots movement comprised of a handful of girls into a sprawling forest of institutions spanning Europe was no facile endeavor. In less than two decades Bais Yaakov encompassed more than 40,000 students. It would have been natural for Sarah Schenirer to assume to the role of superintendent. Sitting behind a desk in her office she would have remained inspiring and farsighted, but distanced from the tens of thousands of young girls.

Yet her primary role remained that of teacher and mentor in the Krakow Bais Yaakov. Though skilled in texts and sources, her principal method

of reaching her young charges was through her example. Her approach, devoid of intellectual proofs and polemic, saturated with passionate conviction, spoke directly to the hearts of her *talmidos*. Her unshakable faith, her unswerving devotion to God and His Torah, the energy and authentic feeling she brought to her own prayer, and her excitement and precision in performing mitzvos generated an unparalleled enthusiasm in girls who had been led to believe that their heritage was not relevant to women.

Sarah's genuine love of God and deep affection for her students clearly was the source of her authority; it was the root of the girls' unswerving loyalty to herself and to all she represented. But the emotions were not merely evoked; they were refocused on greater understanding of the Torah and directed towards the development of each girl. Sarah Schenirer would frequently paste her favorite verses from *Tehillim* on to the walls of the classroom. The posters were not merely decorative calligraphy; she analyzed each *pasuk* with her *talmidos*, so that they would understand not only the sacred words, but also comprehend the importance of having such fundamental verses before their eyes.

For example, on the verse, "*Limnos yameinu kein hoda* — Help us to count our days," Sarah asked, "What sort of help do we need to number our days?" Clearly, the *pasuk* does not mean assistance in adding sums! She then explained that

in order for a day to be counted as an integral part of life, it must be a day of value, that is, a day filled with Torah and mitzvos. A day spent merely eating, sleeping and making small talk would be nothing more than 24 hours of *existence*. How could it be counted as a day of *life*? To have all our days included in the category of life — that is our plea for Divine assistance. Making a motto of such a verse, having it before one's eyes and in one's consciousness always, could help a girl create her own life, a life that *truly* counted.

Fifty-two

THE CLASSROOM was only one of many settings available for lessons. The scheduled curriculum notwithstanding, a pinnacle of learning frequently occurred outside the classroom, and every lesson, formal or informal, was taught with love. The threat of punishment was absent entirely.

Students accompanied Sarah on walks, strolls that inevitably evolved into itinerant instruction. Rebbetzin Chava Pincus recalls how a group was once riding up a hill in a farmer's cart. Frau Schenirer pointed out how difficult was the climb; on the way down she stressed how easy it would be to fall.

YEARS EARLIER, Krakow's most stylish young women had sought Sarah's assistance in dressing themselves to best advantage. In Bais Yaakov, Sarah was the model par excellence of a very different fashion. She owned an expensive coat of Persian lamb, yet the *talmidos* never saw her wear it. It was reserved for her fundraising and recruiting expeditions. She explained the disparity: the elegant garment might result in greater respect for Bais Yaakov, particularly among those who looked askance at the fledgling institution. It might even lead to larger donations, and thus she felt justified in wearing it. But at home — and home for Sarah Schenirer meant Bais Yaakov — among her *banos*, wearing something so extravagant was not only unnecessary, but even distasteful, since the concept of basing opinions upon appearances was antithetical to her sense of integrity.

Prior to the Second World War, synthetic hair was unknown. All wigs were made out of human hair. Frau Schenirer was loath to wear such a wig, contending that it looked too much like the real thing. Therefore she commissioned a "custom wig" made out of pellar — a material that bore only a slight resemblance to hair. It was not especially attractive or becoming. Nevertheless, when in shul Sarah would wear a scarf over this coiffure, asserting that true beauty in God's eyes, was *tznius* — modesty. Similarly, her wardrobe consisted of somber, ankle length gowns that brushed the tops of old-fashioned black shoes.

(Interestingly, the myriad of Bais Yaakov pictures includes not one image of Frau Schenirer. She never allowed herself to be photographed, and the one extant photo is that from her passport. All claim that the picture does not reveal her inner fortitude and dedication.)

Shabbos morning in Bais Yaakov was not a time to sleep in — everyone went to shul. What the girls saw as they accompanied their teacher could never be conveyed in class. Sarah Schenirer approached the Krakow shul with trepidation, her awe visible as she kissed the mezuzah. And while their mentor's deep concentration in prayer was undoubtedly an inspiring model to emulate, what reached the girls' hearts was the clear and obvious reality that they themselves were the subject of her intense entreaties.

Polish winters consume the better part of the school year, and snowy landscapes were the familiar norm. Nonetheless, one Shabbos morning the girls woke nervously to an unusual stillness. The air was clammy and the Krakow skies gray as damp newspaper. Suddenly, gray turned black and fist-sized hailstones pounded on railings and balustrades like a mad glockenspieler out for vengeance. Slowly, the banging subsided as the hail became sleet, but the relative calm was shattered over and over by ever closer lightening bolts, thunder booming in each one's wake.

Krakow streets in winter.

Frau Schenirer, glancing at the clock, reached for her cloak and shawl. It was time to go to shul. The girls watched in silence — they knew it would be futile to suggest davening at home this week. But what most amazed the *talmidos* was that it never once occurred to Frau Schenirer *not* to attend shul in this weather. It didn't even occur to her to wait for a lull in the blinding rain. For *tefillah,* you left on time to arrive on time.

Learning in Bais Yaakov was most intense on Shabbos — but this learning was done without texts. Sarah Schenirer recited *kiddush,* and the *seudah* was spiced with the girls' own *divrei Torah.* Each vort gave way to a chorus of appreciation, "*Haht gezugt a Torah, gezugt a Tora; Haht gezugt a Torah.*" And so the meal went on, Torah and singing, late into the night.

Fifty-three

SARAH SCHENIRER's love of knowledge was contagious. Her youthful zeal for learning did not diminish with age and her greatest joy was a newly acquired idea. She expected her young charges to share her need, and provided for them accordingly. One afternoon Sarah Schenirer rushed into the office of Reb Binyamin Zusman, publisher of the religious newspaper for youngsters, *Kindergarten*.

It was ten days before Passover and she had remembered a particular story that she was certain would inspire the *talmidos*. Sarah had written to the author, requesting a copy, but the holiday was fast approaching. Could Rabbi Zusman be so kind as to search for it in the paper's archives? How could one say no to Sarah Schenirer? Story in hand, Frau Schenirer thanked him profusely, adding, "Now I will finally be able to eat *breakfast.*"

Still, while learning was most beloved, action took precedence. Sarah's energies were not confined to her life's work. Her *shleimus,* the perfection she demanded of herself and of her charges, drove her with the same intensity in performing mitzvos of all types. One student recalled the all-night marathon Sarah devoted to *bedikas chametz,* entailing a meticulous search of each desk in the school to verify that the building had been utterly rid of any trace of leaven.

Sarah's care for her students perhaps stemmed from the fact that she truly viewed them as *banos.* But the *chesed* she displayed for any Jew came from a deeper source, the profound *ahavas Yisrael* that had originally caused her to abandon her seamstress shop. She seemed to embody the maxim of the *ba'alei mussar,* that "*yenem's gashmius iz mein ruchnius* (my spiritual challenges lie in the arena of others' physical needs)." For example, her aforementioned modest black shoes were not only old-fashioned, but plain old, period. New flats were simply a very low priority in her allocation of funds.*

When the balls of her feet were scraping the floor, Sarah finally agreed with her students and colleagues that perhaps it was time to invest in a new pair. Just as she was leaving for the shoe store, a poor man entered the school and explained that his daughter required costly medical treatment. Without pausing a moment, Sarah handed him the money she had scraped together for her purchase.

Those present were distressed by Sarah's generosity, for they knew it would take months to save again for new footwear. "But I did buy shoes," Sarah explained. "I bought eternal shoes that will clothe me even in the World to Come."

---

*Despite her personal frugality, Sarah never neglected the social or financial difficulties of her students, and constantly sought ways to improve their situation. She was as much a social worker as an instructor, and she never failed to remind her audiences, *Im ein kemach ein Torah* — "If there is no flour, there is no Torah;" that is, spiritual goals are not attainable without material backing. Sarah Schenirer considered vocational training and employment assistance one of Bais Yaakov's primary responsibilities.

Fifty-four

IN AN HISTORICAL blink of an eye, Sarah's school had been turned into a teacher's seminary. In addition to the regular courses, classes were devoted to developing teaching skills and techniques, imparting both the arts and the methodologies of education. None of this was theoretical, for positions were available in abundance, each town and city eagerly awaiting the next batch of graduates to staff their own Bais Yaakovs.

The seminary in Krakow became such a prestigious institution that parents were willing to send their very young daughters across Europe to attend. They knew they were doing what was best for their girls, and having a daughter at the Bais Yaakov in Krakow was a source of great family pride. In an era when telephones were a rarity, and transportation cumbersome and slow, the separation, often for a full year, was a difficult hardship. But families bore it willingly, for they knew there was no other choice. If Jews in Lithuania were really concerned that their daughters remain religious, the only sure guarantee was to send them all the way to Galicia.

Their parents' enormous sacrifice was a powerful motivation for the girls to succeed. They were driven to justify their parents' expenditure and renunciation, and to bring them *nachas*.

So great was the honor of acceptance to Bais Yaakov Seminary that the letter of admission was considered to be a tribute to the girl's entire home town. The community would make the young girl a *seudas preidah* and then escort her en masse to the train station.

This warm send-off was just what was needed, for the journey was long and intimidating. For many, tears threatened beneath the surface, risking overflow, from the beginning to the end of their difficult travels. The downpour was only averted through Frau Schenirer's compassionate embrace. Sarah's kindly smile and motherly warmth wiped away their homesickness and filled them with anticipation. Her intelligence, *ehrlichkeit*, and spiritual perfection overcame their fears. Intuitively they felt that, in spite of the miles separating them from their families, they were home.

FOR THE GIRLS who arrived from Western Europe, the Seminary, as well as Krakow, Poland — indeed, everything east of the Danube — produced a tremendous cultural shock. Coming from elegant, spacious homes with parquet floors and luxurious draperies, the girls found themselves housed in an ancient tenement, the main hall separated from the kitchen by a flimsy curtain, with barely room to move, as Sarah Schenirer never turned away an eligible student for lack of space. To Chava Weinberg Pincus, who braved the journey all the way from America, everything must have seemed utterly strange and, well, primitive.

Nevertheless, all of the girls adjusted rapidly, thanks to Sarah Schenirer. The great matriarch greeted each arrival, sincerely expressing her desire to help the young girl. The discussion would first focus on the girl's Jewish knowledge and learning skills, and then cover a host of issues, including where she would sleep, meal times, and advice on coping with local life and customs. Invariably, in the course of that first meeting, Sarah's personal charm would win the girl over, bringing her under her protective wing.

Not long after the initial encounter, Sarah would gather her charges and deliver her pep talk. "My dear daughters, you have come here to join in a sublime, spiritual quest. I know that you are young and have not had much experience in life. Nonetheless I must call out to you, '*Mi l'Hashem eilai* — whoever is for Hashem, follow me.' None of you should think even for a minute, 'Who am I that I can stand against the current that is washing away Judaism?' Such baseless thoughts are the scheme of the evil inclination. You may all take an example from me, a simple Jewish woman who used to be a seamstress. One day I decided to switch from physical to spiritual clothing.

"What motivated me can motivate you. It says in *Pirkei Avos*, 'Where there are no men, strive to be the man.' I saw a field that was wide open, barren and desolate of any education for Jewish women. I made a commitment and have not been afraid to carry it out."

Frau Schenirer's inspiration was not limited

to charismatic speeches. She provided tangible experiences through which her students could enhance their spiritual strivings. The *Yom Kippur katan* prayers on *erev Rosh Chodesh* had great prominence in the Krakow seminary. Sarah Schenirer never explained whether she acted from her own sense of piety, or if she were adopting a kabbalistic practice. Her motivations were private, but the experience for her *talmidos* provided memories for a lifetime.

Sarah would lead all 120 girls to the shul of the Ramah, the illustrious Ashkenazic commentator on Shulchan Aruch, Rabbi Moshe Isserlis, where the special tefillos were recited with deep *kavanah*. They would then walk to the Jewish cemetery, where they would visit the graves of the Ramah, the Bach (Rabbi Yoel Sirkis), the Tosfos Yom Tov (Rabbi Yom Tov Lipman Heller) and other famous *gedolim*. As the students recited their *Tehillim* on that sacred ground, they felt themselves dynamically connected to the luminaries of Krakow's previous glory. The unspoken lesson could not have been more powerful: they too could make a lasting contribution to the Jewish People.

Fifty-five

SARAH SCHENIRER was demanding as a teacher and equally demanding of each girl's spiritual growth. She insisted upon total obedience and this in no way diminished their respect for her. Without exception, the students adored their teacher, and their love only increased over time. So much so, that there was nothing that Sarah could ask from them that they would not gladly fulfill. Whether she was from a wealthy or an impoverished home, from a strictly traditional upbringing or one with liberal tendencies, each girl was completely devoted to Frau Schenirer.

Accordingly, the girls' greatest fear was of disappointing their beloved mentor. One winter night, Rebbitzen Chana Garfinkle recalls, freezing temperatures prevented the girls from falling asleep until very late, and naturally, they overslept. Anxious to begin class at the scheduled time, they hurried through the morning routine that, in the cramped quarters of the old Bais Yaakov building, included converting their dormitory into a classroom. One energetic young lady, in her enthusiastic rush, shoved aside a bed, crashing it through the door. The frenzy of activity froze, and all stared in horror at the expensive shattered glass. Each girl was aware of Bais Yaakov's shortage of funds; surely it would take a small fortune to repair the damage. Everyone stared at the floor; the shards of glass, like accusatory fingers, pointed to their shameful carelessness.

Suddenly, Frau Schenirer appeared. Silence descended as her eyes swept the scene. Finally, she spoke. "Is anyone hurt?" she asked. There was no reply — the girls were simply unable to open their mouths. The teacher once again scanned the room. Satisfied that everyone was safe, she uttered "*Baruch Hashem,*" and began to clean up the broken glass. Not another word on the subject was ever spoken.

The glazier's fee was a bargain tuition for the

lesson of that unspoken rebuke: the feelings of a *bas Yisrael* far outweighed any material loss, and no matter the provocation, it was possible to be in absolute control of oneself at all times.

AFTER an exhausting day of teaching and speaking, Sarah Schenirer would retire to her room, but not to her bed. The light would burn most of the night as she prepared for her classes and replied to everyone who wrote to her, no matter how trivial the query. She also wrote to her *talmidos* when they returned to their families for the months of Nissan and Tishrei. She initiated this correspondence, demonstrating her unceasing devotion and care for them.

Sarah knew her *banos* well, and foresaw what difficulties they would encounter at home. The girls awaited her letters, anxious to hear news from their spiritual home; each dispatch was a treasure of Torah lessons, wisdom and practical advice.

Though fluent in both Polish and German, Sarah Schenirer was particular to speak and be spoken to in Yiddish. The girls naturally spoke Polish among themselves, just as American Jewish girls, even if they know Yiddish or Hebrew, will prefer to converse in English. Sarah realized that if Polish became the mother tongue of Jewish girls, then their outlook would become more Polish and less Jewish, increasing the possibility of being drawn into alien cultural circles. Yet, as critically important as Yiddish was to her, her principles did not override her sensitivity to the feelings of her *talmidos*.

One young woman wrote Sarah a letter, requesting that she reply in Polish, as the girl could not read Yiddish. Frau Schenirer penned her response in the most elegant and refined Polish — in rhyme!

No matter the subject, her style was masterful, each argument bolstered with sources from *Tanach, midrash, Chazal* or chassidic thought. When necessary to illustrate a point, she would even draw on her wide knowledge of secular classics.

How was Sarah Schenirer able to accomplish so much? Her unswerving focus on her overriding goal prevented her from being sidetracked, even momentarily. Serving God was the barometer against which all actions and all plans were measured. What fit this criterion was pursued; what did not was summarily dismissed.

Every school day in Bais Yaakov began with

the prayer, *Avinu Av ha-rachaman*, imploring God for the understanding and the ability to fulfill His will. Yet this simple criterion did not result in narrow parochialism. Sarah Schenirer's breadth of vision kept her world from becoming limited and rigid. She could find a correlation to Judaism in everything, enabling her to offer an inspiring and novel approach to students who had been raised to believe Judaism rejected most of the material world. Psychology and science were meaningful subjects, dovetailing so naturally with *avodas Hashem*. To this teacher, the beauty of nature was all captured in *Tehillim*; stories, a sharp wit, even riddles were all tools to develop an awareness of God.

Fifty-six

SARAH SCHENIRER felt responsible for every single Bais Yaakov; never was she satisfied with merely establishing a school and staffing it with her graduates. She also assumed total responsibility for her students — and their students — during and "after hours." This meant Shabbos, Yom Tov and after the school day was finished.

Sarah invested as much thought in the students' visits to their families and friends as she did regarding their activities during school time. Hence, Shabbos and holidays were not "time-off" at Bais Yaakov — for otherwise the entire week's accomplishments might be placed at risk. Scholastic achievements are often remembered for years — educational achievements in *chinuch* and religion can be lost in a moment.

Thus, it was unheard of for her teachers, former *talmidos* all, to "travel home for Shabbos." It was essential for the teachers to daven with the girls, sing *kabbolas Shabbos* with them, and escort them to shul in the morning. Someone with experience had to oversee the young girls' activities, discussions and games. Most importantly, the aura of *seudah shelishis* would last throughout the week, if the right *niggunim* were sung with the proper spirit way into the night.

Sarah's concern for "after-hours" and "after graduation" were equally shared by the directors of all of the Bais Yaakov schools — numbering some 60 schools according to both Agudas Yisrael and the 1926 Bais Yaakov Journal published by Eliezer Gershon Freidenson. Extracurricular reinforcement of the Bais Yaakov education was deemed essential to protect against the enticements of the surrounding culture. The graduates, most of whom were not more than 14 or 15 years old, were thought to be particularly vulnerable.

Such concerns led to the founding of a complementary youth movement, "Bnos Agudas

Yisrael." Bnos provided the opportunity to ensure that a Bais Yaakov environment and experience continued after school hours and after matriculation. Like its predecessor, Bnos expanded so rapidly that prior to World War II there were 300 different Bnos groups throughout Poland.

Summertime was not a vacation in Bais Yaakov, but it did provide a bit of a holiday. To escape the hot, sultry misery of the Krakow ghetto, where stale and rancid odors from the nearby factories and tanneries thickened the air, the entire school retreated to the nearby mountain villages. There, an altogether different atmosphere prevailed.

Each day was primed with energy, thanks to brilliant sunshine and azure skies. Heavily laden cherry trees and a rainbow of tulips provided a fragrance unimagined in Krakow. At six A.M., the *banos* commenced their school day by doing calisthenics in the meadows.

In fact, the summer courses were the most heavily attended, for the majority of graduates, who had already assumed teaching positions, became *talmidos* once again. They eagerly returned to increase their teaching expertise and regain the inspiration of their mentor.

Also joining the summer retreat were teachers from Germany and Vienna. These seasoned instructors were eager to help Sarah Schenirer fulfill her vision, but were employed during the school year. Despite their good intentions, it is

doubtful if they would have been willing to spend their summer break in a fetid Krakow tenement, but they were eager to join the school on the mountain. Also helping out in the summer was Dr. Leo Deutschlander, of the Bais Yaakov division of Agudah in Vienna. His involvement with Bais Yaakov, as has been described, was year-round.

In 1929, recalls Yaffa Gura, the *talmidos* arrived at the summer resort of Robov just before Shavous. The Torah reading at the beginning of their retreat turned the holiday into an even more festive and meaningful occasion for it included the verse, *"Ko somar l'vais Yaakov,"* from which Bais Yaakov had derived its name. For hours the girls sang and danced *"Ko somar l'vais Yaakov."*

The summer sessions greatly enhanced the camaraderie of the *banos* and strengthened the Bais Yaakov spirit of both the students and the alumnae. The mountain atmosphere was also a boon to their preparations for the *Yomim Noraim*. The weeks of priming peaked on *motzei Yom Kippur*, when the girls would sing and dance most of the night, making *havdalah* only in the wee hours of the morning.

Fifty-seven

REB ASHER SPIRA burst into Frau Schenirer's crowded classroom waving a golden *Holandi* high in the air. "This is the start," he cried. "This money is for the building fund!"

Sarah stared at the man. Of course she recognized one of Krakow's wealthiest Jews, but she had no idea what he was talking about, or what he was doing in her school. Peering around the decrepit classroom as if he were an inspector from the Ministry of Education, the financier finally clarified his statement. "This is for Bais Yaakov's building fund — for the large and impressive building that we will erect. And, *this*," he said, thrusting the Polish coin even higher, "is just the beginning!"

"What a farce!" Sarah Schenirer thought to herself, unable to suppress a smile from her lips. "What is he imagining? Skyscrapers in downtown Warsaw and Lodz or office complexes in Lublin and Katowice? This is a school in its infancy; I would be thrilled if we could rent an additional *room*!"

And yet Sarah guarded Reb Asher's valuable coin. The man disappeared, but his words lingered. Sweet words, like a pleasant dream — but no more substantive. And then, several years later, he reappeared. Reappeared, as if he had never left.

Once again the *gvir* burst into the school, traipsing through the rooms as if he owned the place. Introductions and apologies were still not part of his routine, but he did have this to say: "I have been all over the world, and now, I have finally returned to Krakow. The time has come to make good on my pledge."

"The trip around the world has done wonders for this fellow's imagination," Sarah silently quipped. His idea for impoverished Krakow was no less preposterous today than it had been years ago. What could she do, but return the coin to him, and allow him to continue with his fantasy.

Reb Asher Spira, however, did not make his fortune from hallucinations. He was an entrepreneur, and once he set sights on a project, his well-honed business instincts and natural drive ensured the venture's success. And this project was supremely important to him. As he later explained to Dr. Judith Rosenbaum, of his countless real estate holdings, this was the only one he would be able to take with him.

Thus, a plot of land was purchased at number 10 Stanislawa Street, on the bank of the Vistula River, and it was there that a five-story building holding eight spacious classrooms on each floor would be erected.

On the 16th of Elul 1931 ground was broken for the new seminary in Krakow. The cornerstone was laid amidst a gala celebration, complete with a multi-piece band, and attended by Jews of every stripe. Important rabbis, international notables, communal and business leaders, intellectuals and writers, all crowded onto the site, which overflowed with thousands of Jews coming to witness this historic moment.

Speaker after speaker ascended to the decorated stage to address the gathering. Here was the fulfillment of Sarah Schenirer's dream — but where was the woman who had launched the movement, dedicating every waking moment to its success, the woman who was the sole inspiration for the entire gathering?

Sarah was, as always, in the background. She allowed others, who had built upon the foundations she had lovingly laid, to assume the limelight. Finally they found her. Standing in the last row of the audience, surrounded by some of her students, was Sarah Schenirer, a *sefer Tehillim* clutched tightly in her hand.

It was a moment of great joy, but one of trepidation as well. At this moment of glory, what were her prayers? Sarah Schenirer davened that Bais Yaakov be able to continue and grow. That the wide acceptance which the movement finally enjoyed should not lead to complacency; and that all of its praise, exaggerated as it sometimes was, should not misdirect Bais Yaakov away from its goal of serving God.

Her thoughts were interrupted by cheering, as the multitudes applauded speaker after speaker. The students were very excited. Soon they would not be cramped into one small classroom that doubled as their bedroom — with two girls to a bed. Soon, they would not have to negotiate narrow stairways that functioned as a day-nursery for the many children of the over-crowded tenement. Soon, they would be able to study in peace, free from the chatter of neighboring women resounding through the backyard. Their years of privation would be rewarded when the new building was complete.

Yet, Sarah Schenirer was apprehensive. She feared there might be a price to pay for the modifications. The improved conditions must not be paid for with a decline in *ruchniyus*. Sarah appreciated beauty and admired orderliness, but she was also keenly aware of the dangers inherent in splendor. The seasoned educator remembered how Bais Yaakov had struggled against difficult odds, and how the spirit of self-sacrifice was cultivated as part of the entire educational experience. There had been a blessed simplicity in those early days, when they had all slept together in the dressmaker's workroom, huddling together for warmth, sharing meager slices of bread and lofty dreams.

Fifty-eight

IN JUNE of 1931, with the building nearly completed, a festive *chanukas ha-bayis* was celebrated in the presence of *gedolei Torah*, rabbanim and rebbes, and distinguished guests from Poland and abroad. The true *chanukas ha-bayis*, however, took place the next day when the 120 chosen students, the crème de la crème of the nascent educational system, attended their first class in the new building. Naturally, Sarah Schenirer was called upon to deliver the inaugural lecture. Her emotions on that day are recorded in her diary: "I prayed the prayers of *Yom Kippur katan* with intense conviction and concentration, for this was a Yom Kippur of sorts for me. A fever racked my entire body, but it could not stop me from preparing or delivering my first class."

On opening day, the ground and the first floor were completed, but the upper stories were far from finished. The new home awaiting this eager group of *talmidos* had more the ambiance of a building site than a dormitory. Workmen's tools were strewn all about, amidst buckets of plaster and sacks of cement. Piles of nails, mounds of bricks, blocks of concrete, and forests of planks presented an obstacle course to be navigated each day as the girls rushed to class. Each evening, as they returned to their rooms through doorless doorways, they were greeted by the aroma of fresh dust, a new layer

having been added to the thick coat covering the still boardless floors. Metaphor had been concretized, and Bais Yaakov was truly now, as it had always been, a school under construction.

The work continued for years and, in fact, the building was never completely finished, for Bais Yaakov's ambitions collided with plans of the Third Reich for the Final Solution. The decorative façade was never cast.

On the bank of the Vistula River, at Stanislawa Street Number 10, still stands the five-story building that housed 120 students from all over Poland and Lithuania. Every aspect of the Bais Yaakov

education, the hours of uninterrupted learning, the iron unity forged between students and teachers — fired by Sarah Schenirer's own purity of purpose — took place in that building.*

Down in the earth, below the foundation stone, rests a document describing the lofty ideals of the building and recounting the valiant men who supported Sarah Schenirer and Bais Yaakov over the years. Recorded there is also a prayer for the success of this great endeavor.

High up in Heaven is a matching document recording the heroism and the martyrdom, and the personal agony to which the walls of that building bear testimony. Rabbi Yehuda Leib Orlean, the trustee of Sarah Schenirer's spiritual legacy from the time of her passing, dominated the last phase of the building, the details of which we will never know.

---

*The five-story building was the heart around which the ever growing Bais Yaakov movement continued to revolve and expand. In 1935 the Bais Yaakov Center in Vienna listed 225 Bais Yaakov schools in Poland, numbering 27,119 students; 18 in Czechoslovakia with a student body of 1,569; 18 in Rumania with a student body of 1,292; 16 in Lithuania with a student body of 2,000; 11 in Austria with a student body of 950. Two years later in Poland 250 schools housed about 38,000 students.

Fifty-nine

SARAH SCHENIRER'S extraordinary success in taking a momentary inspiration and turning it into an international movement with thousands of adherents, is attributable to extraordinary *siyata d'Shmaya*, help from Heaven. Whether this assistance was forthcoming as a result of the righteousness of her cause or because of Sarah's own personal piety is a moot point. In reality, the two were one.

Her *ahavas Yisrael*, which drove her to dedicate her life to the future of Jewish women — thus, the future of the Jewish People — fueled her vision of a glorious future in which all would possess her own zeal for mitzvos and love of the Creator. That vision was constantly before her eyes, as illustrated in the following incident.

A prestigious member of the secular community attended a meeting relating to the educational network's infrastructure. He had heard of Sarah Schenirer's revolutionary work and was eager to make her acquaintance. He extended his hand in greeting, but the gesture was not returned. Frau Schenirer politely explained that according to Jewish law she was not allowed to shake a man's hand. The man was flabbergasted.

He exclaimed that she must be the only woman in Poland — and probably in the entire world — who would not engage in this common and accepted courtesy. "Perhaps at present," Sarah Schenirer replied with the fullest conviction, "but in the not-too-distant future there will be an entire generation of women who will meticulously observe Jewish Law."

Sarah Schenirer always seemed to be defending herself against those who sought her good. One afternoon Sarah's own mother was beside herself with worry. In the adjacent room her daughter was counseling two young women and, as yet, had not eaten that day. "What will be with her?" she fretted. Sarah overheard her mother's concern, and excused herself from the meeting. "Mother," she soothed. "Everything is fine. You are worried that they 'are not letting me live'? I assure you, this is the best *living* possible!"

For all her involvement in her students' needs, Sarah never overlooked *chesed* and *tzedakah* outside the confines of the school. In Nissan and

דער קאמיטעט באשטייט פון די פאלגענדע געוועזענע תלמידות
פון שרה שענירער ז"ל, און מסיימות פון קראקאווער סעמינאר:

לויטן א—ב

בתי' בענדער

חו' וואכטפויגעל

בת שבע סאלאווייטשיק

רבקה ספרינגער

חו' פינקוס

רחל ציזנער

וויכנע קאפלאן

חנה ראטענבערג

ווי אויך פאלגענדע אמטירענדע לערערינס אין דעם היגן „בית-
יעקב" סעמינאר און היי סקול:

חנה וויזעל שרה ציילבערגער

Prominent Bais Yaakov educators in America, all disciples of Sarah Schenirer's Krakow seminary.

Tishrei when the seminary was closed, she collected thousands of *zlotys* to distribute to the poverty-stricken inhabitants of Krakow. She drew her students into her *tzedakah* projects and they would join her, climbing and descending the stairs of Krakow's tenements, collecting for the destitute.*

While the Jews of Krakow were rejoicing at their Purim feasts, Sarah Schenirer was out celebrating by distributing *matanos l'evyonim*. Tramping through alleys of the most impoverished neighborhoods, she would deliver baskets of food and money, dispensed to the neediest with encouragement and joy.

The needy outside of Krakow also knew her address, and when she returned home from seminary there were always indigent people waiting — and they never left her house empty-handed.

Sarah once approached Reb Binyomin Zusman and whispered, "I need a favor. A young married man needs monetary assistance desperately, but he is too proud to accept charity. Tomorrow in shul, when he stands up to daven

---

*Vichna Eisen (later to become the famed Rebbetzin Kaplan) was always at Sarah's side during these philanthropic jaunts. Observing Frau Schenirer in and out of class enabled this prize student to carry on the tradition and transplant Bais Yaakov to America in the late 1930s.

shemoneh esrei I want you to place this in his jacket pocket," and she handed him a thick bundle of cash. "I admit this may distract you a bit from your own davening, but it is a small price for the huge mitzvah you will be performing." Reb Binyomin related that he watched this fellow slip his hand into his pocket after davening, and his face lit up with immense relief when he discovered the money.

On a different occasion, Sarah Schenirer approached Rav Zusman again to point out that a girl with whom Rabbi Zusman had some influence was beginning to drift from the right path. The changes thus far had been subtle; only Frau Schenirer's keen eye had perceived the problem. With insight and tact, she was able to deal with it in time.

Late one Sukkos night Sarah knocked on Rabbi Zusman's door regarding a different matter. What was so pressing that it required waking up the rabbi? A *shidduch* had been suggested for one of Sarah's students, but Frau Schneirer had advised the girl to wait for the time being. But now, she had just overheard that the mother of the proposed boy was planning to inquire about a different girl. So Sarah sprang into action. "As soon as I heard this," she told Rabbi Zusman, "I opened up the *Shulchan Aruch* and discovered that one is allowed to propose a match during *chol ha-moed, shema yikadmena acher* — lest a different party come first. I therefore must urge you to pursue the original *shidduch* with my student the first thing tomorrow morning." She then excused herself, saying, "I regret that I cannot personally be of assistance tomorrow, as one of our seminary students is very sick and I must spend the entire day in the hospital praying at her side."

On her way out she apologized to Rabbi Zusman's wife for disturbing her husband. Sarah explained that just as it was acceptable to wake up a doctor in the middle of the night and pay him for his services, she was permitted to disturb a rabbi for the purpose of a *shidduch*. "The payment for this mitzvah," she assured Mrs. Zusman, "will be inestimable." And indeed, the match came to fruition.

Sixty

NOTWITHSTANDING Sarah's enviable professional success, her personal life was a source of constant heartache. As a result of a family tragedy, she was divorced from the man she had married in her youth and remained single for decades. She remarried only toward the end of her life, shortly before her final illness.

Throughout her career, she had imbued her students with her own passionate love for the Land of Israel and for *lashon ha-kodesh*. In the last year of her life, Sarah Schenirer prepared to travel to *Eretz Yisrael* to help open a Bais Yaakov.

Tragically, this was one dream left unfulfilled, for her poor health prevented the journey. Nonetheless, the dream was lost only on the personal level, for the Bais Yaakov movement was eventually transplanted all over the world, especially in Israel, where it grows and flourishes daily. The countless Bais Yaakov schools throughout the country bear witness to Sarah Schenirer's spiritual legacy throughout the land.

Day by day her illness intensified, until surgery was imperative. She wrote, "I suffered horribly Friday night. It was the first time in 23 years that I did not go to shul or eat with the *banos.* This alone was a source of tremendous pain. *Motzei Shabbos* I departed for the hospital and I was comforted by the fullest trust in the Almighty. I am confident that He will aid me, as all of my dear *banos* are reciting *Tehillim* on my behalf. I write these words from the operating theater, and my confidence increases by the minute that my Father in Heaven will send a salvation so that I will be privileged to serve Him in joy with the rest of my *banos.*"

After the operation Sarah experienced some improvement, and planned to resume work at once. But this reprieve was ephemeral, and she was advised to travel to Vienna where Europe's finest medical authorities could examine her.

Their diagnosis was malignant cancer, for which there was no known cure. In critical condition, Sarah returned to Krakow.

Suffering constantly, she was confined to bed, but even her severe infirmity could not prevent her from writing lessons for her *talmidos* and directing and leading her beloved Bais Yaakov. She also composed a spiritual will, instructing her *banos* with the same enthusiasm as she had exhibited in her prime.

> Our job is to educate a new generation. Will you be able to withstand all of the trials that await you? What can I possibly say? Man envisions and plans many things, but the will of Hashem predominates. Now, at this hour of parting, I truly feel the ties so closely connecting me to you, my daughters. I am sure that the force of my feelings is reciprocated. I hope and pray that the tears you shed upon reading this will reach the Throne of Glory, where they will have a profound effect on the future of *klal Yisrael.*
>
> My daughters, I feel it necessary to warn of two things that may hinder you in your efforts to attain fear of Hashem. First, beware of pride — avoid a feeling of haughtiness that can persuade a person to think that she is worthy of praise and honor. Secondly, avoid the other extreme, a feeling of low self-esteem and hopelessness. *Banos,* you have successfully completed your formal schooling. Now, the hardest test awaits you — that of life itself. Life may provide you with many trials and tribulations, but you are well armed.

Your fortification will be fearing, loving and serving Hashem.

Your sainted teacher and mentor, Reb Yehudah Leib Orlean, said, after administering the seminary test, 'You have successfully proven that you have acquired the knowledge to both learn and teach. The question is whether you will be able to implement it and enlighten young Jewish souls.'

זי זאָל זיין געהאָרכזאַם דעם צדיק ווי די ספרים הקדושים שרייבען, אַז דערפאַר האָט דער סוף פון דער תורה אַ חיבור מיטן אָנהייב „בראשית ברא אלקים” צו לערנען אמונת השם און אמונת חכמים.

נביאים ענדיגט זיך מיט ספר „חבקוק”, וועלכער פאַרענדיגט זיין ספר: הנה אנכי שולח לכם את אלי' הנביא. און דער אָנהויב פון זיין ספר: „ד' שמעתי שמעך ויראתי”.

ווי מיר ווייסען, איז חבקוק געוועזן דער זון פון דער שונמית וואָס אלישע הנביא האָט אים לעבעדיג געמאַכט, האָט ער דאָך געזעהן דעם כוח פון צדיקים.

די יראה פאַרן צדיק ברענגט צו יראת השם ווי די חז"ל זאָגען „את ד' תירא”, מיינט מען „לרבות תלמידי חכמים”. און מיר זאָגען דאָך אויך יעדען טאָג **„ויאמינו בד' ובמשה עבדו”.**

דעריבער ענדיגט חבקוק „הנה אנכי שולח לכם את אלי' הנביא” צו ווייזען אַז די גאַנצע גאולה קען קומען נאָר דורך אמונה.

נ.ג. איך ענדיג מיט מיינע אַלטע פסוקים (נישט מיינע, נאָר דוד המלך'ס), וועלכע זאָלען אייך שטענדיג באַגלייטען:

עבדו את ה' בשמחה! שויתי ה' לנגדי תמיד! ראשית חכמה יראת ה'! למנות ימינו כן הודע! תורת ה' תמימה משיבת נפש!

ד' ישמור צאתכן ובואכן מעתה ועד עולם. נ.ג. השם זאָל אונזערע תפלות אויסהערען, אונז שיקען באַלד די גאולה שלימה, אמן.

אייער **שרה שענירער**

קראָקע פ' שמות תרצ"ה.

Strengthen yourselves, my daughters. Never tire of devoting yourselves to the sacred work of Hashem. Do not forget to plant the holy seedling, the pure and perfect souls of our children. You are obliged to sanctify these souls...

אַ מאמר פון פרוי שענירער ע״ה

צוגעשיקט בעת איר קראַנקהייט צום לעצטען סיום אין בית יעקב סעמינאַר

מיינע ליבע און טייערע קינדער לאוי״ט.

מה נאמר, מה נדבר ומה נצטדק, רבות מחשבות בלב איש, ועצת ה׳ היא תקום!

יאַ, שוואַך, זייער שוואַך, זיינען די מענטשליכע חשבונות, אבער ווי השי״ת פירט איז דאָך אַלץ „גם זו לטובה״.

געלויבט השי״ת פאַר זיינע חסדים טובים.

זינט אין דער פרי פון הייגטיגען טאָג, קען איך זיך נישט באַהערשען פון טרערען. איך, וואָס איך האָב זיך אַלע מאָל באַקלאָגט, אַז עס איז מיר אַזוי שווער ביים דאַווענען צו וויינען, פיל איך ערשט איצט ווי שטאַרק עס זיינען די גייסטיגע בענדער, וואָס בינדען מיר מיט מיינע קינדער. איר געדענקט אודאי, ווי איך פלעג צו זאָגען, אַז עס איז דאָ אַ פּויליש ווערטעל: „צאָ קרעוו, טאָ ניע וואָדאָ״ (בלוט איז נישט קיין וואַסער) און איך זאָג... „צאָ דושאַ, טאָ ניע טשאַלאָ״ (נשמה איז נישט גוף). יאַ, גייסטיגע בענדער זיינען דאָך פעסטער, ווייל זיי זיינען אייביג!

דערפאַר פיל איך, אַז אַזוי גוט, ווי מיר גיסען זיך טרערען בשעת איך שרייב צו אייך, אַזוי וועט איהר אויך לאָזען טרערען, בשעת מען וועט לייענען מיינע ווערטער. זאָל השי״ת העלפען, די געגענזייטיגע טרערען זאָלען קומען פאַרן כסא הכבוד און אויסבעטען די גאולה שלימה און דערווייל אַ רפואה שלימה.

נו, און איצט ווענד איך זיך צו אייך, מיינע ליבע קינדער, וועלכע פאַרלאָזען אונזער הויז, גייען אין דער וועלט כדי צו ווערען פירערינס און דערציערינס פון אידישע טעכטער.

&

SARAH was apparently comatose for some time when suddenly, she whispered that she wanted a pen and paper. A query had been received from Eretz Yisrael regarding the role of Jewish women. As long as she was alive, this is precisely what she wished to teach.

Late Friday afternoon Sarah realized that her feeble strength was diminishing. She asked that her candles be brought to her bedside so that she could still perform this pivotal mitzvah of Jewish womanhood. Her energy was waning; there was just enough vigor for one last message.

"Don't worry," she encouraged those around her, "you see that I am not afraid." Like the woman of valor "who laughs at the last day" she really had nothing to fear. The hallmark of the *eishes chayil* is that all of her days are filled with meaningful productivity, so at the end there will be only reward.

"Everything is from Hashem," she said, her voice barely audible. "And just as you must bless for the good you must also bless —" And here she fell silent for she did not wish to complete the statement. Moments later, after a protracted period of suffering, on the 27th of Adar 5695 (1935), her soul departed in sanctity. Sarah Schenirer was 52 years old.

SARAH was gazing at the Shabbos candles when she died. And what did she see if not all the candles that she had kindled throughout her marvelous life — the flame of Jewish vibrancy whose glow would warm countless multitudes and generations. Was this not the intention of the prophet, "***Bais Yaakov*** *l'chu v'nelcha b'or Hashem*" — Come, Bais Yaakov, let us go in the light of the Lord! This was her clarion call: Bais Yaakov, dear Jewish daughters, come with me out of the darkness. Together we will greet the dawn of a new era, the glory of our People, basking in the light of Hashem.

Girls were on their way to their Bnos groups when they heard the news of Sarah Schenirer's passing. They changed direction and converged upon Sarah's home so that they could recite *Tehillim*. The room was illuminated only by the light of Sarah's last two candles. The reflection of the flames danced in the eyes of the *banos*, and they would never be extinguished.

The girls began to recite *Tehillim*, their gaze fixed upon the candles, reflecting upon all that Sarah Schenirer had lit within their hearts. After a while it became impossible to hold back the tears, and cries began to echo throughout the house. The remarkable seamstress, who had woven a glorious garment for every Jewish girl, was no more.

From the adjacent house, Sarah Schenirer's husband, Rabbi Landau, entered and admonished, "Today is Shabbos and it is forbidden to cry. Such behavior would certainly cause anguish to Frau Schenirer." Immediately all of the crying ceased, for no one could bear the thought of causing pain to the *Eim b'Yisrael.*

On Sunday, a funeral of unprecedented proportions took place amid a downpour. The Jews of Krakow and the surrounding towns attended the funeral; all of the shuls, *battei midrashim,* shops and commercial enterprises were closed. When news of Frau Schenirer's passing was transmitted throughout Poland, thousands of Jewish girls tore *kriah;* within the year hundreds of Jewish mothers would name their new daughters Sarah.

Many women in Israel, Zevi Scharstein has noted, were greater than Sarah Schenirer in erudition — but in her high sense of mission, her selfless devotion to her pupils and her dedication to God and His Torah, she had no peer. On this

בית יעקב

ליטעראַרישע שריפט פאר שול און היים
דינט די ענינים פון בית־יעקב שולן און ארגאניזאציעס בנות־אגודת־ישראל אין פוילן
רעדאקטירט דורך א״ג פרידנזאָן

שרה שענירער נשמתה עדן

פרייטיק ערב שבת־קודש פ׳ ויקהל כ״ו אדר א׳ תרצ״ה פאר ליכטצינדן האט נאך א לאנגער קראנקייט אויסגעהויכט איר ריינע נשמה אין עלטער פון צוויי און פופציק יאר די באשאפערן און פירערן פון אונזער באוועגונג, פרוי שרה שענירער זכרונה לברכה!
תנצב״ה

טיף געבויגן שטייען מיר פארן קבר פון דער גרויסער ליכטיקער יידישער פערזענלעכקייט, די באשאפערן פון דער הייליקער בית־יעקב־אידיי, די מאמע פון דער בנות־באוועגונג, די ערשטע מיטגרינדערן און שטענדיקע מיטארבייטערן פון אונדזער זשורנאל

פרוי **שרה שענירער** זכרונה לברכה

גרויס איז פאר אונדז דאס אומגליק און שטארק די ווייטיק.
מי יתן לנו תמורתה?

די רעדאקציע

day, there was no one who could deny that. Even those who had opposed establishing an educational system for girls, could not dispute that a lifeline had been created, and they too joined the funeral cortege.

Drenched and chilled, the procession marched through Krakow's narrow streets, which were crammed with mourners. No one lost the opportunity to pay homage to a woman who had never given birth to a child, yet was called "mother" by thousands. They made their way past the old cemetery, which still had plots available for distinguished citizens and for the affluent who could afford burial there. Sarah Schenirer, however, had left explicit instructions that she be buried in Krakow's new Jewish cemetery.

The old cemetery, as Mrs. Pearl Benisch points out, survived the Second World War miraculously intact. Yet the new cemetery was chosen to be the site of the Plashow concentration camp. Jewish slaves were forced to uproot the gravestones to be used as pavement in the camp. Nothing remains of that cemetery today; clearly it was Sarah Schenirer's desire to be with her *banos* and her nation at the time of their suffering.

Sixty-one

IF TRAVESTY and travail are the true barometer of commitment, then Bais Yaakov's ultimate level was achieved during the unfathomable horror of the Holocaust. It was there that the loyalty of Jewish women to the faith of their ancestors was proven beyond any doubt. Under the constant threat of immediate death, Bais Yaakov teachers disregarded their personal safety in order to deliver their classes.

Graduates sent letters to Rabbi Orlean — who until the liquidation of the Warsaw Ghetto remained at the helm of the movement — and almost without fail, never referred to their personal suffering or distress, focusing exclusively on spiritual matters: how to explain a difficult verse in Proverbs, a problematic paragraph in *Chovos Halevavos*, or a pedagogic inquiry.

IN MIRIAM DANSKY's biography of Rebbetzin Grunfeld she records:

> Bais Yaakov girls who walked through the valley of death kept their purity in the face of immoral filth and degradation, who, although worn and weakened by terrible hunger and suffering, desolate and bereft, taught children whom they came across in the camps. They dispensed comfort to those around them, buried the dead wherever possible and prevented desecration of the bodies. They, who saw no glimmer of hope, found the courage to infuse others with hope.
>
> Cilla [a student of Sarah Schenirer] carried buckets to be emptied at the perimeters of the death camp. One day, in the execution of this task, she passed three women sitting outside the building from where people would be taken the next day to the gas chambers. They had not been commanded by the camp authorities to sit there, they had not been specifically chosen for death, but they were weary of life and wanted nothing more than to be led to their end.
>
> Cilla, with all the energetic enthusiasm of her youth, shouted at them: "What are you doing here? Go back. I have reliable information that tomorrow liberation

will come. And you will not be there to be freed! Just one day — and you are choosing to die?! What kind of madness is this?! Come back immediately!"

Liberation did not arrive the next day. It was just a ploy used by Cilla to draw these poor women back to life. And today, these women are alive and have families!

JOSEPH FRIEDENSON relates his own personal experiences that demonstrated how the light that Sarah Schenirer kindled in the hearts of Jewish girls never ceased to flicker and shine.

In the ghettoes of Lodz and Warsaw they secretly maintained schools, kitchens for children and youth groups. I saw how they starved [yet] carried food to Jews who were ill and to lonely *talmidei chachamim.* I saw them studying *Mishlei* and *Chovos Ha-levavos,* in times when others could no longer think about anything other than bread. I saw how they felt the sorrow of the community, when others proved incapable of seeing more than their own 'I'.

In Birkenau they were the only ones who remembered when it was Shabbos and Yom Tov, when others forgot the sequence of days. Several candles were somehow lit every Friday evening and they whispered a *tefillah.* Some no longer had for whom to pray. They no longer had their husbands or parents, and they wept in prayer for their tortured people.

Somewhere in the Auschwitz women's camp — on a

Chanukah evening in a dark horse stable which the Germans called a barrack — several Chanukah candles were lit. At first a mere handful of girls gathered around the candles. But soon the group grew in size, and the light spread over the entire barrack. And in a few minutes several hundred Jewish women were singing a deathless song of contempt for their tyrants: "*Maoz Tzur Yeshuasi* — Mighty Rock of my salvation, to praise You is a delight," and listening to addresses filled with trust in the ultimate vindication of God's purpose. Who were the girls who thought of the sacred, heroic deed? They were several pupils of Sarah Schenirer's school in Tarnow.

A young woman stood near an old Jew who had just arrived in Birkenau. He was deathly hungry, and she stood near him with a bowl of soup, which she begged him to eat. He would not touch the soup because it was *treife*. But she proved to him with *pesukim* and citations from *Chazal,* that it was permissible for him to have the soup, that he *had* to partake of the soup, that it was a mitzvah for him to eat whatever he was given. She was a former instructor of Sarah Schenirer's Bais Yaakov seminary in Krakow. And it later became known to me, that so long as that young woman was in Auschwitz — she spent *four years* there — she herself never ate *treife* food.

MOST OF THE STORIES of these examples of Bais Yaakov fortitude have tragic conclusions. It was common for the pupils to take comfort before the end and encourage each other by saying, "Don't worry, we will all soon be going to Mama Schenirer — *shrek sich nisht.*" The girls' physical and spiritual martyrdom stand out as among the most inspirational stories of bravery in the face of adversity.

One episode of such heroism is the alleged martyrdom of 93 Bais Yaakov students from the Krakow seminary, which took place in the summer of 1942. Although this event has been immortalized in Hillel Bavli's famous Hebrew poem, Agudas Yisrael now contends that the event did not take place. Regardless, it has become, as Judith Tydor Baumel and Jacob Schacter point out, "a symbolic parable woven into the tapestry of Jewish heroism, taking its place in the historical/legendary chronicles of the Jewish People."

For three years, according to this account, 94 students and teachers of the seminary went underground, as all Jewish schools had been closed by decree of the German army in 1939. Yet, clandestine lessons in a host of subjects continued throughout this period.

On July 27, 1942 the Nazis discovered 93 students studying together and transferred them to an unlit basement in the ghetto. They remained there for two weeks, unaware of what lay in store. On August 9th the girls were permitted to bathe in warm water for the first time since their capture.

The next day they were led to a large building with well-lit rooms and beautiful beds. They were ordered to bathe again, while they did so their clothing was removed from their rooms and replaced with nightgowns. On the evening of August 11th, they were told, German soldiers would come to visit them. The meaning of this "visit" was not lost upon them, and they decided to take their own lives with the poison they had prepared for such a contingency.

One of these 93 young girls was Chaya Feldman. Before returning her soul to her Maker, she penned a letter to the secretary of the World Beth Jacob Movement in New York, which was smuggled out of the ghetto. The report, a classic of unswerving faith and trust in the Lord, is a testimony to all that "our mother Sarah" — as she refers to Frau Schenirer in her letter — taught them.

Corroboration of Feldman's testimony, as described in Drs. Tydor Baumel and Schacter's essay, comes from Hannah Weiss, the 94th girl, who had been called away to care for her sick aunt just prior to the group's capture. Hannah was unsuccessful in her attempt to rejoin her schoolmates, but she hid in the yard outside the building and heard in great detail the words of encouragement spoken by the girls' teacher. She was also able to hear their fateful decision.

The 93 girls, and countless others, took their inspiration from one unpretentious woman. It was "mother Sarah" who led them to realize their full and glorious potential as Jewish women, even in the face of unspeakable torture and degradation.

Epilogue

IN 1918 SARAH SCHENIRER opened her first class in her sewing shop at Catachina No 1. In this cramped room 25 enamored girls sat on boxes and took notes, resting their notebooks on their laps.

Based upon her initial experiences with older girls, Sarah's hopes were tame and hardly ambitious. She was certain that she would be able to exert influence only on the very youngest, for, after delivering one of her earliest lectures to about forty young women, Sarah noted the looks of boredom, the rolling eyes and the cynical smirks which met her presentation.

Slowly, however, a transformation occurred and girls of every age sat raptly under her spell. A dynamic was set in motion, a spiritual rags-to-riches story. In a matter of a few short years there was hardly a Jewish community in Poland that Sarah had not visited, and in hundreds of towns branches of Bais Yaakov were founded. These schools did not merely instruct Jewish girls in their heritage; the renaissance they heralded restored self-respect and pride to Jewish women everywhere.

The Rabbis teach, *Yosef michayev es harisha'im, Hillel michayev es ha'aniyim* — no matter what state you are in, there was always someone in a more desperate situation who did not abandon his commitment to Torah. Appended to this teaching could be the lesson, *Sarah Schenirer michayeves es ha-rabbanim v'es ha'askanim.*

Before Sarah emerged on the scene, the loss of daughters to assimilation was all but inevitable. Before the leaders had adequately grasped the scope of the problem that was decimating our People, Sarah Schenirer had set a solution into motion. Bais Yaakov created a new reality and a new environment. The Jewish girl who had found her home outmoded, disconnected and stifling, was now proud of her heritage. The void in her life had been filled with a vibrant Jewish existence that included school life, clubs, communal affairs, well-organized activities and an entirely new literature that was based on Torah ideas.

Sarah Schenirer did not create the Bais Yaakov movement; she gave birth to it. She nurtured it as a young child, and she guided it into its maturity. Even after it expanded and developed — even after she was no longer living — she would forever be its mother.

Glossary

The following glossary provides a partial explanation of some of the foreign words and phrases used in this book. The spelling, tense, and explanations reflect the way the specific word is used in *BUILDERS*. Often, there are alternate spellings and meanings for the words. Foreign words and phrases which are immediately followed by a translation in the text are not included in this section.

AGUDIST – adherent of the philosophies of Agudas Yisrael

A GUTTEN TUG – (Yid.) good day

AHAVAS HA-TORAH – love of Torah

AMORAIM – later sages of the Talmud

APIKORUS – heretic

ATTA HARESSA – lit., "You have shown"; prayer said line by line at the beginning of Simchas Torah. Each line is traditionally auctioned to the highest bidder

AUFRUF – (Yid.) the custom of calling up a bridegroom to the Torah on the Sabbath preceding his wedding

AVODAH – service

AVODAS HASHEM – service of God

AVREICH – young married yeshivah student

BAALEI MUSSAR – masters of ethics

BAAL HABASTA – (Yid.) an efficient housewife

BAAL HABOSS (pl. BAALEI BATTIM) – (Yid.) a layman; one who has an occupation other than full-time Torah study or education

BAAL MIDOS – person of exceptional character

BOCHUR(IM) – unmarried yeshivah student

BARUCH HASHEM – thank God

BEDIKAS CHAMETZ – the search for leaven preceding Passover eve

BEIN HA-Z'MANIM – yeshivah intercession

BEIS MIDRASH – yeshivah study hall

BENTCHING – (Yid.) prayer after meals

BIRKAS KOHEN – priestly blessing

BLATT – (Yid.) folio

BEN (BNEI) TORAH – learned, observant Jew(s)

BNEI ZEKUNIM – children that have been born when their parents were older; children that are especially precious; connotes an especially warm and emotional bond

BOIMELAH – (Yid.) little tree

B'RAMA – on high

BRIS – the ritual of circumcision; the celebration held in honor of the event

CHACHAM – wise man

CHAG SIMCHASEINU – lit., festival of our joy, Sukkos

CHAIM – life

CHALILAH – God forbid (idiom)

CHAMETZ – leaven

CHANUKAS HA-BAYIS (building dedication

CHAREIDI – devout

CHAZAL – 1. acronym for "our Sages, of blessed memory"; 2. a statement by the Sages

CHEDER (pl. CHADORIM) – elementary school for religious studies

CHESED – deeds of loving kindness

CHIDDUSH(IM) – novel insight(s) in Torah interpretation

CHILLUL HASHEM – desecration of God's name

CHILLUL SHABBOS – desecration of the Shabbos

CHOL HA-MOED – the Intermediate Days of Sukkos and Pesach

CHOZRIM B'TSHUVAH – those who have returned to religious observance

CHURBAN – Holocaust

DA'AS TORAH – the opinions and decisions of Torah leaders which are relevant to the issues and problems of the times and are accepted by the Torah community as authoritative

DAF – page of the Talmud

DAF YOMI – a Talmudic study regimen in which the same folio of the Talmud is studied internationally, one folio each day, the entire Talmud being completed in about seven and a half years.

DARSHENED – (Yid.) gave a learned discourse

DAVEN – (Yid.) pray

DAVKA – (Yid.) purposely

DIN TORAH – case brought to a Jewish court for adjudication according to Torah law

EIM B'YISRAEL – a mother in Israel

EINEKLACH – (Yid.) grandchildren

EMMES – truth

EMUNAS HA-CHACHAMIM – belief in the [authority of the] Sages

ERETZ YISRAEL – the Land of Israel

EREV – eve

EISHES CHAYIL – 1. a woman of valor; 2. a song composed by King Solomon, sung every Friday night

GABBAI – 1. a beadle; 2. a synagogue officer; 3. overseer of charity funds

GADOL (pl. GEDOLIM) – lit., "great one"; used in reference to outstanding Torah scholars

GADOL (pl. GEDOLEI) HADOR – the greatest Torah scholar(s) of the generation

GAON – genius

GEMATRIA – numerical equivalencies of the Hebrew alphabet

GORAL HA-GRA – Vilna Goan's method of casting lots to indicate a particular Scriptural verse as a solution to a personal or communal problem

HAVDALAH – the ceremony marking the end of the Sabbath, in which blessings are recited, separating the holy day from the other days of the week

HECHSHER – authoritative certification that food is kosher

HISLAHAVUS – excitement, passion

ISH HA-CHAZON – man of vision and foresight

ISRU CHAG – the day after Passover, Sukkos, and Shavuos

IYUN SHIUR – a discourse clarifying the deeper meaning of a Talmudic text

KALLAH – bride

KAVOD – honor, respect

KAVOD SHOMAYIM – lit., "the heaven's honor," the respect given to God

KASHA(S) – (Yid.) question(s)

KIBBUDIM – ceremonial honors, often the recitation of various blessings, given to respected people on important occasions

KIDDUSH – blessing sanctifying the Sabbath, usually recited over a cup of wine

*KI LO TISHAKACH MIPEE ZARO – verse in the Bible promising the Jewish nation that the Torah will never be completely forgotten

KINDERLACH – (Yid.) children

KLAL YISRAEL – the Jewish nation

KOLLEL – institution or organization of full-time Torah study for married men

KOL TORAH – the sound of Torah learning

KRECHTZ – (Yid.) a mournful sigh

L'HALACHAH AVAL LO L'MAASEH – in theory but not in practice

LAMDAN(IM) – Torah scholar(s)

LATKES – (Yid.) pancakes

LEIL – eve, night

L'HAVDIL – lit., "to separate"; this word is.inserted in the sentence to indicate a separation between the holy and the mundane

MAARIV – the evening prayer service

MACHMIR – one who is stringent in matters of Jewish law above the letter of the law

MAGGIDEI SHIURIM – Torah lecturers

MALACHEI HASHARES – ministering angels

MANHIG HADOR – leader of the generation

MAKKAH – a plague

MAIKEL – one who interprets the halachah leniently

MARA D'ASRA – (Aramaic) communal Torah authority

MASHGIACH – 1. dean of students in a yeshiva who also acts as guide and advisor; 2. kashrus supervisor

MASMID(IM) – diligent student(s)

MATANOS L'EVYONIM – charity to the indigent given on Purim

MECHANECH – educator

MECHIRAS CHAMETZ – the selling of one's leavened bread before Passover

MECHUTTANIM – the parents of one's son-in-law or daughter-in-law

MESHUGEH L'OSO DAVAR – (Yid.) someone who has committed himself to a cause to the point of insanity

MESHULACH – lit., "messenger"; itinerant fundraiser for a charitable institution

MESORAH – tradition

*MICHAYEVES ES HARABBANIM V'ES HA'ASKANIM– lit., "obligates the rabbis and the community lay leaders"

MISPALLELIM – v. pray; n. those who pray

MIZRACH – east; front wall of the synagogue housing the ark

MIZRACHIST – adherent of the philosophies of the Zionist movement

MUSSAR – ethical instruction

MIN HASHOMAYIM – heaven-sent

NACHAS – (Yid.) pleasure; pride; satisfaction

NARISHKEIT – (Yid.) foolishness

NE'ILAS HA-CHAG – concluding celebration of a holiday

NIGGUN – tune; song

NITZAVIM – lit., "standing"; the prominent

NOCH – (Yid.) more

NU NU – (Yid.) oh, well

PESUKIM – verses from Scripture

PIDYON SH'VUYIM – the mitzvah of ransoming captives

PIKUACH NEFESH – lit., "life threatening"; a situation in which one is obligated to disregard Torah law in order to save a life

PIRKEI – chapters

REFUAH – healing

ROSH CHODESH – beginning of the Jewish month

ROSH YESHIVAH – yeshivah dean

SANDAK – (Yid.) individual who holds the baby during the circumcision

SEFER (SEFARIM) – book(s)

SEUDAH SHLISHIS – third Shabbos meal

SEUDAS HODA'AH – a festive meal in celebration of thanks to God

SEUDAS MITZVAH – a festive meal connected with the performance of a mitzvah

SEUDAS PREIDAH – lit., "a meal of separation"; a good-bye party

SHACHARIS – morning prayers

SHAILOS – halachic queries

SHALIACH TZIBBUR – lit,; "messenger of the congregation"; prayer leader; cantor

SHAIMOS – worn out holy writings that need burial

SHAMASH – attendant

SHEMONEH ESREI – lit., "eighteen"; the central prayer in Jewish liturgy which is recited three times daily

SHIDDUCH – a (matrimonial) match

SHIUR(IM) – Torah lecture(s)

SHIUR KLALI – Torah lecture for the entire yeshivah, usually given by the rosh yeshivah

SHMUEZ – mussar discourse

SHOSHBINIM – escorts of a bridegroom as he walks to the marriage canopy

SIDDUR(IM) – prayer book(s)

SHLEIMUS – completion; perfection; wholeness

SHTENDER – (Yid.) a lectern

SHULCHAN ARUCH – the authoritative Code of Jewish Law, written by Rabbi Yosef Karo in the sixteenth century

SIYUM HA-SHAS – conclusion of the study of Talmud, accompanied by a celebratory meal

SVARA – (Aramaic) rationale; line of thinking

TALMID(IM) – student(s)

TALMID(EI) CHACHAM(IM) – Torah scholar(s)

TANACH – Scripture

TENAIM – engagement agreement

TEFILLAH – prayer

TORAH LISHMAH – Torah learning purely for its own sake

TREIFE – (Yid.) non-kosher

TZADDIK – righteous man

TZEIDAH LA-DERECH – provisions for the journey

TZEILIM – (Yid.) object of religious worship other than Jewish

UDIM MUZALIM M'AISH – lit., "firebrands snatched from the burning fire"; survivors

VIDUY – confession

YAAKOV AVINU – our patriarch Jacob

YIDDISHE KINDERLACH – (Yid.) Jewish children

ZEH SEFER TOLDOS ADAM – a verse in Genesis; "this is the book of Adam's life"

ZT"L – acronym for, "may his memory be a blessing," commonly said after mentioning the name of a righteous man who has passed away

Edifying BIOGRAPHIES, *thought-provoking* ESSAYS *and entertaining* STORIES FOR YOUTH — *quoted by religious leaders and laymen, politicians and the man on the street. For a truly unique reading experience there's nothing like a book by*

HANOCH TELLER

BIOGRAPHIES

SUNSET. Instructive and dramatic episodes in the lives of ten contemporary Torah luminaries. Revised and enlarged edition. 288 pp.

THE BOSTONER. Stories and recollections from the colorful court of the Bostoner Rebbe, Rabbi Levi I. Horowitz, whose philanthropic and outreach endeavors have earned international acclaim. 209 pp.

BRIDGES OF STEEL, LADDERS OF GOLD. The rags-to-riches story of philanthropist Joseph Tanenbaum, who endowed over 1,000 Jewish educational institutions.

A MATTER OF PRINCIPAL. The fascinating biography of the renowned educator, Rabbi Binyamin Steinberg, z"l, principal of Bais Yaakov of Baltimore and champion of women's education in the U.S. 296 pp.

AND FROM JERUSALEM, HIS WORD

An inspiring tribute to the beloved gadol ha-dor, Rabbi Shlomo Zalman Auerbach zt"l, whose vast scope and legacy of Torah knowledge, humility and love of chesed affected Jews the world over. 399 pp.

PARSHAS HASHAVUA

A MIDRASH AND A MAASEH. An anthology of insights and commentaries on the weekly Torah reading, including hundreds of old favorites and new stories. 2 volumes, slip-cased, 1,006 pp.

YOUNG READERS

THE BEST OF STORYLINES. Over two dozen inspiring stories that convey Jewish values and Torah concepts. 224 pp.

WELCOME TO THE REAL WORLD. The story of a young girl's rite of passage as she faces the first real challenges of her life.

The Sound of Soul

For years **Hanoch Teller** has delighted the Anglo-Jewish reader with inspiring tales of ordinary people who do extraordinary things. With a cast of fascinating characters and modern spiritual heroes and heroines, these true, contemporary stories touch the soul of readers everywhere and strike a responsive chord in their heart. Joy and drama, laughter and pathos combine to create a new genre of Jewish literature: "soul stories."

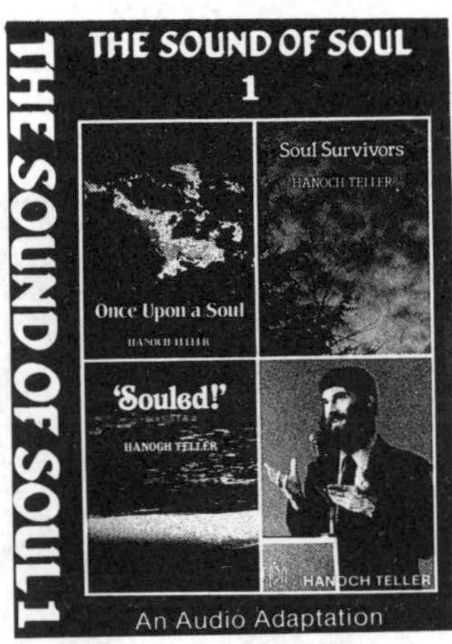

Each one of Teller's cherished tales of Jewish souls from all across the globe, skillfully written with powerful, image-evoking prose, conveys the timeless precepts of Judaism to young and old alike.

Now, in response to requests from countless educators, commuters, housewives, students, and program directors, these masterpieces have been reproduced on audio cassettes, fully dramatized with musical accompaniment and vivid sound effects.

The ***Sound of Soul*** volumes I & II provide over two hours of listening enjoyment for the entire family. The most heart-warming, enlightening, hilarious, and poignant of Teller's tales have been transformed into an audio classic. Each cassette also contains new enchanting stories not featured in any of Hanoch Teller's books.

These high-quality tapes are not available in book stores, but may be ordered directly from:

Media Education Trust
143 Hoyt St. # 2B
Stamford, CT 06905-5741

Each tape is only $9 each, plus $2.75 for postage and handling. Connecticut residents: please add sales tax.